Safeguarding and Promoting the Well-being of Children, Families and Communities

Child Welfare Outcomes

Series Editor: Harriet Ward, Centre for Child and Family Research, Loughborough University, UK
This authoritative series draws from original research and current policy debates to help social work managers, policy makers and researchers to understand and improve the outcomes of services for children and young people in need. Taking an evidence-based approach, these books include children's experiences and analysis of costs and effectiveness in their assessment of interventions, and provide guidance on how to develop more effective policy, practice and training.

of related interest

Approaches to Needs Assessment in Children's Services
Edited by Harriet Ward and Wendy Rose
Foreword by Professor Al Aynsley Green
ISBN 1 85302 780 4

Assessing Children's Needs and Circumstances
The Impact of the Assessment Framework
Hedy Cleaver and Steve Walker with Pamela Meadows
Foreword by Al Aynsley Green
ISBN 1 84310 159 9

The Child's World
Assessing Children in Need
Edited by Jan Horwath
ISBN 1 85302 957 2

Child Neglect
Practice Issues for Health and Social Care
Edited by Julie Taylor and Brigid Daniel
Foreword by Olive Stevenson
ISBN 1 84310 160 2

Developing Good Practice in Children's Services
Edited by Vicky White and John Harris
ISBN 1 84310 150 5

Child Welfare Services for Minority Ethnic Families: The Research Reviewed
June Thoburn, Ashok Chand and Joanne Procter
Introduction by Beverley Prevatt Goldstein
ISBN 1 84310 269 2

Supporting Parents
Messages from Research
David Quinton
Foreword by Right Honourable Margaret Hodge, Minister for Children, Young People and Families
ISBN 1 84310 210 2

Fostering Now
Messages from Research
Ian Sinclair
ISBN 1 84310 362 1

Safeguarding and Promoting the Well-being of Children, Families and Communities

Edited by Jane Scott and Harriet Ward

*Foreword by Maria Eagle MP
Parliamentary Under Secretary of State
for Children, Young People and Families*

Jessica Kingsley Publishers
London and Philadelphia

First published in 2005
by Jessica Kingsley Publishers
116 Pentonville Road
London N1 9JB, UK
and
400 Market Street, Suite 400
Philadelphia, PA 19106, USA

www.jkp.com

Parts of Chapter 6 are reproduced from 'Catching children as they fall: mental health promotion
in residential care in East Dunbartonshire' by M. van Beinum, A. Martin and C. Bonnet (2002)
in *The Scottish Journal of Residential Child Care 1*, 19–20. Reproduced here with permission from
The Scottish Institute for Residential Child Care.

Library of Congress Cataloging in Publication Data
Safeguarding and promoting the well being of children, families, and their communities / edited by Jane
Scott and Harriet Ward.
p. cm.
Some chapters based on papers originally given at the Fifth International Looking After Children
Conference held in Oxford, England in Sept. 2002.
Includes bibliographical references and index.
ISBN-13: 978-1-84310-141-3 (hardcover : alk. paper)
ISBN-10: 1-84310-141-6 (hardcover : alk. paper) 1. Child welfare. 2. Children with social disabili-
ties—Services for. 3. Social work with children. 4. Family social work. I. Scott, Jane, 1968- II. Ward, Harriet,
1948- III. International Looking After Children Conference (5th : 2002 : Oxford, England)
HV713.S22 2005
362.7—dc22

2005020179

British Library Cataloguing in Publication Data
A CIP catalogue record for this book is available from the British Library

ISBN-13: 978 1 84310 141 3
ISBN-10: 1 84310 141 6

Printed and Bound in Great Britain by
Athenaeum Press, Gateshead, Tyne and Wear

Contents

List of Figures

List of Tables

Foreword

This book demonstrates the value of international collaboration in exploring ways to improve the developmental outcomes of vulnerable children. It highlights some of the challenges and shows how solutions can cross countries and cultures.

This book is published against the backdrop of the ambitious British Government change programme for children's services in England set out in Every Child Matters: Change for Children, designed to ensure that every child develops his or her full potential in achieving the five outcomes of being healthy, staying safe, learning and achieving, making a positive contribution and achieving economic well-being. These outcomes are closely linked to the Millennium Goals, to which all the signatories of the United Nations Convention on the Rights of the Child aspire.

Yet the evidence in this book highlights the obstacles that even the wealthiest countries face in meeting these objectives. It shows how considerable effort has been spent on identifying need and monitoring outcomes, but less is known about which interventions are effective in safeguarding and promoting wellbeing. The book contains examinations of the impact of national policy initiatives, such as poverty reduction, set alongside examples of specific interventions which can make a difference to vulnerable children and their families, and it is therefore relevant to researchers, policy makers and practitioners.

As national and local governments focus increasingly on the introduction of routine service evaluations and outcome monitoring in child welfare agencies, this book also helps us to explore what we mean by outcomes and provides practical methodologies for their measurement in the context of organizational culture. It is through a continued collaboration across countries to develop knowledge and skills that we will be able to promote the well-being of children, families and their communities.

*Maria Eagle MP, Parliamentary Under Secretary
of State for Children, Young People and Families*

Preface

One of the major concerns of contemporary social policy in Western societies is to improve outcomes for children in need. As the final section of this book demonstrates, considerable effort has been spent on identifying need and monitoring outcomes, but less is known about which interventions are effective in promoting and safeguarding well-being. This book uses examples from the UK, US, Canada and Australia to explore both the evidence of need and the effectiveness of interventions in improving well-being and therefore outcomes. Children's well-being depends on that of their parents and the environment in which they live: chapters also explore issues such as poverty, racism or poor housing which reduce the ability of individual families or communities to provide an environment in which young people can develop to their full potential.

The book is divided into five parts. Part I explores the evidence of need, its effect on well-being and the impact of national policy initiatives aimed at addressing poverty and improving outcomes. Parts II, III and IV explore specific interventions aimed at improving the health and well-being of children, families and communities. The concluding chapters (Part V) consider how the outcomes of such interventions can be monitored.

The chapters have been written by policymakers, researchers and senior managers in child welfare agencies, all of whom have been directly involved in constructing, evaluating or implementing the programmes they discuss.

Some of the chapters in this book are based on papers originally given at the Fifth International Looking After Children conference on Promoting Wellbeing and Monitoring Outcomes for Vulnerable Children, held in Oxford, England, in September 2002. Other papers from the conference have been published in a special issue of the journal *Child and Family Social Work* (vol. 9.1, February 2004).

A book of this nature takes considerable effort to produce and, as editors, we are indebted to the many people who have been involved in the process. We would like to thank the authors, many of whom have, with great forbearance, revised early drafts to ensure that they reflect recent changes of policy and practice which have emerged while other chapters were being written. We are extremely grateful to Suzanne Dexter and Sophie Astwood, whose administrative support has proved invaluable, and Sarah Lawrie's work on the glossary was greatly appreciated. We also wish to acknowledge the help and advice provided by Leonie Sloman at Jessica Kingsley Publishers. Finally we owe an enormous debt to Graeme Gidney and Christopher Ward without whose patience and support this book would never have been completed.

Jane Scott and Harriet Ward

A Note on the Book

Different chapters of this book have been written by authors from Australia, Canada, England, Scotland and the United States of America. In each of these countries there are differences in the way in which the English language is both spoken and written. We have made no attempt to impose a degree of uniformity on spellings and sentence construction; however, differences in terminology and definitions of key terms used by the authors are indicated in the glossary at the back of the book.

Chapter 1

Safeguarding and Promoting the Well-being of Children, Families and Communities

Harriet Ward and Jane Scott

Despite their affluence, Western societies nevertheless experience difficulties in safeguarding and promoting the well-being of vulnerable children. This book uses examples from Australia, Canada, the United States and the United Kingdom to explore evidence of need and its consequences; the effectiveness of policies aimed at reducing need; and specific interventions which seek to address those factors within children, their families and their communities that prevent them from achieving a satisfactory standard of health and well-being. Methodologies for routinely monitoring the outcomes of interventions are also discussed.

Introduction

The definition of 'well-being' used in this book draws from the work of the United Nations Convention on the Rights of the Child. Acknowledged as 'the most universally embraced human rights treaty in history', and ratified, acceded to or signed by 192 countries, the Convention specifies a comprehensive set of legal standards for safeguarding and promoting the well-being of children. The Millennium Development Goals (1990–2003) translate these standards into specific targets that can be monitored to demonstrate how far well-being is achieved: these include reducing poverty and child mortality rates and increasing literacy. Later documents reiterate the commitment to the Convention and describe how children's well-being will be safeguarded and promoted by creating a 'world fit for children' in which 'all children get the best possible start in life' and all 'have ample opportunity to develop their individual capacities in a safe and supportive environment' (United Nations 2002, p.5).

This book is about safeguarding and promoting the well-being of children in Western societies. Examples are drawn from four English-speaking jurisdictions: Australia, Canada, the United States of America and the United Kingdom. One might assume that these societies are all sufficiently wealthy to ensure that the Millennium Goals have all long since been met, but this is manifestly not the case. Over three million children in Great Britain are currently living below the poverty line (Department for Work and Pensions 2003a); 388,200 are defined under the Children Act 1989 as unable to achieve or maintain their full potential without the provision of services (Department for Education and Skills 2003a); 37,900 are looked after away from home because of abuse or neglect (Department for Education and Skills 2003b). There is similar evidence of need in Canada, where there were an estimated 61,201 substantiated child maltreatment investigations in 1998 (Trocmé *et al.* 2001), in Australia, where the life expectancy of the indigenous population is twenty years below that of the majority culture (Clare and Noonan 2002), and in the US, where 4.3 million (11%) children have no health insurance (National Center for Health Statistics 2003). The purpose of this book is to explore how the well-being of these children can be better safeguarded and promoted by initiatives that address those factors that make it harder for them to achieve a satisfactory standard of health and development.

A world fit for children

The United Nations describes a world fit for children as one in which 'We will promote the physical, psychological, spiritual, social, emotional, cognitive and cultural development of children as a matter of national and global priorities' (United Nations 2002, p.5). The designated areas where action is needed to bring this world into being are identified as: promoting healthy lives; providing good quality education; protecting against abuse, exploitation and violence; and combating HIV/AIDS. Similar objectives and action areas form an essential component of policies designed to safeguard and promote the well-being of children in all signatories to the UN Convention.

The well-being of children cannot be promoted in isolation, for they will not flourish unless their needs are met both by parents, or other primary carers, and by the environment in which they live. This book is therefore about promoting the well-being of families and communities as well as that of children. While 'the primary responsibility for the protection, upbringing and development of children rests with the family' (United Nations 2002, p.5) it is also acknowledged that parents, families and legal guardians require support and assistance from institutions of society. All children will require support from universal services, such as education and health; some will need extra help in achieving well-being through targeted and specialist services, such as speech therapy or emotional and behavioural programmes. Some adults will be unable to nurture children sufficiently to promote their well-being because of problems which diminish parenting capacity, such as poor mental health or substance abuse; others may be impeded by family and environmental factors such as poor housing or a hostile neighbourhood. Still others will encounter difficulties in a combination of these domains. It may therefore prove more appropriate and effective to provide services aimed at supporting parents and/or wider communities rather than focusing solely on the children themselves.

In the UK considerable attention has been devoted to constructing conceptual frameworks that facilitate social workers' assessments of children's needs and progress across a range of developmental dimensions. A number of chapters of this book refer to the Looking After Children initiative, a comprehensive methodology for gathering information, identifying needs, making plans and assessing outcomes for children looked after away from home. Key features of this initiative are that outcomes are measured across a spectrum of seven dimensions of children's development: health, education, identity, family and social relationships, emotional and behavioural development, social presentation and self care skills; that the progress of all children, including the most vulnerable, towards age-specific goals is compared with that of their peers so that deficits can be identified and addressed; and that children's progress is firmly linked to the quality of care that they receive. The materials developed to support this initiative have now been adapted for use in many parts of Western and Eastern Europe, and implemented with varying degrees of success in several countries, including the UK, Canada and much of Australia.

The *Framework for the Assessment of Children in Need and their Families* (Department of Health, Department for Education and Skills and Home Office 2000) builds on this initiative to construct a comprehensive map to help social workers gather information about children and families that facilitates the identification and assessment of need. The seven key dimensions of children's development that form the focus of Looking After Children are complemented by six dimensions of parenting capacity (stability, basic care, ensuring safety, emotional warmth, stimulation, guidance and boundaries), and seven key family and environmental factors (community resources, social integration, income, employment, housing, wider family, family history and functioning). By focusing on the interplay between these domains and dimensions, practitioners should be able to identify those factors within the child, the parents or the wider environment that support or inhibit the achievement of well-being. Materials from this system are designed to help social workers identify and understand need. After gathering information in each of these domains, they are more likely to conclude that a combination of services that address factors within the parents and the environment as well as the child might provide appropriate interventions to meet children's needs.

The Assessment Framework has been implemented throughout England and Wales; it is also being piloted in Australia, Canada and Sweden. In Britain it has been linked to the Looking After Children project to form a comprehensive system for assessment, planning, intervention and review for all children in need (see Chapter 17). With increased integration of services the interface with other assessment programmes used by professionals who undertake related work in heath, education and the criminal justice system is also being explored (see Cleaver *et al.* forthcoming; Jones, Chant and Ward 2003). Similar programmes to gather and report on information that facilitates the identification of need and the assessment of outcomes are being implemented in parts of the US (see Chapters 16 and 17).

Our understanding of the process of identifying need and assessing outcomes has advanced considerably over the last decade or so; we are also clearer about the consequences of unmet need. Cleaver, Unell and Aldgate's (1999) review of the impact of parental problems such as mental illness, domestic violence and drug abuse on children's development; Tomison's (1996) work on the relationship between child maltreatment and mental disorder; and Knapp's (2000) work on the long-term costs of persistent behaviour problems are among many studies that have contributed to improved understanding of the rationale for interventions.

However, while information about need and its consequences is improving, we still know little about the effectiveness of specific interventions (see Law and Joughin 2005; Macdonald 2001). This book aims to advance the discussion in this area by exploring a number of initiatives that are intended to improve children's well-being by addressing potential or actual difficulties within the three domains of child development, parenting capacity and the family and environment. These are all programmes that have been introduced in the UK, Canada, Australia or the US, some on a national and some on a local basis. All the chapters provide valuable insights into the effectiveness of the initiatives they describe. We do not know how successfully specific interventions can be transplanted from one society to another, but there are sufficient similarities within the cultures of these jurisdictions to assume that the lessons learned from evaluating these programmes would be of value to a wide range of practitioners, policy makers and researchers who seek to safeguard and promote the well-being of children, families and communities in any of these societies.

Reducing poverty

The inter-relationship between need and poverty is one of the primary issues to be addressed in any attempt to safeguard and promote well-being:

> Chronic poverty remains the single biggest obstacle to meeting the needs, protecting and promoting the rights of children. It must be tackled on all fronts, from the provision of basic social services to the creation of employment opportunities, from the availability of microcredit to investment in infrastructure, and from debt relief to fair trade practices. Children are hardest hit by poverty because it strikes at the very roots of their potential for development – their growing bodies and minds. (United Nations 2002, p.5)

As both Chapters 2 and 12 point out, in affluent countries of the industrialized world there are no valid excuses for child poverty, yet all the four societies reflected in this book are marked by substantial inequalities, with large numbers of children being brought up on insufficient incomes. In Chapter 2, Bennett spells out the consequences for children of being brought up in poverty, both in terms of their current childhood experiences and the long-term impact into adulthood. Poverty does indeed strike at the very roots of children's well-being, affecting their health, their cognitive development, their educational opportunities and their self-esteem. Bennett explores the link between poverty and social exclusion, demonstrating how insufficient family income restricts children's opportunities for social interactions and prevents families from participating fully in the life of their community. In Chapter 14 Leslie adds a further dimension to this discussion, tracing the links between poverty, poor housing and child abuse.

Far-reaching issues such as poverty are largely structural, and should primarily be addressed through broad scale government policy agendas. National initiatives introduced by the New Labour government in Britain, with the aim of eradicating child poverty in twenty years and halving it in ten, have tackled the issue on a number of fronts and form an integral part of the government's policy agenda for children and families. However, while the programmes have achieved considerable success in some areas (see Chapters 2 and 3) concerns have been raised at proposals to make entitlement to income conditional on particular behaviours (see Chapter 2).

The key question is whether coercive measures, such as conditionality of income, improve well-being. The American programme of welfare-to-work, intended to reduce poverty and dependency and increase employment, income and self-esteem by encouraging parents back to work is explored in Chapter 4. While there have been some positive findings relating to improved incentives for employment, and more interest from family-friendly employers, the programme has failed to take account of the absence of stable employment opportunities, the low earning potential of most participants and their need for transitional arrangements if they join the workforce. As a result, families have tended to move off welfare but not out of poverty, with damaging consequences for children's (and parents') well-being.

Promoting the well-being of parents and children

While addressing poverty is a core requirement in promoting children's well-being, there are many other areas to be addressed on both a national and a local basis.

The United Nations acknowledges a commitment to: 'recognise and support parents and families or, as the case may be, legal guardians as the primary caretakers of children...[and] strengthen their capacity to provide the optimum care, nurturing and protection' (United Nations 2002, p.2). Supporting parents is also high on the British government agenda. A major research programme to identify the type of support that parents find helpful and the ways in which it can best be delivered is described in Chapter 10. Findings from many of the studies discussed in this chapter have formed the basis for policy development in this area.

Physical and mental health problems, misuse of drugs and alcohol, domestic violence and social exclusion are among the many reasons why some parents find it difficult to provide children with a sufficiently nurturing environment. Such parents may require extra help in accessing universal services such as ante-natal care or early years education. They may also benefit from more focused specialist services. Programmes such as Head Start in the US and Canada (Chapter 7) and Sure Start in the UK (Chapter 3) focus on at risk populations with the aim of breaking negative cycles of deprivation and disadvantage by offering early childhood development Program to parents and very young children. The Canada

Pre-Natal Nutrition Program (Chapter 11) offers intensive support to pregnant women in at risk groups to improve their opportunities of achieving well-being both for themselves and their children.

Such intensive programmes can bring positive results. One of the individual studies in the Canadian federal programme found that there were significant benefits in both foetal and maternal outcomes, with reduced pre-natal substance exposure, higher birth weight, better post-natal health and fewer mother–infant separations (see Chapter 11). Children's opportunities for achieving long-term well-being were thus considerably enhanced.

One of the major difficulties encountered by parents who have been disadvantaged themselves is that they are unlikely to have adequate or appropriate parenting experiences. An American programme, Shared Family Care (Chapter 13), places very vulnerable parents with their children in the homes of mentors where they are re-parented themselves and learn to model more appropriate parenting and home management skills. Positive outcomes include greater independence and stability, increased parenting capacity and reduced likelihood of separation.

Preventive programmes, designed to reduce the likelihood of problems in high risk populations, have been found to produce more sustainable long-term benefits than later interventions, introduced to address difficulties which have already arisen (MacLeod and Nelson 2000). One possible consequence has been that, while much of the focus is on early intervention programmes for very young children, the needs of adolescents are often overlooked. Chapters 5 and 6 both discuss specific programmes aimed at improving the well-being of teenagers. Chapter 5 reports on a quasi-experimental study that explored the benefits of providing specialist adolescent support teams, which offer intensive, structured interventions to help young people address behavioural problems and improve communication and relationships with parents. Chapter 6 describes a closely related initiative – the development of a dedicated mental health service for children in care or accommodation in Scotland. Both such initiatives were aimed at improving the well-being of young people with extensive, deep-seated problems, and they both showed positive results. The involvement of support teams appeared to reduce conflict between young people and their families and prevent the need for placement away from home. Residential staff were involved in the development of the mental health service, which was seen to facilitate greater understanding of the needs of the young people concerned, and to contribute to improved stability of placements.

Strengthening communities

While a number of interventions can be shown to improve the well-being of individual parents and children, there is some evidence that benefits are most likely to be sustained if whole communities can be engaged in the process of change (see Chapters 12 and 16). Comments from very poor families (Chapter 2) underline the relationship between poverty, powerlessness and poor self-esteem. Helping a community to shape and direct its own programme for improved well-being is a powerful generator of change, allowing its members to take control of their lives and develop the confidence to improve their circumstances and those of their families. The Highfield Community Enrichment Project in Toronto (Chapter 12), for instance, showed significant improvements in children's behaviour patterns, and in adults' parenting skills and social and emotional functioning; perhaps the most interesting findings relate to parents' improved perceptions of their neighbourhood and their local school, in which they became involved. However, as Chapter 15 shows, such programmes are difficult to evaluate and do not always produce such clearly positive findings.

In both Canada and Australia, the populations at greatest risk are the indigenous native peoples, whose opportunities for achieving well-being have been severely limited by a long history of discriminatory and damaging policies (see Chapter 7). Engaging indigenous peoples in the development and implementation of programmes to promote well-being is essential to their success. Aboriginal Head Start in Canada (Chapter 7), which includes Aboriginal culture and language as integral components, provides a blueprint for engaging this hard to reach population.

Conclusion: Monitoring the effectiveness of services

If services are to be effective, the extent to which they serve their purpose needs to be constantly assessed and evaluated. Many findings from the programmes explored in this book emphasize the importance of establishing strong communications between the users and providers of services. Service users need to be engaged not only in the planning and construction of services, but also in their evaluation. It is, however, all too easy to overlook their views, particularly if they are young or disabled. And yet it is only those who receive a service who can really know what it was like, or how far they benefited (see Chapter 8). For instance, young people's reflections on their experiences in care (Chapter 9) provide valuable insights about the exceptional demands made of care leavers as they make the transition to adulthood and indicate how this difficult period could be better managed. Their views of their experience while looked after should surely inform planned changes to the delivery of services. Communication with service users is often an integral part of government policy.

The final two chapters in this book explore more formal methods of routinely evaluating services. The United Nations has identified a series of objectives for improving the well-being of children, and progress towards them is routinely monitored. Friedman and colleagues (Chapter 16) demonstrate how setting similar objectives and deciding how they can be achieved can provide a framework for identifying the contribution each agency needs to make to ensure that targets are reached, and thus provide incentives for better inter-agency co-operation. Chapter 17 shows how the data required to monitor progress towards these objectives forms an integral part of interactions between practitioners and service users, and should inform the development of services to improve well-being at an individual as well as an aggregate level. It is only by constantly assessing progress and questioning the effectiveness of services that we can create a world that is truly fit for children.

Part I

Evidence of Need

Chapter 2

Promoting the Health and Well-being of Children

Evidence of Need in the UK

Fran Bennett

This chapter highlights the implications of poverty and social exclusion, both for children's well-being in the present and for their life chances in the future; the increasing quality and quantity of evidence available now is extending the volume and depth of our knowledge about the damaging effects of poverty and social exclusion on children themselves, on families and communities, and on society as a whole. Both parents and children are active agents in trying to minimize the impact of poverty on everyday life, although their best efforts can be overwhelmed. Powerlessness and 'voice poverty' are important components of their exclusion. We need an alternative to the 'deficit model' of people living in poverty, which values the experiences and insights they can bring, and the contribution they can make to society. We also need to avoid determinism, whilst retaining our awareness of the largely structural causes of children's experiences of 'ill being'. These considerations may help shape the nature of policies to combat poverty and social exclusion amongst children and their families, and of interventions to support children in need.

Introduction

There are several reasons why those working with children in need in the UK should be aware of the poverty and social exclusion they have experienced, and the potential impact on their childhood and future life chances. First, a high proportion of social services users, including families with children, live on social security benefits or tax credits and/or in poverty (Becker 1997). Social services departments also have some practical powers to ameliorate that situation, even if only at the margins, via discretionary powers to give small payments to families and young people under the Children Act 1989 in England and equivalent legislation in the devolved administrations of the UK. In some parts of continental Europe social assistance and social services have traditionally been much more closely connected; but in the UK, social workers do have to liaise on a regular basis with the benefits authorities about social security benefits. In particular, they may be helping low-income families to apply for grants or loans to meet the costs of one-off items such as cookers or beds under the discretionary 'social fund'.

The extent and nature of child poverty

Bijon Chaudhuri, aged eight, from Lowestoft, winner of an essay competition for children and young people run by the Child Poverty Action Group in 1989, was cited in *Poverty* Summer 1989:

> My name is Bijon. I am coming up to nine years of age. I feel more like a teenager because I'm coming out of the little-boy box into the outside world of busyness...
>
> I used to enjoy the funny bits of being poor, like doing homework with a torch or having Christmas dinner in candlelight when the electricity meter ran out. But now I'm fed up and bored with poverty...
>
> My mum's friend has always had poverty. Her little baby got ill. The doctor said, 'if it gets worse, telephone me'. That night, it got really worse – but they hadn't got a telephone, so her husband ran outside to a phone. It was broken. When he found one that worked the ambulance came, but their girl was dead. Mum says that poverty is like slowly bleeding to death. It kills people all the time, all over the world.

In the UK in 2001/02, about 30 per cent of children (some 3.8 million) lived in poverty, defined as living in households with under 60 per cent of median contemporary income after housing costs (Department for Work and Pensions 2003a). Research suggests that one in three families suffers a deterioration of living standards on the birth of a child, and 10 to 15 per cent fall into poverty as a result (HM Treasury 1999a). The relationship of these statistics with the Department of Health's 'census' of children in need, published in 2000, and covering England only, is complex. The Department of Health defines some 3 to 4 million children as in vulnerable families, including those living in poverty; but of that number, only some 300,000 to 400,000 are 'in need', i.e. unlikely to achieve or maintain a satisfactory standard of health or development without additional support (Department for Education and Skills 2003d). Low income is cited as the primary reason for being 'in need' for only 6 per cent of these children (Becker and Ward undated). These figures sit somewhat oddly with the data cited above on the high proportion of social services users as a whole living on benefits and/or in poverty. However, which factor is counted as 'primary' is perhaps less important than the recognition that low income interacts with, and exacerbates, other difficulties facing families.

'Deprivation' is distinct from, though related to, poverty defined as low income (Department for Work and Pensions 2002). The Poverty and Social Exclusion Millennium survey (Gordon *et al.* 2000), based on evidence about deprivation of 'socially perceived necessities' – defined as such 'democratically', or by consensus – found that some 2 million children in Great Britain, or 18 per cent, had to do without two or more items which the majority of the population regard as necessities. These include fresh fruit or vegetables at least once a day and new, properly fitted clothes (p.34). This rises to 23 per cent for two- to four-year-olds. Thirty-four per cent of children do without at least one such necessity (in many cases a holiday away from home for one week a year). Low income and deprivation were found not to correlate exactly with each other; some families had only been living on low income for a short time, for example, and so still possessed some items regarded as necessities, or were able to draw on savings to help meet their needs.

Different groups of children in Britain are more, or less, at risk of experiencing poverty and social exclusion (Howard *et al.* 2001). There is a disproportionate risk for those in minority ethnic families. In 1999/2000, for example, a third of children in total lived in poverty (defined in this case as living in households with below half average income after housing costs); but this was only just over one in four for white children, whereas for Indian and black children it was over two in five, and for Pakistani and Bangladeshi children it was a massive two thirds (Department of Social Security 2001). The Poverty and Social Exclusion Millennium survey also showed that doing without two or more 'socially perceived necessities' was more likely for those children in minority ethnic families (Gordon *et al.* 2000). Berthoud discusses the multiple reasons for the high risk of poverty for Pakistani and Bangladeshi children (Modood and Berthoud 1997), and Platt uses the most recent figures to explore differences between minority groups as well as those between minority ethnic groups and the majority white population (Platt 2002). The government has also recently examined more closely the circumstances of large families (Willitts and Swales 2003), since half of all poor children live in families with three or more dependent children (Department for Work and Pensions 2003b).

The current UK government has also consistently highlighted worklessness as a cause of poverty. Using a nine-point summary score of 'hardship' based on 80 items (including problem debts, poor housing and essential items families had to do without), researchers found in one recent study that over eight out of ten of all children in non-working households were living in hardship (Marsh *et al.* 2001). Significant factors associated with hardship included not only low income, but also longstanding ill health or disability, caring responsibilities, larger families and belonging to a non-white ethnic group. One in four lone parent families were experiencing 'severe hardship', as were many of those living long term on income support. In 1999/2000, nearly eight out of ten children in workless families were also living in households living below 60 per cent of median income after housing costs (Millar and Ridge 2001).

Depending on the level of social protection given to those out of work, worklessness does not necessarily have to correlate with poverty (Bradshaw 2001a); and paid employment in itself is, of course, no guarantee against poverty, particularly for part-time workers, many of whom are lone parents or disabled people. However, the government's increases in benefits for families on low incomes out of work, as well as the improvements in tax credits for those in work but still on low incomes, have made a real difference to the well-being of both groups. 'Severe hardship' had been reduced amongst families with children by 2001 to only 8 per cent in total – though this still amounts to almost one million children (*Guardian* 2003).

Longitudinal research studies such as the British Household Panel Study, started in 1991, are increasingly adding to our understanding of the dynamics of poverty. Children, especially those of pre-school age, have been found to be particularly at risk of persistent poverty (Berthoud 2001). Almost one in five children were in the bottom 30 per cent of the income distribution for four consecutive years in the 1990s (Department of Social Security 2001). But even short spells in poverty can be devastating, especially at certain times of child development; and recent research has found that children who had experienced income volatility as a result of their parents' transitions in and out of work and benefit were much more likely to be in persistent and severe poverty (Adelman, Middleton and Ashworth 2003). Recurring spells of poverty, even if not continuous, can prevent the accumulation of assets which research shows are important in families keeping their heads above water if their living standards are threatened (Millar and Ridge 2001). And, whilst poverty may persist for many children, it touches many more. The conclusion of a recent comparative study of child poverty was that post-war welfare states in industrialized countries had been better at protecting elderly people from poverty than children (Vleminckx and Smeeding 2001). However, it is clear that performance varies across countries: the reduced risk of poverty for children compared with adults in some European countries demonstrates that an increased risk of poverty is not an inevitable attribute of childhood (Eurostat 2000).

The current UK government is also concerned about social exclusion which, whilst closely connected to poverty, may not overlap entirely with it. Ministers have recently preferred to talk of social exclusion rather than of an 'underclass'. Their preferred definition emphasizes cumulative disadvantage (see, for example, Social Exclusion Unit 2001). The Centre for Analysis of Social Exclusion tried to discover whether all dimensions of social exclusion overlapped for adults, and concluded that a definitive group suffering from all the dimensions and cut off from the rest of society did not exist; on the other hand, many people are affected by each of its components, and some by several, including many children (Hills, Le Grand and Piachaud 2002).

The impact of poverty and social exclusion on children during childhood

It is often argued that the impact of poverty and social exclusion on children is important because of the implications for adulthood, or because it is important to build up the human capital of the country, or because of a problem affecting the future of society as a whole, such as a fertility crisis. Investing in children for any or all of these reasons may be crucial. But unless we are also concerned about the impact of poverty and social exclusion on children's experience of childhood now, we will not be taking the children's rights approach recommended in the United Nations Convention on the Rights of the Child, and we will not be valuing our children in and of themselves (Ruxton and Bennett 2002). The UK government has highlighted the need to focus on children's current poverty, although more frequently it tends to emphasize the longer-term impact of poverty and social exclusion on children's life chances as adults (HM Treasury 2001).

In 1973, the authors of a summary of research about the first cohort study in Britain, the National Child Development Study, wrote:

> This book…shows that the adversities of some boys and girls can extend into almost every aspect of their health, their family circumstances and their educational development. It shows the enormous inequalities of life for 'disadvantaged' compared with 'ordinary' children. (Wedge and Prosser 1973, p.9)

This quotation could just as easily describe the situation today.

There are, however, some problems even in assessing the current impact of poverty and social exclusion on children. We tend to count what we can measure, and what we can measure counts. The 'necessities' in the Poverty and Social Exclusion Millennium survey (Gordon *et al.* 2000) largely focus on consumption. But investment for children in, for instance, family environment, local community, and wider economic and social environment (Piachaud and Sutherland 2001, p.154) may be as, if not more, important, although less easy to measure. It may also be more difficult to measure the more intangible, qualitative aspects of children's well-being, though some efforts are now being made in 'quality of life' assessments (Piachaud 2001). Moreover, data on health, such as low birth weight, are often analysed by social class, rather than by poverty or deprivation. It is also frequently difficult to disentangle whether a particular aspect or dimension of poverty is a cause or a consequence; often, it may be both.

Health is one of the clearest dimensions of the experience of poverty for children. Poverty and social exclusion affect children's physical, mental and emotional state of health, from low birth weight to shorter height and accidents in the home and on the roads (Howard *et al.* 2001). One study revealed that some one in three lone parents and low to moderate income couples had at least one child with a disability or long-term illness (Marsh *et al.* 2001); the researchers were reportedly shocked at the extent of ill health amongst lone parents and their children living on income support, and at the way in which this appeared to increase with length of time spent on benefit.

Poverty and social exclusion also have important implications for child development. Sustained experience of poverty may be particularly damaging for cognitive ability (McCulloch and Joshi 1999). Much research on brain development draws attention to the importance of stimulation and human contact during the first year of life, but also to diet and living standards during pregnancy (Shonkoff and Phillips 2000). Research has found that children from social classes I and II have a 14 per cent advantage over children from social classes IV and V by the age of 22 months (Feinstein 1998). In general, there is increasing emphasis on the impact of poverty and deprivation in the very earliest stages of life (Harker and Kendall 2003).

There are also differences in educational opportunities and attainment between children living in poverty and their peers, including rates of staying on at school, which are emphasized by the government (HM Treasury 2001). Up to 75 per cent of the difference between the highest and lowest attaining GCSE pupils can be explained by factors affecting the pupil intake, including low income; and both children who regularly truant from school and those who are permanently excluded are more likely to come from poorer backgrounds (Howard *et al.* 2001).

There is very often also a link between income poverty and insecure housing conditions. Shelter has reported that 100,000 children in Britain were homeless in the twelve months to July 2002 (*Guardian* 2002), with damaging consequences for their education, behaviour and health. Shelter reported that two in five children had to move schools when they became homeless, and over half of these were bullied for having no friends. Some organizations working with people in poverty have called for more focus on the impact of frequent house moves on children – which may be common for very poor families in particular (Tardieu 1997).

Traditionally, children themselves have not often been asked about their experiences of poverty and social exclusion, even when researchers have investigated adults' experiences (Ruxton and Bennett 2002). Neither have they often been asked about how their well-being, or its opposite, should be measured (Barnes 2001). But innovative research by Tess Ridge (2002) has emphasized the importance of seeing poverty through children's eyes, and has looked at social exclusion from the world of children, not just that of adults. For example, when children living in low-income families miss out on school trips, this can mean not just losing out on educational stimulation, which adults might focus on, but also on shared memories of fun, and on collective social experiences. This can result in such children beginning to feel different, left out, isolated and excluded. Ridge discusses the importance of social participation and inclusion for children, and focuses on the two key concepts of 'fitting in' and 'joining in'.

These insights need to be combined with the better-known quantitative data about deprivation and low income (Millar and Ridge 2001). Focusing on the exclusion from the world of childhood experienced by children living in poverty is *not* the same as comparing the living standards of children in poverty with those of other children (as mooted, for example, in Vleminckx and Smeeding 2001).

This would result in their poverty appearing less serious, for families with children as a group are worse off than other groups in the UK (HM Treasury 1999b). This relative disadvantage of families as a whole should not be used as an excuse to minimize the degree or impact of poverty amongst children (Ruxton and Bennett 2002).

Research from the Family Budget Unit has shown the difference between weekly income support rates and 'low cost but acceptable' family budgets for a series of 'typical' lone-parent and two-parent families with children of different ages (Parker 1998). However, since 1997 the British government has more than doubled the amount paid in income-related benefits for under-11-year-olds in real terms (Department for Work and Pensions 2003b). By October 2000, the differences between income support rates and 'low cost but acceptable' budget for families with young child/ren had already been significantly reduced (Bradshaw 2001b); by now, they are likely to have narrowed even further, or may even have converged.

However, the Family Budget Unit also calculates a more generous budget standard, which it calls 'modest but adequate', for the same 'typical' families. This is likely to exceed means-tested benefit and tax credit rates despite the recent improvements. In addition, the income levels often taken as a 'poverty line' – 60 per cent of contemporary median income after housing costs – were still significantly above income support rates in 2001/02 for a range of families with children (Howard *et al.* 2001, p.65).[1]

The current government has therefore done much to combat child poverty in the UK. The latest available figures show that by 2001/02, it had managed to reduce child poverty measured in terms of relative income by about half a million since it came to office in 1997 (Department for Work and Pensions 2003a; see also Brewer, Clark and Goodman 2002). Hardship, and severe hardship, measured in a broader way also seemed to have declined by 2001 (Marsh and Perry 2003). There is still a long way to go, and child poverty is still much higher than it was in the late 1970s (Barclay 1995); but the trend is clearly in the right direction.

The impact of poverty and social exclusion on children's life chances

An increasingly important area of research in the UK concerns the dynamics of poverty (Walker 1999). Analysis of the circumstances of a cohort of children born in a certain week in March 1958, via the National Child Development

Study, shows that they were more likely to be jobless and to have lower wages at 33, and that teenage pregnancy or early parenthood was also more likely, if they had been poor in childhood (Howard *et al.* 2001, p.139). Other long-term effects of poverty, social exclusion and disadvantage include lower educational attainment and qualifications (Hobcraft 1998; see also Gregg, Harkness and Machin 1999).

However, it is difficult to disentangle cause and effect, especially the impact of income versus family background, and whether and how family, neighbourhood and the quality of local services can intervene between income and outcomes (Plewis *et al.* 2001). It does appear, for example, that educational attainment is an intervening mechanism between parent and child outcomes: income matters, but there is nonetheless quite a wide variation in outcomes leaving this aside (Gregg and Machin 2001). Moreover, there is not necessarily a critical time period for all subsequent outcomes (Plewis *et al.* 2001). Income and other aspects of disadvantage in childhood may affect different outcomes in adulthood. For example, family income levels at ages nought to five may have a strong influence on educational progress, but much less impact on some health and behavioural outcomes (Duncan *et al.* 2001); and subsequent events also undermine, or build on, earlier influences (Plewis *et al.* 2001).

In addition, some commentators on brain science have begun to warn against determinism, and emphasise the multiple factors that influence child development (Wilson 2002). The fact that not all outcomes are inevitable (Hobcraft 1998) is a hopeful finding – and also means that, while acknowledging the weight of the structural factors underlying poverty, it is also important to recognize that pulling policy levers in a mechanistic way does not guarantee success.

However, the relationship of family income in childhood to outcomes in adulthood appears to have increased in importance between the two British cohorts born in 1958 and 1970 (Gregg and Machin 2001). It is difficult to know what effect the massive increase in inequality between the late 1970s and early to mid 1990s had on parents living in poverty and their children – following, as it did, a period of increasing social mobility. However, it is likely that parents were no longer able to believe that, even if they themselves had not escaped poverty, their children might be able to do so. What impact would this have had on the hopes and aspirations of families?

In parallel to the child-centred research on children's current experiences of poverty and social exclusion (Ridge 2002), recent research based on the British Youth Panel has also started to examine the feelings and thoughts of children and young people living in poverty about their own futures. Living in poverty at the time made it more likely that 11- to 15-year-olds would play truant, expect to leave school at age 16, not want to become parents themselves, think that health was a matter of luck, be inclined to feel a failure, and have low self-esteem (Ermisch, Francesconi and Pevalin 2001).

The impact of poverty and social exclusion on parents and families

Low-income parents often feel that bringing up children is their most important role in life. But they often feel undermined in that role, because of the lack of resources with which to give their children what they regard as a decent upbringing (Cohen *et al.* 1992). As one author puts it succinctly, 'Living on low income in a run-down neighbourhood does not make it impossible to be the affectionate, authoritative parent of healthy, sociable children. But it does, undeniably, make it more difficult' (Utting 1995).

One project run by an international human rights organization working with families living in poverty tried to investigate what working in partnership with parents might mean in practice. It described participating parents as those

> ...whose lives seemed...to have been shaped by a long history of poverty that had sapped their health, limited their horizons, and greatly affected their capacity to learn. Their poverty had brought exclusion from school life, from employment and training, from secure housing and – when children were put in care and then often placed for adoption – from family life itself. (ATD Fourth World 1996, p.12)

These characteristics of parents living in poverty who were in touch with social services were echoed by a speaker at a meeting of the All Party Parliamentary Group on Poverty, which creates an avenue for people with direct experience of poverty to engage in dialogue with ministers and members of the Westminster parliament. She was taking part in an exercise designed to contribute to the current government's consultation about the future definition and measurement of child poverty (Department for Work and Pensions 2002). Participants were asked to start by saying 'poverty is...'. She said:

> Poverty is...
>
> ...seeing foster-parents get so much money to buy my children the things I could never afford to buy them;
>
> ...having all the same dreams for the future that everyone else has, but no way on earth to make them come true;

…having no choice of where we live, what school the kids go to or what kind of job we get;

…needing help, but being too scared of being judged an unfit mother to ask for it;

…telling my whole life story over and over again, just to get what I'm entitled to;

…having not one person to talk to who isn't paid to listen;

…being told that I have nothing to offer my own child, and believing it – then. (Participant in a meeting of the All Party Parliamentary Group on Poverty, 18 June 2002)

Child welfare policy in Britain promotes partnership and co-operative relationships with parents or other caregivers, though rightly keeping the focus on the child. It also recognizes that services and support to parents are often the best way of helping children in need; and it emphasizes building on the strengths and resources within the family, as well as identifying difficulties (Department of Health, Department for Education and Skills and Home Office 2000). This echoes the messages coming from these parents.

Poverty and social exclusion: Communities

British social workers are advised that the assessment of children in need should extend to take account of wider family and environmental factors (Department of Health, Department for Education and Skills and Home Office 2000). But is it clear what the 'neighbourhood' or 'community' might mean in this context? Recently, some researchers have suggested that factors such as travel to work – or travel to school – may be more appropriate than the traditional administrative entities when considering issues of child poverty (Plewis *et al.* 2001). Academic analysis may be made more difficult if researchers use area boundaries of greater relevance to children living in poverty themselves. But these may be the very areas (the 'run-down neighbourhoods' mentioned by David Utting (1995, p.41) which people living in poverty often say are labelled and criticized, thereby negatively affecting their identity and self esteem.

It is widely believed that family influences on child outcomes are stronger than the influence of areas – though the evidence is in fact not very strong (McCulloch and Joshi 2001). However, the polarization of neighbourhoods in the UK is generally agreed to have been one of the most damaging consequences of the increase in inequality between the late 1970s and the early to mid 1990s, creating a 'divided Britain' (Barclay 1995). Researchers who have devised an index of childhood deprivation have found that it varies from a few percentage points in some of the richest areas in England to over 90 per cent in some of the poorest areas in Scotland (Noble *et al.* 2001). They describe the latter as 'intense geographical concentration of poor children'.

It may be assumed that children living in such 'intense geographical concentration' have a more difficult childhood. However, our understanding of the relative importance of this 'area effect', compared with the importance of family background and/or income level, is not yet very advanced; and the impact of the 'area effect' is controversial (Kleinman 1999). Within the complex collection of factors associated with 'area', it is also difficult to know whether it is the neighbourhood itself that is more important, or more specific issues such as the quality of the local school, or services more generally (Plewis *et al.* 2001). Certainly the current government has begun to pay more attention to the marked pattern of poor neighbourhoods getting a poorer quality of services. This has been a particular focus of its national neighbourhood renewal strategy for England (Social Exclusion Unit 2001) and associated policies for the devolved administrations. Disadvantaged areas have also been the beneficiaries of the government's programme of Sure Start projects for boosting the health, cognitive abilities and social skills of pre-school children and the more recent plans for bringing a range of children's services together in new children's centres (HM Treasury 2002).

It is important to remember, however, that many children living in poverty do not live in poor areas (Kleinman 1999). Moreover, a 'community' can be a community of interest, and/or a social grouping, rather than a collection of people living in a particular geographical area. The initial and core assessment records (Cleaver and Walker 2004) introduced to support the implementation of the Framework for the Assessment of Children in Need and their Families require social workers to explore the relationship between the child's developmental needs (based on the seven dimensions used in the Looking After Children (LAC) schedules), the dimensions of parenting capacity, and family and environmental factors. Whilst these records prompt questions about ethnic and immigration status, and about 'community' (Department of Health, Department for Education and Skills and Home Office 2000), they do not enquire into (for example) the idea of a 'community' of people from a particular ethnic background, and what impact belonging to such a community may have on a child or family. The experience of poverty may in practice be very different if lived through a certain filter of culture and/or ethnicity, as well as varying in different regions of the country, and in urban versus rural areas (Plewis *et al.* 2001).

Parents and children as active agents in trying to combat poverty

The term 'poverty' is itself often rejected by people living in poverty themselves, in part because of its negative connotations – as is the label of 'deprived' or 'disadvantaged' area (Beresford *et al.* 1999). At a more practical level, however, the real extent of child poverty depends on how effectively household income reaches children – and hence is dependent on parents' actions (Plewis *et al.* 2001).

Evidence on the efforts of parents, especially mothers, to try to protect their children from the impact of poverty is well known (Howard *et al.* 2001, p.136). Parents have been found to spend far more on their children than allowed for in the income support scale rates at the time (Middleton, Ashworth and Braithwaite 1997); they were therefore spending less on themselves. The Poverty and Social Exclusion Millennium survey showed a higher percentage (26%) of the population in general experiencing poverty (defined as being deprived of two 'socially perceived necessities') than was the case for children (18%) – confirming other evidence that children may be protected to some extent, though not completely, from poverty by their parents or other care givers (Gordon *et al.* 2000). This research suggests that mothers also try to protect their partners (see also Millar and Ridge 2001), and often take on the burden of restricting parental spending on themselves (Goode, Callender and Lister 1998). The depth of parental poverty that results from these efforts will not be highlighted in the official statistics on low income, because the figures assume equal sharing of resources within the household between its members (Department for Work and Pensions 2003a). This is a useful reminder that every coping strategy has costs – and that these often fall on women.

Middleton and her colleagues (1997) also point out that contributions to children's standard of living are also made from outside the immediate family. Even if this may of necessity be more limited for those on low income, grandparents and others may also be trying to cushion the impact of poverty on children. The wider family is rightly recognized as a potential resource in the Framework for the Assessment of Children in Need and their Families (Department of Health, Department for Education and Skills and Home Office 2000).

However, children themselves can also be involved in attempting to mitigate the impact of poverty on the family. Whilst the moderation of demands and expectations ('pester power') by children in low-income families because of their knowledge of their parents' financial situation has been called 'learning to be poor' by some researchers (Shropshire and Middleton 1999), Ridge sees this as a more active process. She describes children trying to manage the situation and protect their parents, just as their parents try to protect them; so, for example, they may 'self censor' the delivery of letters from school proposing expensive trips or asking for so-called 'voluntary' contributions towards school expenses (Ridge 2002; see also Tanner *et al.* 2003).

Of course, such strategies by parents or children may backfire. For example, parents want to ensure that their children are not seen as different, and so they try hard to maintain a 'mainstream' diet. In addition, they cannot afford to experiment, because they will be unable to afford to replace uneaten food (Dobson *et al.* 1994). Both these factors may result in a more restricted, less varied diet for their children. Parents may keep their children at home, to try to protect them from being bullied at school, perhaps because they do not possess the latest brand label clothes, or because they smell; they and/or their children may then be punished for truancy.

And despite their best efforts, children and their parents can, of course, be overwhelmed by poverty. An overview of 31 qualitative studies of low-income families showed that most people progressed from acute worry to 'coping', and did learn to budget their money with experience. But it also showed that often the wear and tear of the sheer daily grind of living in poverty led in the long term to depression and even despair (Kempson 1996). In this context, it is useful to be reminded that both parents and children are actively engaged in a constant struggle to cope with, and minimize, the effects of poverty on their own lives and on those of the people nearest and dearest to them.

An alternative to the 'deficit model'

This is a useful reminder in part because it acts as a corrective to the 'deficit model' of parents living in poverty and involved with social services, which is all too easily adopted – though also resisted strenuously – in social work practice and elsewhere. In other words, families in this situation can often be seen as having nothing positive to offer, but instead are seen as 'people in endless need, many of whom end up believing that they have nothing to say and nothing to contribute, even to their own future' (ATD Fourth World 1996).

This view may also be extended to people living in poverty as a whole. Tony Blair, addressing the National Council for Voluntary Organizations, once talked of his desire to 'rehabilitate do-gooding'. But his speech was solely about one-way traffic, with no hint of potential reciprocity. Those living in poverty were not seen as having anything to give to society as a whole, or anything to teach – about the effects of the denial of human rights, about endurance, about the tenacity of family links and love across enormous gulfs, about the sheer bloody-mindedness of keeping going in the face of overwhelming odds.

This is not to deny that people living long term in poverty may be very damaged by that experience, as well as by others. The Chancellor of the Exchequer, Gordon Brown, is fond of saying that child poverty is a 'scar on Britain's soul' (Brown 1999). But poverty can scar the souls of those living it as well. In addition, it may not be easy for professional workers to recognize and build on the positive qualities of families involved with social services, especially when child protection issues are involved – though, as the Department of Health itself says, partnership is possible even in these situations (Department of Health, Department for Education and Skills and Home Office 2000).

A wider and highly topical issue is at stake here, too: user involvement in services. As Chapters 7, 8 and 9 show, this is beginning to be taken more seriously – though it is often more in evidence, and more familiar, in services for disabled people, in part due to pressure from the disabled people's movement (Beresford 2002). It is less common in family and children's services to date, although some initiatives are now under way (by, for example, such groups as the 'Making Research Count' network: www.uea.ac.uk/swk/research/mrc/welcome.htm). This trend is very welcome, and its momentum is now irresistible: 'evidence-based' policy and practice must now increasingly include evidence from users in order to be credible.

It is important also, of course, to see people living in poverty in the round – not only as users of social services, but with something to say about their poverty and about other issues in society, and with a right to culture, and beauty, and political participation, as well as a right to a 'user' voice in the development of the services they use.

Powerlessness and 'voice poverty'

The perspective described above is similar to the view taken by those involved in international development. As Dereje Wordofa, an Oxfam staff member, told the All Party Parliamentary Group on Poverty in 2002, following innovative work in Uganda which focused clearly on the perceptions of people living in poverty themselves: 'We found that poverty is about powerlessness most of all – more than about not having money, jobs, services, or meeting basic needs. It is the inability to do anything about it…' Powerlessness is a key element of poverty – as is 'voice poverty', the experience of not having one's voice or views taken into account by policy makers and decision takers with power over one's life. The Commission on

Poverty, Participation and Power – a unique commission, made up of half people from 'public life' and half people with direct experience of poverty – was set up recently by anti-poverty organizations to investigate barriers to participation in decision-making processes faced by those living in poverty in the UK. It found that the extent of alienation and distrust of the 'powers that be' felt by people in poverty cannot be underestimated.

Trying to tackle that alienation and sense of powerlessness, however, requires not just overcoming many practical barriers but also basing any strategy on respect for those living in poverty. Such respect is not always apparent in public rhetoric, which includes statements about 'dependency', the 'something for nothing welfare state' and other such phrases. As one grassroots member of the Commission said with grim humour: 'it's not just that these voices are harder to hear; some people have got their fingers in their ears' (Commission on Poverty, Participation and Power 2000).

The Commission was an experiment involving adults with direct experience of poverty. There are also increasing numbers of initiatives, however, which involve children defining their well-being and happiness for themselves, rather than just via measures for adults or whole families (Currie 2001). In addition, children's voices are increasingly being heard. Many voluntary organizations, especially those with a longstanding children's rights perspective, are encouraging children to voice their views about standards of services and about their own futures (see examples cited in Ruxton and Bennett 2002). The current government has supported a national organization for young people in care organized by young people in care themselves (A National Voice). And the Children and Young People's Unit has developed a positive stance on participation which should be disseminated across government departments (Children and Young People's Unit 2001): see Chapter 3. Whilst progress is still patchy and inconsistent, the principle that children should be involved in the development of services and in wider debates, which is recognized within the United Nations Convention on Children's Rights, is gradually gaining acceptance.

Conclusions

Social services staff may be drawn in by the current government to help it achieve its targets on reducing child poverty – targets which, whilst recognizing low income as key, also cover much wider areas (Department for Work and Pensions 2003b). In particular, social workers may be asked to help increase the take up of means-tested benefits and tax credits. The Framework for the Assessment of

Children in Need and their Families already draws attention to the importance of checking that families have access to all the benefits to which they are entitled (Department of Health, Department for Education and Skills and Home Office 2000). The government will need to overcome the traditional wariness among social workers in the UK about involvement in social security provision and welfare rights activities if it wishes to coopt them in this endeavour.

However, another way in which social workers and others working with children in need may be drawn into cooperation with the government's strategy is through the increasing emphasis within current policy initiatives on behaviour – especially parenting skills. There is a growing number of examples in which entitlement to income is, or may become, conditional on fulfilling certain parental or other roles. In current pilots, educational maintenance allowances are given only to those over-16s who attend classes regularly. The Sure Start maternity payment (not in practice linked to the Sure Start initiative described above) is only available to those women who make contact with a health professional; so, for example, anyone hiding a pregnancy for fear of the baby being taken into care may not receive a lump sum until at least after the birth. A proposal was put forward recently that child benefit be withdrawn from parents whose children persistently truant from school, though this was eventually dropped. (*Observer* 2002). In this respect, social policy for children and families in the UK is drawing closer to the North American model (see Chapter 4).

Proponents of conditionality would argue that the arguments supporting it are particularly compelling when the welfare of someone else, rather than solely the recipient of payments, is at stake – and that therefore parents are a particularly appropriate group for this approach. In addition, they would argue that the conditions imposed are intended to increase freedom and choices in the longer term for parents and/or their children, even if these may be restricted in the short term.

On the other hand, there is a tension between the paternalistic nature of conditionality (Deacon 2002) and the emphasis by many people living in poverty on their sense of powerlessness, and their view that their lives are already controlled by those who wield power (Commission on Poverty, Participation and Power 2000).

The government may be more likely to wield the weapon of withdrawal of benefits when it is finding it difficult to affect outcomes by other means. If social services workers are uneasy about any role they may be asked to perform in relation to the implementation of such measures or their monitoring for compliance, it is therefore in their interests to demonstrate that other ways of working together in cooperation with children in need and their parents can be effective.

These relationships will need to be rooted in respect (Lister 2002), and based on listening to children and parents living in poverty. Building the kind of partnerships envisaged by the Children Act 1989 requires trust, and truth, but also time. Many people in poverty feel betrayed by an endless series of short-term projects, and need funding and structures which have been set up to continue (Utting 1998). Many feel let down by professionals who, however understandably, have moved on and out of their lives. Long-term commitment – in the good times, too, as well as in the bad – is crucial (ATD Fourth World 1996).

Moreover, these initiatives can also go beyond individual relationships. Those working with children in need and their parents could encourage the coming together of people in touch with social services, and support wider groups of people living in poverty and their organizations to develop a collective voice. Coming together, rather than having to deal with professionals as isolated individuals, is the crucial ingredient for a shift in power. This should include methods of holding the authorities to account in constructively critical ways and extending the principle of user involvement in services to include an ongoing input into the monitoring of professional practice.

There is also a key role of witness. Professionals, together with the people in poverty with whom they work, could help convey core messages to the government and the general public. These messages would include both a clear picture of the impact of poverty and social exclusion on children, and evidence of how exclusionary mechanisms work. They would include the need for a multi-pronged strategy to tackle child poverty successfully, which recognizes both the centrality of income and the relevance of the wider dimensions of powerlessness and 'voice poverty'. These messages would emphasize that prevention is better than cure and highlight the need to value the voice of people in poverty and their organizations in influencing the overall shape and priorities of action against poverty and social exclusion, including the nature of interventions affecting the lives of children in need and their families. Finally, and just as importantly, such messages would need to continue to ensure that government spokespeople and others with a public platform maintain their responsibility to show respect in their public pronouncements about people living in poverty and struggling to combat it every day. 'Especially in the affluent countries of the industrialised world, there are no valid excuses to prevent governments from having a low child poverty rate' (Vleminckx and Smeeding 2001, p.543).

Acknowledgements

Many thanks to Saul Becker and Ann Buchanan for valuable information and guidance; the opinions expressed and any errors are, of course, my responsibility.

Note

1   The McClements equivalence scale used in official government statistics of low income is often said to underestimate the extent of poverty amongst younger children; it may also therefore underestimate the impact of recent government measures on reducing that poverty (Berthoud 2001; Brewer *et al.* 2002; Sutherland 2001). Equivalence scales are a way of trying to ensure that like is compared with like – adjusting income levels to take account of how many people have to share that income in different households or families. But there are different equivalence scales in use, which give different weights to additional adults and/or children of different ages.

Chapter 3

Policies in the UK to Promote the Well-being of Children

Gillian Pugh

This chapter reviews the very considerable policy agenda introduced by the New Labour government in Britain since 1997. It identifies a growing focus on children's overall well-being and an understanding of the risk and protective factors to be taken into account in meeting children's needs. Driven by a commitment to reducing child poverty, a number of other policy themes are discussed, particularly those which are central to the Green Paper *Every Child Matters* published in 2003: prevention, early intervention, a focus on families and parenting, better accountability and integration nationally and locally, and reform of the workforce. Some specific initiatives are discussed and policy outcomes assessed.

The well-being of children

The New Labour UK government, elected in 1997, is one that has put children, young people and families high on its agenda. It also claims to be developing policies and services on the basis of evidence of 'what works'. This chapter therefore starts with a very brief review of current trends in relation to the well-being of children, before going on to explore policies and what, if any, impact they have had.

In many respects, children in the UK have never had it so good. Compared with their parents children are, on average, better educated, physically healthier and taller, they have fewer accidents, go on more holidays and have more spending money. They live in a time of rapid and accelerating change, when television and the internet create instant access to all parts of the globe, when long distance travel is commonplace, and when the media creates a universal youth culture to which millions of children and young people aspire.

But the news is not all good. Not all children benefit equally from this increased wealth, and the gap between those who have and those who do not is only slowly reducing, with nearly one in three children still living on or below the poverty line (Bradshaw 2002). There are heavy pressures on children and young people to conform and to succeed, and increasing levels of depression and mental illness. The growing requirement for skills and qualifications in the employment market further disadvantages those who have left school with few of either. There are worrying increases in asthma and obesity. Parents are so concerned about the dangers of traffic and possible abduction that many have become over-protective of their children, limiting opportunities for them to play outside or walk to school on their own.

Family life is also changing. Two thirds of children are born outside marriage, and one in five live in a lone parent family. One in four children will experience their parents' divorce, and two thirds of these children will lose touch with their fathers. Families are getting smaller, and more geographically dispersed, often leading to a sense of isolation for parents and children alike.

A national consultation recently showed that children and young people saw their family and friends as the most important influence on achieving good outcomes (Department for Education and Skills 2001). They wanted more play and leisure facilities in local communities; to be free from bullying; to be and feel safe, but not to feel restricted; to be consulted on issues that affected their lives, but not formally involved in community life. They said they valued life skills as well as formal educational qualifications; that they wanted childhood valued for itself and not just as a preparation for the future; and that they wanted to be listened to and respected. A survey of children in London raised many of the same issues, together with the wish for cheaper and better public transport; cleaner and safer streets; someone there for them when they wanted help; more say in what happens in schools; and the wish to be taken more seriously (Sharpe 2002).

What these children's views illustrate very clearly is that wellness or well-being is both an individual and collective concept, something that is measured in terms of individual lives, but is very often delivered through families and communities. This ecological approach, which grounds work with children and young people in their families, and within the community and the culture in which they are growing up, has been central in informing policy. An analysis of key risk factors that are likely to have an adverse effect on children's development, and the corresponding protective factors that we know can help to develop the resilience that they will require if they are to thrive were key to the Green Paper *Every Child Matters* (Department for Education and Skills 2003d). These can be summarized as:

- an adequate standard of living

- a temperament/disposition for a child that encourages care giving, leading to high self esteem, sociability and autonomy, the ability to solve problems, and an internal locus of control

- dependable care givers, where children can grow up in a family with one or two caring adults, who have positive and appropriate child-rearing practices

- networks of community support, including a pro-social peer group, high quality early education, and schools where children are valued and learning is encouraged.

Better outcomes for all children

Although the primary focus of this book is the well-being of vulnerable children, it is preferable to start from a concept of entitlement for all. What do we want to achieve for *all* children, and what do we then need to do to facilitate access for more vulnerable children to these entitlements? Drawing on promising examples from both the US and the UK, a report published in 2001 outlined an approach which focused on the outcomes or results that we wanted services to deliver, and on the processes by which this could be done (Utting, Rose and Pugh 2001). Central to these processes was a much clearer understanding of what overall outcomes should be sought and what quantifiable improvements in children's welfare and well-being would be required in order to achieve them (outcomes rather than inputs or outputs). This approach also built on community collaboration and participation by families and children in achieving these results, and innovative ways of creating joint budgets to fund the strategies. It was argued that for this approach to work, it would be necessary to move away from the silos in which people currently work, the individual departmental targets and the separate collection of data, towards a centrally collected set of high level data, and a set of overall outline indicators that could be worked towards in local communities' young people.

This work has informed the 2003 Green Paper *Every Child Matters* which is discussed below and the 2004 Children's Act and Friedman, Garnett and

Pinnock (see Chapter 16) describe in some detail how this approach has been implemented as a specific programme in an English council.

The UK government agenda

Since 1997, a considerable number of priorities in the government's policy agenda are those which impact on the lives of children and families. These include:

1. *Reducing child poverty.* The target set in 1999 was to eradicate child poverty in twenty years and halve it in ten through additional financial support for all families and targeted benefits for those most in need. The reduction of poverty is absolutely fundamental to achieving improvements in other areas. The strong association between poverty and poor physical and mental health, low educational attainment, behavioural difficulties, truancy and criminal activity has been proved through numerous studies. Because of its importance, this key policy area has already been discussed in some detail by Bennett in Chapter 2 and is not explored further here.

2. *Improving support for families. Supporting Families* (Home Office 1998) outlines policies in this area. It is based on an understanding of children's need for stability and security, and on the government's role in helping parents to support their children. The paper pursued a number of different policy directions:

    - access to support (through the establishment of schemes such as Sure Start)
    - better financial support
    - helping families balance work and home
    - strengthening marriage
    - better support for serious problems.

    Quinton (see Chapter 10) discusses the role of parents and describes the findings of a major national research initiative designed to explore how they might best be supported. Parents are integral to any discussion of children's well-being. The UK Government's 2002 spending review recognized this when it established a new £25m Parenting Fund (Department for Education and Skills and HM Treasury 2003). There is, however, some concern at the strong emphasis within the government's support of parenting programmes on punishing parents for their children's misbehaviour or 'anti-social behaviour' (see also Chapter 2).

3. *Strengthening communities.* There is a focus on strengthening communities through local neighbourhood renewal strategies, and through many of the child and family centred programmes noted below.

4. *Reducing social exclusion.* Reducing social exclusion focuses on the regeneration of inner city areas, truancy, homelessness and teenage pregnancy. The 2002 spending review included a cross-cutting review of children at risk of social exclusion – and there is now an even stronger emphasis on prevention, with the requirement on all local authorities to establish preventive strategies by autumn 2003.

5. *Improving health.* This is primarily to be achieved through the implementation of the National Health Service Plan (Department of Health 2000b). In relation to children this has included setting up a Children's Taskforce at central government level with a remit to create a National Service Framework for Children (Department of Health 2004), and linking into other policy initiatives such as Quality Protects (www.dfes.gov.uk/qualityprotects), child and adolescent mental health services, adoption, and children with disabilities. These are discussed further below.

6. *Raising education standards.* The commitment to raising standards is through expanding nursery education, through reducing class sizes, and through introducing standards for literacy and numeracy.

7. *Improving access to work.* This is seen as a key plank in the anti-poverty strategy, and is a key driver behind the expansion of childcare provision as a means of enabling more parents to return to work.

8. *Basing services on:*

    (a) what consumers want, rather than what service providers think they should have

    (b) evidence of what works, with a strong emphasis on the evaluation of new initiatives.

9. *Joined up thinking and joined up services.* This has driven all policy development in the New Labour government, and was emphasized again in the 2002 Spending Review. It underpins most of the initiatives discussed below, and is a central focus of the Green Paper *Every Child Matters* (Department for Education and Skills 2003d).

10. *Participation of children and young people in decision making.* This is building on the commitment within the Children Act 1989 to promote the best interests of the child and giving children a voice in decisions that affect their lives.

How is the government's agenda being taken forward?

During the first seven years of a New Labour government there has been a veritable blizzard of new initiatives and programmes emanating from every department that has even a passing interest in children. Amongst the most notable of these have been the National Childcare Strategy, including Sure Start and Children's Centres, the Children's Fund, and Quality Protects, the Connexions service and broader programmes such as New Deal for Communities and Neighbourhood Renewal. But it is the Green Paper *Every Child Matters* (2003), described by the Prime Minister at its launch as the most important document relating to children for over 30 years, and the 2004 Children Act that is likely to have the biggest impact on changing both the culture and the organization of children's services in the UK.

The Green Paper team was set up in response to the Laming report (2003)[1] and the team was charged with focusing their attention on children at risk. However, following active dialogue with those working in the field, the report has taken prevention as its starting point, and has accepted the view that to support *all* children better through well coordinated mainstream services is more likely to benefit those in need and at risk than a separate child protection service. The five key themes of the report are strong foundations in the early years; a stronger focus on parenting and families; earlier intervention and effective protection; better accountability and integration locally, regionally and nationally; and reform of the workforce.

The proposals are far reaching in a number of ways, underpinned as they are by a commitment to more effective coordination at every level, from government, through commissioning of services, to delivery in local communities. A Minister for children, young people and families now heads up a children and families directorate within the Department for Education and Skills, which has brought within its remit government responsibilities for children's social care, family policy, childcare law, Sure Start, the Children's Fund and Connexions, though not as yet children's health, youth justice or schools. At local level, some 35 local authorities are piloting children's trusts, bringing together education and social services and, in time, health, the police and the voluntary sector to commission services across the board. These will build on the children and young people's strategic partnerships that have already been set up in many parts of the country (see Association of Directors of Social Services 2002b). There are to be directors of children's services in every local authority, and an elected politician with responsibility for the children's agenda.

The model of 'joined up' service delivery which has been pioneered through children's centres is to be extended into schools, which will be central to the multi-agency teams which are intended to ensure that children do not fall through the welfare net. There are to be a common assessment framework and inspection system, a single identification number for each child, and a lead professional for any child known to more than one specialist service.

The very considerable shortfall in staff appropriately qualified to work with children and young people is being addressed through the establishment of a Children's Workforce Development Council, which will also look at the potential of common core training and continuing professional development for all those who work with children.

From the perspective of children and young people perhaps one of the most encouraging developments is the recognition that five key outcomes really matter for their well-being. Building on the work of Utting *et al.* (2001) and the Children and Young People's Unit (2001), the five areas identified by the Green Paper, to which service providers must respond in an integrated way, are as follows:

- being healthy: enjoying good physical and mental health and living a healthy life style

- staying safe: being protected from harm and neglect and growing up able to look after themselves

- enjoying and achieving: getting the most out of life and developing broad skills for adulthood

- making a positive contribution: to the community and to society and not engaging in anti-social or offending behaviour

- economic well-being: overcoming socio-economic disadvantages to achieve their full potential in life.

The Green Paper also responded to intensive lobbying by announcing the appointment of a children's rights commissioner for England, in line with similar appointments in Scotland, Wales and Northern Ireland.

Prior to the publication of the Green Paper, the Department of Health had been leading on the Framework for the Assessment of Children in Need and their Families (Department of Health, Department for Education and Skills and Home Office 2000). This significant piece of work to support professionals assessing children under Part III of the Children Act 1989 has already been described in Chapter 1. The assessment triangle (see Figure 3.1) demonstrates the interrelationship of the three domains of children's developmental needs, parenting capacity and family and environmental factors. It provides a powerful statement of the need to recognize the full context of children's lives, which is now the basis for a more integrated approach to work with children and their families (Department of Health 2002c) and which will feed into the work required by the Green Paper *Every Child Matters* and the Children Act 2004.

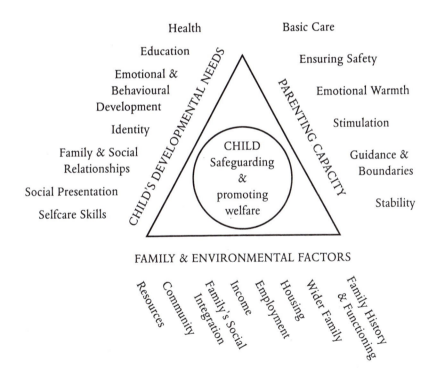

Figure 3.1: The Assessment Framework

Another 'joined up' solution is being driven by the Department of Health, which has set up the Children's Taskforce to oversee the implementation of the NHS Plan for children and to work towards achieving the Public Service Agreement targets which seek to improve the life chances of children in care.

One of the means by which this taskforce hopes to meet its objectives is the publication of a Children's National Service Framework (NSF) to improve the lives and health of children and young people through the delivery of appropriate, integrated, effective, evidence-based and needs-led services and to improve the experiences and satisfaction of children, young people and their carers with the services provided for them. The NSF (Department of Health, Department for Education and Skills 2004) will lay down standards, drawing on a substantial group of external experts, in a number of key areas: children needing acute/hospital services; maternity; mental health and psychological well-being; children in special circumstances; disabled children; and healthy children and young people.

It will be critical to the ambitious intentions of the Green Paper that this work on children's health is fully integrated into the increasingly joined up mainstream children's agenda.

So there has been no shortage of childcare experts sitting in darkened rooms thinking about children's services. But what has been delivered on the ground?

Three key initiatives

Three of the most substantial initiatives, all of which reflect a number of the strands of the policy agenda, are worthy of a closer look.

National childcare strategy

Given the importance of effective support and, if necessary, intervention in the early years, the increased commitment of government to funding mainstream services for young children is very welcome. In the past five years nursery education has been made available to all three- and four-year-olds, a network of 'early excellence centres' (now renamed children's centres) has been set up providing nursery education, day care and support for parents, there has been a huge expansion of after school provision, and some additional childcare support for parents wishing to return to work. The 2004 Spending Review substantially increased the budget and targeted the creation of 2,500 children's centres and an extended role for schools.

The longitudinal Effective Provision of Preschool Education (EPPE) project, following the progress and development of 3,000 children from three to eight, is coming up with some compelling evidence on the effectiveness of high quality early years centres on children's educational attainment and on their behaviour and social adjustment (EPPE 2004). There is still a long way to go, but progress has been substantial.

But it is probably the Sure Start initiative that has attracted the most attention, with its overall aim of improving the health and well-being of families and children under four, particularly those who are disadvantaged, so that children have greater opportunity to flourish at school. There are over 500 Sure Start schemes in the most disadvantaged areas of the UK, each providing services for about 1,000 children, about 16 per cent of children under four, and a third of all children living in poverty. All programmes are built on existing statutory and voluntary sector services, are developed by partnerships of local professionals and parents, and are working towards the same public service agreements:

- improving social and emotional development
- improving health
- improving children's ability to learn
- strengthening families and communities.

Sure Start was set up as a direct result of the government's first cross-cutting spending review – of services for children under eight – and in almost every respect built on the advice that those working in the field gave to an initially sceptical Treasury. There was also a long process of consultation, involving huge numbers of people across the country and with different levels of responsibility, and it really was multi-agency, from Cabinet Ministers down to grass roots workers.

Although a national programme, each scheme is required to develop in response to local need, but to deliver a number of core services – outreach and home visiting, support for families, support for play and learning experiences for children, community-based health care, and support for children with special needs. There is a also a substantial evaluation programme in place, which has recently published its first report (Department for Education and Skills 2002), pointing both to early successes but also the challenges of working in this multi-agency way to reach the most disadvantaged families. There is also a commitment to affect the way in which mainstream services are delivered.

Children's Fund

The Children's Fund, available to every local authority for schemes for children aged 5 to 13, is also part of the government's drive towards better coordinated preventive services. This Fund also puts an emphasis on joint working, with a local partnership taking responsibility for planning and delivering the services. Most of the new funding has gone into services aimed at parents or families; these include parent education, home–school liaison, information and advice services, advocacy support and family learning.

There is also a strong emphasis on crime prevention, particularly since the Children's Fund incorporated the 22 On Track projects, another initiative to fund local services, originally set up by the Home Office to reduce delinquency. Crime prevention was re-emphasized following the 2002 Spending Review, and 25 per cent of funding is now required to target reducing offending behaviour.

The selection criteria for all of the projects within this Fund include partnership with the voluntary sector, consultation with parents and children, and the promotion of community cohesion and proven benefits to a multi-cultural society. In time, all partnerships must have in place identification, referral and tracking systems for all children and young people at risk.

There is an extensive evaluation programme in place, but it is too early to make any claims for its success. There have been challenges in getting the projects up and running and some have already closed due to cutbacks in funding. However, the Every Child Matters agenda should ensure that the experience of the projects set up under this Fund are built on, and discussions are already underway as to how the projects can be 'mainstreamed'.

Quality Protects

This five-year programme, established by the Department of Health in 1999, aimed to improve the life chances of children in care. As Frank Dobson, Secretary of State with responsibility for social services, said in his letter to the leaders of all councils, 'You should care for these children as if they were your own.' This concept of corporate parenting included specific targets for reducing the number of placement changes for children in care, ensuring annual health assessments, improving levels of education, training and employment, and improving educational qualifications.

There is some evidence of progress (see *Children Act Report 2002* (Department for Education and Skills 2003c). There is new legislation – the Children (Leaving Care) Act 2000 and the Adoption and Children Act 2002. The numbers of children in care at any one time have not decreased over the last ten years, but there has been some reduction in the frequency of moves. There has been some increase in the number of children adopted, particularly younger children, and fewer registrations on the child protection registers. But the educational achievement of looked after children continues to be unacceptably low, and the little data that there is provides disturbing reading in relation to the mental health of children and young people in care or accommodation (Meltzer *et al.* 2003).

Participation

The other area in which there has been considerable debate and some movement is participation of and consultation with children and young people. Pioneered in the field in which there is the greatest need – children and young people looked after – government policy has over the past five years included an increasingly strong commitment to seeking the views of all young people, for example the Children and Young People's Unit document *Learning to Listen* (Department for Education and Skills 2001) and the standards for advocacy services (Department of Health 2002d). There is also a Children's Rights Director, although in England this post has until recently only been for looked after children. The proposals for a children's commissioner, similar to those in Wales, Scotland and Northern Ireland, have been welcomed.

Outcomes

The government's agenda is an ambitious one and, as has been noted above, it is early days to be able to make any definitive judgements about whether or not policies have been effective. Looking specifically at the impact of New Labours' policies for children and young people, the journal *Children & Society* (Pugh and Parton 2003) includes articles from a number of distinguished academics and policy commentators. It points to the many tensions and ambiguities in current policy and confirms that, whilst there has been no shortage of activity, it is still too early to assess the effectiveness of much of what has been put in place. In some areas, notably education and youth justice, Tomlinson (2003) and D. Smith (2003) argue that the policies leave much to be desired and are actually increasing existing divisions within society.

In other areas, notably early education (Pugh 2003) and children with disabilities (Russell 2003), there is a greater sense of achievement. Kurtz (2003) points out, in relation to children's health and well-being, how difficult it is to relate changes in health to specific policies in the short term, but she applauds the government's attempts to base policy on evidence of what works. Perhaps most interesting for this chapter is the paper by Axford, Little and Morpeth (2003) on services for children in need. They note that most of the new initiatives are not headed up by the Department of Health, whose responsibility these children have traditionally been, and that it is teachers and health workers rather than social workers to whom families refer themselves. They also conclude that there are limits to what can be achieved by these interventions in the short term, and argue that if there is to be real change for the most disadvantaged children, then the current widespread but low level intervention will need to be replaced with more limited but more intensive provision.

A broader assessment, describing trends overall rather than a commentary on the New Labour government, is given in Bradshaw's *The Well-being of Children in the UK* (2002). He argues that in most respects the well-being of children in the UK is improving, but there are some areas of deterioration. His findings are summarized in Table 3.1.

Table 3.1: The well-being of children in the UK

Improving	*Deteriorating*	*No change*
Child poverty	Overweight and obesity	Diet and nutrition
Infant and child mortality	Immunization rates for measles	Child homicide
Breastfeeding	Parents reporting longstanding illness	School test scores for 13-year-olds
Survival rates for cancer and cystic fibrosis	Diabetes, asthma, HIV/Aids	Recorded crime
Children entering care	Length of time in care	Truancy rates
Child injury death rates	Traffic volumes	
Day care, nursery, out of school clubs, holiday schemes	Children's use of public spaces	
Teenage pregnancy rates	Homelessness	
Housing conditions	Free play	
Educational qualifications	Smoking, alcohol and drug use	
Post-16 staying on rates		
Sporting participation		
Permanent exclusion from school		
Suicides		

Bradshaw also makes the point, however, that there are considerable variations between countries in the UK, and by region. Whilst well-being is improving overall, it is also becoming more diverse. There is also a lack of comparative data in many key areas, including children; as carers, child labour and the mental health of children.

With regards to the Convention on the Rights of the Child, the United Nations response to the government's most recent submission (United Nations 2002) welcomed a number of developments, but also identified a wide range of concerns. These included the continuing high level of child poverty; the fact that the UK locks up more children than any of our European partners; the fact that we criminalize children at an earlier age than almost any other country in Europe; our poor treatment of asylum seeking children; and the perpetuation of parents' right to hit their children.

Concluding thoughts

The New Labour government in the UK has made a huge investment in services for children, and although it will take some years before the outcomes are evident, many of the plans are beginning to deliver – particularly for young children and their parents. Children are increasingly being seen within the context of their families and communities, there is a very real commitment to consulting with children and young people, and there is a strong and explicit emphasis on improvements in health and educational attainment and gainful employment. The social inclusion agenda and the promise of reducing poverty underpin all of this, and there is also evidence of improvements in collaboration between service providers from different agencies. The Green Paper *Every Child Matters* provides an ambitious agenda of very real reform and a commitment to seeing children and young people at the centre of the frame, rather than the professional agendas of people working in their separate silos.

But there will be very real challenges if the Green Paper proposals and the new Children Act do not bring with them sufficient funding to implement them. There is, for example, evidence of reduction of funding in some mainstream services, so that whilst the icing (or special initiatives) is getting thicker the cake itself is diminishing. This is particularly the case within social services, where the funding for preventive work and family support has in many areas reduced substantially, and where it is proving very difficult to shift the emphasis away from crisis intervention and towards prevention. Within health there are competing agendas between children and families and, for example, the elderly. And notwithstanding the work on the National Service Framework for children, there is little mention of children within the National Health Service, where the targets are improvements in hospital waiting lists, reducing death rates from cancer and heart disease, tackling drug abuse, and helping more older people live independently at home. A real challenge for government now is where children fit in the Department of Health agenda, and where health fits in the new Children and Families Directorate at the Department for Education and Skills.

There is a very proper emphasis on evidence-based practice, and all the programmes and initiatives are investing in substantial evaluation programmes (see for example, Barnes *et al.* 2003; Department for Education and Skills 2002). But this is putting very heavy and sometimes unmanageable demands on those running the programmes – particularly those who have applied to four or five different funding streams and are now having to account separately to each accountable body. And despite the lip service paid to evidence, political conviction often turns out to have the stronger pull. The rhetoric required by politicians to take the electorate with them sometimes flies in the face of the actual facts.

A major stumbling block to implementation or delivery of this agenda, which would merit a further chapter in itself, is the lack of suitably trained staff, and an absence of both forethought and investment in training for those who work throughout the statutory and voluntary sectors with children and their families. This is very rightly a key priority for Every Child Matters, but it will take considerable resources to make a real difference.

And finally – how easy will it be to change the culture? Can the UK become a society that listens to and respects children, and really promotes their well-being?

Note

1   The tragic death of Victoria Climbié in 2002 was the result of appalling abuse at the hands of two people who were supposed to be caring for her. However, Victoria's case was known to social services, the police and the National Health Service who all failed to protect her, as Lord Laming's report made clear.

Chapter 4

The Impact of US Welfare Reform on Children's Well-being

Minnesota Focus

Anthony A. Bibus, Rosemary J. Link and Michael O'Neal

This chapter presents what is known about the impact of welfare reform on children's well-being in the United States (US). Trends in the US and Minnesota since national welfare reform was introduced in 1996 are reviewed. Then outcomes in the Phillips neighborhood of Minneapolis (Hennepin County), Minnesota, where the authors have been exploring perceptions of parents who use services at Southside Family Nurturing Center, are discussed. The chapter concludes with discussion and recommendations.

Welfare reform = welfare-to-work

Until 1996, the US welfare program for poor families was called Aid to Families with Dependent Children (AFDC). It was funded with federal taxes and administered jointly with the states. Although states could set their own threshold for the income below which families would become eligible for cash assistance, and many set this level far below poverty, all eligible families were guaranteed some income. In the UK, the Department of Work and Pensions defines poverty as household income below 60 per cent of median income after housing costs. By contrast the formula used in the US is not tied to median income, but is a measure of need; in 2003, for a family of three, the poverty line using this measure was $15,260 or 36 per cent of the median annual household income, which in 2002 was $42,409.

Over time, AFDC had presented difficulties since federal rules often failed to support parents' employment goals or move families out of poverty. In the early 1990s, Minnesota experimented with reforming AFDC by initiating the Minnesota Family Investment Program (MFIP). The MFIP provided supports, encouragement and requirements for parents to move off public assistance and into gainful employment (Hage 2004b). The original MFIP pilot maintained publicly funded financial aid, health care, childcare, and other services until families' earnings reached 140 per cent over the poverty line. The MFIP was also evaluated to determine its impact on children's well-being, i.e. their academic, cognitive, mental, and physical health, overall development, and social, emotional, and behavioral outcomes (Crichton 2003; Crichton and Meyer 2003; Hage 2004b; Hollister *et al.* 2003; MDRC 2003; Minnesota Department of Human Services 2001, 2003, 2004). The results from the pilot were positive. For example, parents in the original experimental program enjoyed significant increase in income and employment compared to the control group with AFDC, and their children performed better in school and had fewer behavior problems. Incidents of domestic violence also declined.

In 1996, President Clinton signed the Personal Responsibility and Work Opportunity Reconciliation Act (Public Law 104.193). This repealed AFDC. The primary responsibility for administering the new legislation devolved to states. New time limited financial aid programs were introduced through Temporary Assistance to Needy Families (TANF), but financial assistance to poor families was no longer guaranteed. Now parents on welfare are referred to as 'job seekers' (Link and Bibus 2000, p.36). This historical policy change transformed the US welfare system 'from one focused on eligibility and cash assistance to an employment based program' (McPhee and Bronstein 2003, p.34).

Under TANF, states receive grants from the federal government designated up to a certain amount for cash assistance to eligible parents. The grants can also fund training (which could include education to a limited extent), preparing parents for employment, and childcare while parents are working. States are also encouraged to use the grants to support marriage and prevent teenage pregnancy. Other welfare programs, such as food stamps, can be added on top of the monthly assistance that a family receives. TANF rules, however, require clients to seek work first before receiving cash assistance. In addition, cash assistance is limited to no more than 60 months during a parent's lifetime. Able-bodied adults without children are not eligible for federal cash assistance through this program and state general assistance programs for adults have been cut back or eliminated entirely.

Tighter eligibility requirements have meant that assistance may only be available to parents with young children, for example, and tougher penalties for not complying with the rules include reductions in or complete elimination of cash assistance. While food stamps and medical assistance for the children might remain available, parents who lose their cash assistance face subsequent loss of housing and other basic family needs which could in turn become factors leading to neglect of their children and potentially to voluntary or court ordered placement of their children in foster care.

Minnesota modified its MFIP program in 1998 to conform to the new federal requirements. However, in contrast to other states, it tried to reduce child poverty as well as increase parents' employment. The MFIP program supports parents seeking jobs by providing transportation, childcare, health insurance coverage, or educational assistance, casework services, budgeting advice, and job training (see below) as well as cash, but also imposes sanctions such as a 30 per cent reduction in monthly cash grants for failing to comply with rules. While many MFIP families successfully moved from welfare to work under this combination of incentives and inducements, a substantial proportion are still in poverty.

Since the 2000 economic recession, state budget cuts have resulted in less financial aid for MFIP participants and increased sanctions. Moreover, parents receiving housing subsidies have had their MFIP grants cut by $50 per month; those receiving Supplemental Security Income (SSI) for family members with a disability now have their grants cut by $125 per month. To set this in context, a family with one child and two parents, one of whom is disabled, would have received $564 per month in SSI benefits plus $532 in MFIP cash assistance. This total of $1098 per month plus food stamps has been reduced to $973 per month due to the new cuts; an amount far below the poverty line. And there is no longer increased aid for an additional child.

Globally, faith in the market rises while families' income drops

The 'welfare-to-work' strategy is the hallmark of welfare reform worldwide. Welfare policies increasingly require parents to find employment rather than rely on public assistance. The underlying shift in philosophy introduced in the United States has also influenced the provision of state benefits in the UK (see Chapters 2 and 3). Goldberg and Rosenthal's 2002 study of nine countries, including the US, found that 'benefits are more closely tied to past and present employment or denied altogether. This...is concurrent with deteriorating employment opportunities' (p.339). 'Nonetheless,' they concluded, 'faith in the market has risen at the very time when market income leaves more people impoverished' (p.347). This market-based strategy leads to adjustment programs, such as the International Monetary Fund and the World Bank requiring countries to reduce social service spending in favor of dependence upon the marketplace.

In the US, trust in the market has resulted in many parents remaining poor even when working full time (Center on Budget and Policy Priorities 1999). Requiring parents to 'work first' and rely on public assistance only as a time-limited last resort has become the dominant feature of welfare policies. Consequently, poor parents must attempt to meet their families' needs within unpredictable job markets while state budget cuts strain neighborhood resources. Between 1996 and 1998, the financial resources for lone parents declined, and the number in extreme poverty increased (Weil and Finegold 2002).

In the first six years following the introduction of the Personal Responsibility and Work Opportunity Reconciliation Act of 1996, the percentage of children whose family income was below the official poverty level (less than $15,020 for a family of three) increased from 16.4 per cent to 17.2 per cent (United States Census Bureau 2003). There is now a wide gap between the well-being of children in low-income families and that of children from higher-income families (Weil and Finegold 2002). For example, in 2002 children in low-income families were three times more likely to be in poor health (Vandivere, Gallagher and Moore 2004).

While the number of parents receiving welfare has fallen by half nationwide, one in four of those leaving the welfare rolls are not finding work (Mathematica Policy Research 2003) and 'the number living in poverty has fallen by only 11 percent' (Hage 2004a, p.AA9). In Minnesota, three quarters of those parents who expend their eligibility for public cash assistance have incomes below $15,202; less than half of that needed to meet children's needs (Crichton 2003, p.21, footnote 18). As elsewhere in the US (Finegold and Staveteig 2002), children of color are over-represented among those living in poverty. For example, 32 per cent of African American children live in poverty compared with 6 per cent of white children (Children's Defense Fund Minnesota 2003).

In Hennepin County, Minnesota, the percentage of children in poor families increased from 12.9 per cent in 2001 to 15.5 per cent in 2002. In the Phillips neighborhood, child poverty is even more pervasive. Of the 5958 children, 2348 (39.4%) are living below the poverty line. The study discussed later in this chapter explored the perceptions of parents in this neighborhood regarding the effects of welfare reform policies – an issue that is clearly critical.

However, before their views are considered in detail, this chapter reviews more broadly the impact that welfare reform has had on children's well-being. The authors focus particularly on the experience of parents leaving welfare and trying to rely on the labor market to meet their children's needs.

What we know

If the main purpose of welfare reform was to reduce the number of parents receiving cash assistance, welfare-to-work policies appear successful. Hays (2003) documented a decline by over half in welfare rolls 'from 12.2 million recipients at the start of reform to 5.3 million in 2001' (p.221). However, she also pointed out that poverty levels have not declined at a corresponding rate: 'half of working parents were not making wages sufficient to raise them out of poverty' (p.8). Acknowledging the positive results of welfare reform such as TANF-funded 'wage supplements and funds for education, training, childcare and work-related expenses' (p.237), Hays concluded: 'Yet in the long run and in the aggregate, poor mothers and children are worse off now than they were prior to reform' (p.226).

Duncan and Chase-Lansdale agreed: 'Caseload declines have been dramatic, but caseload declines do not necessarily translate into enhanced family and child well-being' (2001, p.3). Indeed, data on the number of former recipients not employed or returning to the rolls, reviewed by Loprest in 2003, suggested 'that early employment successes in welfare reform have not been sustained' (p.1). 'Employment is more difficult to find and to keep, and for some families unemployment is a precursor to a return to cash assistance' (p.2). Haskins (2001), who viewed welfare reform as generally positive, also urged policy makers to 'help floundering families' with extensions on time limits, continuing food stamp eligibility, and expanded use of tax credits (pp.284–5).

Increased income is key to children's well-being

Dunifon, Kalil and Danziger (2003) summarized welfare reform's impact: 'Overall, then, existing research supports that the movement from welfare to work may have benefits for children, and that such benefits are most likely to be found when the transition off of welfare is accompanied by an increase in total family income' (p.61). However, many parents moving from welfare to work experience a loss of income, not an increase.

In 2002, Zaslow and colleagues completed an integrative review of several studies of states' programs, including MFIP. While they reminded readers that findings provide evidence only of particular programs' impact on children's well-being, their analysis calls attention to important potential effects of welfare-to-work policies on parents' ability to meet children's needs. They determined that 'children in families currently receiving welfare and children in families that have left welfare within the past two years were at consistently greater risk than children in high income families (200% of the poverty level)' (p.92).

In her review of welfare reform effects in the US and Canada, Hardina (2003) found that many former recipients experienced substantial economic hardship. Findings that some parents moving from welfare to work are not better off financially are troubling in the light of the evidence now that increased family income, not just parental employment, is key to improving children's well-being (Morris and Gennetian 2003). Gennetian and Miller (2002) used a rigorous experimental design to examine results of the original pilot MFIP program. Gathering lone mothers' reports on children's well-being (such as academic achievement, engagement in school, and behavior), they found that children whose parents received income supplements only, without being required to participate in the other program elements (such as casework services, budgeting advice, and job training), had consistently more positive outcomes than children whose parents relied solely on welfare or on work that did not raise family income 140 per cent above poverty: 'These experimental impacts suggest a strong link between increases in income and improved child well-being' (p.726). After a similar study in Michigan, Dunifon and colleagues (2003) concluded that 'results from these two studies suggest that children benefit, particularly in terms of behavioral adjustment, when welfare policies are such that women are able to combine welfare and employment' to maintain income above poverty (p.77).

As summarized by Weil and Finegold (2002), 'parental work appears to yield better outcomes for children only when it results in additional resources for the family and then only in some subgroups' (p.xxii). For example, 'programs that resulted in increased maternal education were also sometimes associated with favorable impacts on young children's cognitive development' (p.81).

Just having a job is not enough if parents are to be successful in meeting their children's needs (Billings, Moor and McDonald 2003). To meet their children's needs, parents who move from welfare to work must have access to transition services such as food stamps, health coverage, childcare, transportation, and housing subsidies. Health coverage is particularly critical in the US, since there is no universal national health service and many employers do not pay for employees' health care, especially in part-time positions. Even if parents are working, children face increased risks for maltreatment and foster care if families lose income or medical benefits.

The MFIP program conforms to federal requirements by introducing a 60-month (five-year) time limit on eligibility over a parent's lifetime, no matter how many children they may have. In a study on the effects of these time limits, half of the parents surveyed were working, but 72 per cent lived below the poverty line (Crichton 2003). Most of those employed did not have health insurance. Over 80 per cent reported that their lives were the same or worse than when they were participating in the MFIP; only 18 per cent reported that their lives were better. Forty-four per cent had experienced discrimination in seeking jobs. African American parents are over-represented among those who are reaching time limits in Minnesota and represent 32 per cent of MFIP recipients compared with 3.5 per cent of the general population. The Office of the Legislative Auditor (2002) found that income gains for MFIP recipients first moving from welfare to work soon disappear as their increased earnings are offset by decreased welfare assistance. Despite the hardships, parents often retain a hopeful attitude, as summarized in the Minnesota time limit study: 'When asked to name what helps them to get along each day, the number one response to this open-ended question was that their children keep them going, as they take care of them and provide for them (38 percent)' (Crichton 2003, p.19; see also Crewe 2003; McPhee and Bronstein 2003; Rank 1994; Tweedie 2001).

Health care coverage loss

Programs such as the MFIP may include health coverage for participants for the 60 months that they receive welfare assistance and for a year after they have found employment; however, few employers offer health insurance for casual workers and so coverage often ceases once participants move from welfare to work. The US Department of Health and Human Services (2002) reports that one in four children in families moving off welfare are without health insurance. Evidence related to the lack of health care coverage for parents moving from welfare to work and other systemic discrimination is also emerging from the longitudinal, random sample study that Hollister and colleagues (2003) conducted in Hennepin County. MFIP participants who were employed most extensively during the study period also were most likely to be without health care coverage. In addition, 'nineteen per cent of all participants studied stated that there was at least one time when their children did not get needed medical attention – especially dental care' (p.4).

Impact on vulnerable children

Parents in the Hennepin County study 'found their work and training experience to be helpful, with immigrant groups reporting the greatest appreciation' (Hollister *et al.* 2003, p.4). However, participants of color earned much less per hour (and $200 less per month) than white participants: 'Children of color on average live in households where the full-time wages their parents earned were more than $2 (full-time) and $3 (part-time) an hour less than the wages white parents earned on average' (p.15). Children of color were also more likely to be in poverty. Moreover, children whose parents worked most experienced more disruptions in their schooling. In addition, 'there were concerns about the lack of evening, early morning, and special needs childcare' (p.4). These families were better off financially when working, but they also reported that 'the children's well-being had been affected by the MFIP experience and stated that family time together and household routines had been compromised' (p.4). Some of the parents who were working extensively indicated that not receiving income support to stay home and raise their children and instead being required to work outside their home resulted in '"lack of time for family routine", "less time with the children"…and "parents stressed"' (p.15).

Summary of what we know

In summarizing the results of the earlier review of research on welfare reform in the US (Link and Bibus 2000, pp.114–24), the authors identified positive results such as heightened public awareness of child poverty, promotion of public/ private partnerships, workforce development, and encouragement of family friendly employers. They were troubled by the inadequate minimum wage, policies that did not recognize parents' care of children as legitimate work, the lack of choice for low-income parents to be homemakers, and punitive rhetoric reflecting a deepening conviction that welfare was a question of morality instead of social obligation or human rights. We now know that millions of US children whose parents move from welfare to work are at risk of 'social exclusion' (Elliott and Mayadas 1999). This risk increases when parents are not able to realize earnings gains through steady, well-paid work with benefits and when transition supports diminish or are absent altogether. For a closer glimpse through parents' eyes of the impact of welfare-to-work policies, this chapter now returns to the study of the perceptions of mothers attending the Southside Family Nurturing Center in the Phillips neighborhood of Hennepin County, Minnesota, mentioned above.

Parents' perceptions: Focus group at Southside

The Phillips neighborhood is one of the oldest sections of Minneapolis and is located just south of the central business district. As a result of the physical 'walling off' of the neighborhood by highways and the movement of many middle class families to the suburbs, the neighborhood's population declined about 30 per cent from 1960 to 1990 (24,776 to 17,272). However, the 2000 Census showed the population had risen again, by 14.8 per cent since 1990, due to an increase in Black/African American and Hispanic groups and those reporting 'some other race,' while the White, American Indian, and Asian/Pacific Island populations had declined. This recent population increase has contributed to a population density in Phillips that is over 68 per cent higher than the rest of the city as well as sharply contrasting in racial and ethnic population. The number of children has also increased since 1960; in the 2000 Census dependent children accounted for over one third of the population in Phillips (35.8%) in contrast to only 25.69 per cent for the city. While the region has experienced economic prosperity, Phillips has experienced increasing poverty, as shown in Table 4.1.

Table 4.1: Phillips poverty rates, 1970 through 2000

	1970	1980	1990	2000
Families below poverty (%)	12.7	20.3	53.8	42.2 (est)
Individuals below poverty (%)	31.7	33.8	49.6	34.2

Even though the 2000 Census indicates that poverty rates in Phillips had abated to a degree, many individuals and families are still experiencing deep and persistent poverty. Four of the eight census districts (or tracks) in Phillips have poverty rates exceeding the city's threshold goal of 33.5 per cent of residents (O'Neal and Marano 2003).

Today's 'jobless recovery' does not bode well for those Phillips residents who have reached the MFIP/TANF time limits. Even more foreboding are 1998 health statistics indicating that:

- 42.1 per cent of mothers in Phillips had less than a high school education
- only 30.5 per cent of mothers received first trimester prenatal care
- 67.3 per cent of mothers were unmarried women
- the infant mortality rate in Phillips was 23.9 per 1000 live births.

Table 4.2: Contrasting Phillips to the City of Minneapolis and the region (using 2000 US Census)

Phillips: Census tracts	White/People of color* (%)	Total population below poverty (%)	Families' incomes less than 30% MMI* (%)	Median family income
5902	19/81	42	43	$23,444
7301	12/88	42	58	$17,045
7302	18/82	27	26	$31,563
7802	29/71	31	34	$31,172
7900	26/74	28	25	$28,512
106,000	29/71	34	37	$25,949
107,100	46/64	40	47	$22,266
107,200	25/75	27	31	$30,843
City of Minneapolis	65/35	16.9	17.3	$48,602
Twin Cities	90/10	7.3	9.9	$63,600

*rounded to nearest whole number

These statistics reveal the dramatic impact on low-income women and their children who live in an inner-city community such as Phillips. With its patterns of persistent and concentrated poverty, the neighborhood is a vivid representation of the transformation affecting many US inner cities. It is within this community context that the focus group participants live and must attempt to provide for their children's well-being.

Southside Family Nurturing Center

Entering its thirtieth year, Southside Family Nurturing Center is based in the Phillips neighborhood. Southside believes in the strength of families and in co-operative strategies to prevent child abuse and neglect. The agency was established to work with whole families rather than identified 'problem' members and has been recognized as innovative in its holistic systems approach. Most of the 150 adults and children receiving services have experienced neglect, poverty, drug abuse, child protection inquiries, housing, and transport concerns.

Southside offers three main areas of service: The Center-based Early Childhood Education Program, Home Based Services, and the Fathers' Program. Set in a Victorian four-storey house, the agency is a welcoming place: a site visitor recently commented: 'If I were a child, I would want to be here.'

In January 2004, two focus groups were convened of parents who used MFIP services and the supports offered at Southside. Parents were invited to share perceptions on how moving from welfare to work had helped them support and raise their children and were asked if they had encountered difficulties. Particular attention was given to neighborhood supports and barriers such as access to jobs, childcare, housing, education, financial institutions and banks, social services, health care, and transportation (Zedlewski 2003).

Focus group findings

Two focus group sessions were conducted. Sixteen mothers participated, five in the first group and eleven in the second; all volunteered from two of the support groups at Southside Family Nurturing Center. Most of the mothers lived in the Phillips neighborhood and all used the services of Southside as well as the MFIP. In a survey participants completed afterwards, respondents indicated an age range from 22 to 40 years old (mean = 27.9; median = 26). They identified themselves as American Indian (11); as Black, African American or African (2); as White, Caucasian or European American (1); as Asian (1); and as Hispanic (1). All but one of the women from the second group identified themselves as American Indian. Fifteen of the respondents rented and one was a homeowner. Thirteen estimated their yearly household income at below $10,000. Fourteen were lone parents, raising between one and eight children (average total number of children = 3.1; average under six years old = 2.0). Eleven parents did not have a high school education, but four had been to community or technical college and one had a college degree.

In the parents' responses to questions about their experience with welfare reform, the following themes emerged.

INTRUSION

MFIP rules require participants to document job-seeking efforts. The mothers shared a sense of intrusion into their private lives related to using the MFIP. They objected to having to write down what they did all day, as if they were on parole and their job counselor or eligibility worker were their probation officer. Some MFIP staff brushed mothers off, treated them rudely, or seemed to enjoy reporting to the mother that she was cut off assistance.

NEGATIVE, PUNITIVE CHANGES

Even though we asked the mothers about positive changes in their lives, they focused mostly on negative changes such as the recent housing subsidy penalty whereby if a parent on the MFIP also receives rental assistance, $50 per month is deducted from his or her cash assistance. They called this and the similar reduction in grants if they received supplemental income for family members with a disability (SSI) 'not fair,' and they experienced these cuts as punishing. They resented:

- the pressure to work first and insinuations that if they did not move off welfare and into full-time jobs, their children might be removed

- having to ask permission to attend school as part of their plan to seek gainful employment

- the new co-payments wherein parents must now contribute money from their own pockets to cover a portion of the costs required for medical assistance and childcare

- having less money

- sanctions (punitive reductions in income, for example for not documenting 40 hours per week of work or job-seeking activities).

POSITIVE SUPPORTS

Participants agreed that life is 'much tougher now' both for themselves and others they know on MFIP. Nevertheless, they shared some positive aspects:

- rental assistance and once a year emergency cash assistance ($300)

- referral to transitional housing

- medical assistance and childcare coverage sustained during the first year after MFIP.

EFFECT ON CHILDREN'S WELL-BEING

Some participants had more difficulty identifying changes in the children's lives resulting from welfare reform. At first they could not see how being on MFIP was relevant to their children's lives. They explained that welfare reform concerned adults, not children. One said that she tried to shield her child from having to worry about how she supported the family. When asked if their children were better off, worse off, or the same since welfare reform, some replied 'the same,' 'not bad,' 'in between'; others replied 'worse'; and some found the question irrelevant. Then, after exchanges among participants, some suggested that the cuts in childcare funding, losses in children's interaction time with other children in childcare, and reduction in family income did harm their children despite their desire to buffer them from these effects. They called the time limits 'crazy,' though some thought that other new rules encouraging work were helpful and should have been in place earlier. Others commented on how stress on parents due to budget cuts led to stress on children; and not being able to purchase clothes or shoes or toys contributed to parents being 'stressed out.'

EFFECT ON PARENTS' WELL-BEING

Participants wanted to respond to a similar question about whether they as parents were better off, worse off or the same. They stated vehemently 'worse off' and gave examples of rising prescription costs resulting in less money for other needs, reductions in family income resulting from the new deduction of $125 SSI benefits, and the rule prohibiting additional cash assistance to care for new children. The sentiment expressed by one mother: 'I'd rather be working' was met with affirming nods. One mother reported that she had just been laid off her job, due in part to discrimination. Some wished that they had more opportunity and support for further education. Some noted that food shelves (stocks of donated goods, located in neighborhood agencies or centers where staffers distribute them to people in need) were closing. However, they added that more supports were available through Southside and other resources in the Phillips neighborhood than elsewhere.

WHAT IMPROVEMENTS WOULD PARENTS RECOMMEND TO LAWMAKERS?

The mothers recommended the following improvements in welfare reform policies:

- Explain the time limits and reductions of housing assistance and SSI.
- Enforce the work rules, but lift the time limits; provide more extensions on the time limits; 'Since there is a five year limit, at least make [sure] that families or single parents are able to maintain themselves on their own. While they are receiving assistance, definitely help them to be prepared.'

- Although the rules and expectations of welfare reform might not have a direct impact on children's well-being or success, an increase in cash assistance and food stamps would help.

- Parents should be able to make a living while off welfare and at least $9.45 per hour at work; money that parents receive from their tribe or reservation should not be deducted from welfare grants.

- Make sure there are jobs out there with living wages.

- Childcare should be available at more times, more flexibly, and for extended hours.

- Encourage ('push us toward') more and better education and job training.

Finally, one group asserted that researchers should 'Bring a group of mothers to testify at the legislature!'

Implications of the focus group findings

This case study helps assess the impact of welfare reform in the US. The mothers in the focus groups are pragmatic, resourceful, and responsible, just as those in other ethnographic studies (Almgren, Ymashiro and Ferguson 2002; Lengyel 2001; McPhee and Bronstein 2003; Seccombe 1999). Parents see the benefits of moving from welfare to work, if jobs can be stable and bring in adequate income. However, they also value transitional support services such as childcare, extended health care coverage, access to higher education, and help with transportation. Evidence from welfare reform experiments, such as MFIP, supports these parents' conclusions regarding the importance of transitional services. But funding these services, which typically cost more than cash assistance, will require more government investments and continuing partnerships between government, private foundations, and businesses. In its most successful form as a pilot project without time limits, without drastic sanctioning, and with a high threshold of 140 per cent of the poverty level before parents needed to rely entirely on their wages, MFIP cost between $1900 and $3800 more per family per year than AFDC (Minnesota Department of Human Services 2000). Research on MFIP's impact on children's well-being bolsters earlier findings related to the detrimental effects of poverty and the conversely beneficial effects of increases in income for children of working poor parents (Gennetian and Miller 2002). These increases, beyond what many families will be able to find in the employment market, require substantial investment of public money.

In an economy where most families need two adult earners in order to meet children's needs, lone parents deserve to have the government as their partner to supplement their earnings and benefits (Hage 2004b). Beyond income increases, the provision of comprehensive and on-going transition services such as support groups has been found to be associated with parents being less likely to return to welfare (Anderson-Butcher, Khairallah and Race-Bigelow 2004). The mutual aid observed among the parents at Southside Family Nurturing Services and their process of providing information and encouragement to each other demonstrate that support groups should be part of any comprehensive welfare reform package.

Summary and recommendations

This chapter has discussed implications for practice in neighborhoods that are most vulnerable to seemingly intractable poverty. Narrated experience of parents who are poor puts a human face on the interaction between people and place and highlights the barriers to successful employment. These include lack of affordable housing, unreliable transportation, inadequate childcare, health difficulties, low wages, acute stressful events, discrimination, and insufficient experience and preparation (Carnevale and Desrochers 1999; Nightingale 2002; Strawn 1998; Weil and Finegold 2002; Wilder Research Center 2003). Immigrants and refugees encounter particularly challenging obstacles (Pinto 2002; Shelton and Roy 2001). When parents face lack of education services, sanctions for unsuccessful job search, employers 'unfriendly' to families, and poor quality childcare, children often suffer (Sherman 1999). 'Family friendly' employers are scarce but can be found, and their qualities include attention to family needs, including child sick leave, childcare, flexible maternity leave, fast-track re-entry after negotiated family leave, and the willingness to stay abreast of the balancing act between family and work life.

Conditions such as unsuccessful job searches and poor quality childcare facilities can be anticipated and buffered by progressive social policies. This chapter offers several recommendations for improvements in welfare reform including more universal and substantial income maintenance for parents without arbitrary time limits; continuing health care coverage; childcare assistance; food, housing, and transportation subsidies; and social services such as the support groups at Southside Family Nurturing Center. With this information, lawmakers, administrators, practitioners, and neighborhood residents can join in a united effort to lift children out of poverty (Banerjee 2002; Lens 2002).

However, we must not underestimate the uphill nature of this effort, given the characteristics of American society that Goldberg (2002, p.34) cites as potentially impeding improvements in social welfare policies: 'persistent, entrenched individualism; deep racial and ethnic cleavages; marked regional differences; and a labor movement that is relatively weak and, for much of the post WWII period, ideologically conservative' (see also Katz 2001). In order to advocate for welfare reform that meets children's needs and their human rights, social workers, professional advocates, and policy makers will need to tap resiliency, stamina, and fortitude like that manifested by the parents and staff at Southside Family Nurturing Center.

Acknowledgements

We owe a debt of gratitude to the parents and staff at Southside Family Nurturing Center, whose dedicated participation in our study enriched this chapter. Special thanks also to Professor Karen Robards and her students.

Part II

Effective Interventions to Promote Children's Health and Well-being

Chapter 5

Support Teams for Adolescents

Nina Biehal

Concerns about high rates of placement change for older children and teenagers in the UK have led to the development of specialist support teams, which typically offer an intensive, short-term service with the aim of preventing unnecessary placement. This chapter compares outcomes for 11–16-year-olds referred to six support teams to those for a similar group of young people who received a 'service as usual' from mainstream social workers. The study found that the majority of young people had extremely high levels of need. At six-month follow-up many of those in both groups showed improvement on measures of child and family functioning. However, those receiving the specialist service were less likely to be placed and, in particular, were less likely to enter what was anticipated to be long-term care.

Introduction

Part I of this book has explored poverty and its effects on the well-being of children, families and communities. The effectiveness of policy agendas to address poverty in the UK and US has also been discussed. We now consider a number of more specific interventions; this part of the book presents some of those aimed at promoting the health and well-being of children.

Over the last 15 years or so there has been a rapid expansion in the number of specialist support teams working with teenagers and their families in the UK, variously referred to as community support teams, adolescent support teams or simply family support teams. These community-based teams have developed principally in response to concerns about high rates of placement for older children, the high costs involved and the possible damaging effects of placement.

Typically, they offer an intensive, short-term family support service whose principal aim is to divert young people from the care system, although some have additional aims such as the prevention of placement breakdown.

Most support teams have been established following the closure of children's homes and the diversion of resources to establish an alternative, community-based service to work with older children and teenagers (Brown 1998). This chapter describes an evaluation of six support teams working with older children and adolescents in England, in which outcomes for young people were compared with outcomes for a similar group receiving a mainstream social work service (Biehal 2005).

Background to the study

While there have been a number of studies of family support services in the UK, there has been a tendency to focus on forms of provision targeted at families with younger children, such as family centres or day care (Gibbons, Thorpe and Wilkinson 1990; Smith 1992). Other studies have included children with a wider age range but have not paid specific attention to work with adolescents (Gardner 1992; Gibbons 1991; Macdonald and Williamson 2002; McCauley *et al.* 2002). One study that did give some separate consideration to older children and teenagers found that few family support services were available for this age group (Tunstill and Aldgate 2000).

Research which has focused more generally on social work with teenagers has also suggested that they are less likely to receive family support interventions than younger children. Three studies undertaken in the mid-1990s found that teenagers received little attention and that cases were only allocated once a major crisis occurred. By this time it was often too late for preventive strategies to avoid placement (Packman and Hall 1998; Sinclair, Garnett and Berridge 1995; Triseliotis *et al.* 1995).

In the US, the principal objective of the family preservation services that have developed since the 1970s has been the prevention of placement in care. Intensive family preservation services (IFPS) are time-limited support services which are crisis-oriented and are targeted at children thought to be at imminent risk of placement. In this respect, they bear some similarity to the specialist support teams that are the subject of this chapter, although many of the IFPS evaluated have been demonstration projects which were far better resourced than UK services. In recent years, the evidence of experimental studies on the effectiveness of these services in preventing placement has been mixed. Some studies found no evidence that IFPS were more effective than mainstream services in preventing the placement of children, in some the evidence was inconclusive while in at least one it appeared that IFPS perversely led to higher placement rates (Schuerman, Rzepnicki and Littell 1994). Even where IFPS were apparently effective, any positive effects were often found to have dissipated over time.

There has also been much debate as to the validity of placement prevention as a measure of effectiveness, as this may indicate system-based changes as well as, or indeed instead of, family-based changes. Accordingly, later studies have turned their attention to other outcomes. From the limited evidence available on outcomes other than placement, it appears that IFPS may produce modest, short-term improvement in some aspects of child and family functioning, but the North American evidence on the effectiveness of these intensive family support services remains inconclusive (Feldman 1991; Pecora, Fraser and Haapala 1991).

As with family support services in the UK, the majority of IFPS have focused on providing services to families with younger children referred for reasons of abuse or neglect. Although only a few of these intensive services have been targeted at adolescents (for example, Feldman 1991; Schwarz, Au Claire and Harris 1991), one review of the research evidence in the US concluded that they may be moderately effective with older children and those in early adolescence, where child behaviour is identified as a major problem (Fraser, Nelson and Rivard 1997). Some of the preventive services developed in the US that have been more directly aimed at teenagers have targeted specific subgroups, such as young people with serious mental health problems or young offenders (Evans and Boothroyd 1997; Henggeler, Melton and Smith 1992). Wraparound services (sometimes referred to as individualized services) have been developed for children with severe emotional and behavioural disturbance in an attempt to provide flexible support. These aim to co-ordinate mental health, education, welfare and other services into a network to meet the individual needs of children in their home environment. However, there has been little published evaluation of these to date and existing studies have been criticised as lacking in method-ological rigour (Bates, English and Kouidou-Giles 1997).

Although there has been a rapid expansion in the number of support teams for older children and teenagers in the UK, there has been very little research on these services. Only five small-scale, largely qualitative studies have been conducted, each focusing on a single team (Biehal, Clayden and Byford 2000; Brodie *et al.* 1998; Cliffe and Berridge 1991; Frost 1997; Fuller 1989). These studies suggest that such teams may help vulnerable young people to be supported at home and may prevent inappropriate placement in care. However, samples have been small and most of these studies have focused principally on questions of process rather than outcomes, so there is little available evidence on the effectiveness of these teams.

Method

The evaluation of the service discussed in this chapter employed a prospective, quasi-experimental design, in which young people using specialist support teams in six English local authorities were compared with others receiving a mainstream social work service in three authorities. The main focus was on individual outcomes, specifically, changes in child and family functioning. However, since the principal aim of support teams is to prevent unnecessary placement, service outcomes with regard to placement rates were also examined. Young people were included in the study if:

- they were 11–16 years old
- they had just been referred for a service, and
- *either* the young person or the parent had requested placement *or* the social worker who assessed them considered that there was a risk of placement within four weeks if a service was not provided.

Young people, parents, support workers and social workers were interviewed at referral and again at follow-up six months later. Both quantitative and qualitative methods were used and a number of standardized measures were employed to assess outcomes. These included the Strengths and Difficulties Questionnaire (SDQ), a measure of children's emotional and behavioural difficulties, and the Family Assessment Device (FAD), a measure of family functioning, which were completed by both parents and children (Epstein, Baldwin and Bishop 1983; Goodman 1997). Cantril's Ladder, a measure of well-being, was also completed by young people and the General Health Questionnaire (GHQ), a measure of adults' mental health status, was completed by parents (Goldberg and Williams 1988; Huxley *et al.* 2001). A Severity of Difficulties scale for adolescents was also designed for the study. This checklist, completed by parents and young people, aimed to measure the severity of specific difficulties in child behaviour and parent–child relationships upon which social work interventions might reasonably be expected to have an impact. Support workers and social workers provided data on their interventions as well as on the young people's difficulties at referral and their histories of involvement with social services and other agencies.

Data were collected on 209 young people at referral. At follow-up a full data set, including questionnaires from at least one family member and at least one professional, was available on 62 per cent (129) of the sample, but some information was available on a further 31 per cent (66) for whom questionnaires either from family members or professionals were received. As a minimum, data on case events, such as placement or child protection registration, were therefore available on 93 per cent of the sample. Sample attrition was similar for young people using both types of service and there were no significant differences between the samples at referral and at follow-up in terms of child and family characteristics or the severity of problems (as measured on the SDQ and the Severity of Difficulties scale).

The qualitative component of the study covered a sub-sample of 50 cases selected from those that professionals had rated as being at high risk of placement at the point of referral. The first 50 cases to meet this criterion were selected and in-depth interviews were conducted with young people, parents and professionals at follow-up.

Answers to pre-coded questions and self-completion checklists were analysed using the statistical programme SPSS-11 and all associations between variables reported below are statistically significant at $p = 0.01$ or less. Analysis of qualitative interviews allowed for the exploration of themes that emerged across cases as well as the detailed consideration of individual case studies. Qualitative data were also used to explore how, why and in what circumstances interventions appeared to be more, or less, successful.

The young people

The majority of the young people (88%) were aged 12–15 years and just over half (56%) were male. Despite attempts to over-sample children from minority ethnic groups, just 4 per cent were of mixed ethnic origin, 1 per cent were black and none were known to be from any other minority ethnic groups. Just under half (46%) were living with a lone parent, 25 per cent in a step-family and just 16 per cent with both birth parents. The remaining 13 per cent lived with adoptive parents, grandparents or other relatives. Families were far more fragmented than in the wider population, in which 65 per cent live with both birth parents; family composition was in fact similar to that for children who are looked after (National Statistics 2003; Sinclair, Wilson and Gibbs 2000).

A substantial minority of the young people had high levels of need due to physical or learning disabilities or emotional and behavioural difficulties. A total of 27 per cent had one or more of these, the most common being learning disabilities (15%) and emotional and behavioural difficulties (14%). Again, this proportion is similar to that for children who are looked after, among whom it is estimated that 25 per cent have physical or learning disabilities, sensory impairment or emotional and behavioural difficulties (Gordon *et al.* 2000). A further 8 per cent were reported to have mental health problems and 11 per cent were reported to have Attention Deficit Hyperactivity Disorder, although it was unclear how many of these had a formal diagnosis of this condition. Over one fifth (22%) had a formal statement of Special Educational Needs, in the majority of cases due to their emotional and behavioural difficulties.

Many of the young people also had a history of long-term difficulties. Nearly three quarters had been in contact with social services at some time in the past and for one third there had been episodic contact over three or more years. Furthermore, one quarter had been looked after at some time in the past, another indicator that family stress was not new. There had been past concerns about abuse in relation to one third of the young people, including physical abuse (16%), emotional abuse (9%) and sexual abuse (7%), and one eighth were said to have experienced neglect at an earlier stage in their lives. Many (43%) also had experience of domestic violence and some expressed continuing distress about this, even several years after it had occurred. Domestic violence has been found to be a correlate in a substantial minority of cases of child abuse (Gibbons, Conroy and Bell 1995), and there is also evidence that children who witness this violence are significantly more likely to display emotional and behavioural problems (Humphreys and Mullender undated).

The SDQ was used as an objective measure of the young people's emotional and behavioural difficulties and this revealed that an extremely high proportion of those referred had severe difficulties. SDQ scores indicated that between 42 per cent (on young people's own rating) and 76 per cent (when rated by parents) had severe emotional and behavioural difficulties indicating high levels of need, whereas scores at this level would be anticipated in only 10 per cent of the wider community (Goodman 1997).

Many of the young people referred therefore had multiple and often serious difficulties which, for a substantial minority, had persisted over a considerable period of time. The groups referred to support teams or mainstream services were well-matched in terms of child and family characteristics, past placement in care, family functioning and sense of well-being (according to the FAD and Cantril's Ladder). However, those in contact with support teams were more than twice as likely to have long-term problems (44%) than those using mainstream services

(20%), to have experienced abuse in the past (40% compared with 17%) and to have seen a child psychiatrist or psychologist in the past six months (44% compared with 17%). On young people's own ratings of their emotional and behavioural difficulties on the SDQ, scores were higher for those referred to support teams, but scores on parent versions of this measure revealed no difference between the groups. In contrast, scores for mental health status on the GHQ suggested that psychological problems were worse for the comparison group using the mainstream service.

Difficulties at referral

Both young people and parents reported multiple problems at referral. They were each invited to rate a range of potential difficulties as being a 'major' or 'moderate' problem, or 'not a problem'. The problems reported to be 'major' by young people and parents are shown in Table 5.1.

Table 5.1: Difficulties rated as 'a major problem' at referral (n=209)

	Parents (%)	Young people (%)
Young person's behaviour at home	85	37
Parents upset about behaviour outside home	64	29
Parents' concern about young person's friends	51	26
Stays out late	36	17
Parent/child arguments	78	34
Child/parent 'doesn't listen'	63	22
Child/parent 'can't talk things over'	54	32
School problems	59	34
Drug problems	12	3
Alcohol problems	10	4
Offending	22	12

Problems at home and at school were mutually reinforcing and raised levels of stress within families, particularly when children were out of school. One fifth of the sample had not attended school at all in the six months prior to referral and 42 per cent had truanted in the previous month. Over three quarters were reported to display behaviour problems at school and 35 per cent had been temporarily excluded in the month prior to referral. Only 80 per cent attended mainstream schools and, worryingly, 14 per cent of the sample had no alternative educational provision.

Running away from home was also common, as 60 per cent had run away in the previous year. Other studies have shown that children often run away in response to serious family conflict and that running away may sometimes be prompted by abuse (Biehal and Wade 2000; Safe on the Streets Research Team 1999). In addition, parents were often concerned about their children's peers, fearing that they were 'getting into bad company' (51%), and about their involvement in the criminal justice system (22%).

Parents were also worried about young people's violence to themselves and to others, reporting that 20 per cent had attempted to harm themselves in the past year, including 8 per cent who had attempted suicide. Over half (55%) of the parents reported that their child had been violent to them in the past six months and even more young people (69%) were reported to be violent to others. Interviews with parents revealed their real sense of desperation:

> Drinking, drug abuse, violent temper, he's on a short fuse all the time and extremely volatile. My other daughters are frightened of him… It's like a living bomb, a miniature volcano. (Mother of boy, aged 15)

The young people were distressed too by their own behaviour and many explained that they wanted help to change it. They hoped that workers would 'calm me down, help me stop being angry' or 'help me with my behaviour – telling me different ways to react'. Others felt that they were not the only ones who needed to change. As one girl explained, she wanted the worker to: 'try and stop me and my mum arguing more, by having a word with my mum, tell her not to shout at me'.

Professionals reported similar behavioural and emotional problems, but were also concerned about abuse and neglect in respect of over half (54%) of the young people. They reported concern about the emotional abuse of over one third (34%) of the young people, neglect (17%) and also physical (11%) and sexual (3%) abuse. There were no significant differences in the number, nature and severity of problems reported at referral between the young people referred to each type of service.

The interventions

For those young people referred to support teams, professionally qualified social workers assessed families and then passed on much of the direct work with them to support workers who, for the most part, held vocational rather than professional social work qualifications. In most cases social workers acted as case managers and had a largely administrative role. Of course this pattern varied, with some social workers engaging more directly in work with families, but the general pattern was for them to oversee work undertaken by other, less qualified, staff. Sessional staff were sometimes used by support workers, and occasionally by social workers, to befriend young people and try to engage them in positive social activities in their local communities.

The support teams carried out predominantly task-centred work and drew on a range of approaches including solution-focused brief therapy, which was popular with all the support teams, and family systems theory. They made much use of structured resources such as parenting and anger management programmes, worksheets and videos. Social workers working with the mainstream group were also eclectic in the methods they used but did not normally use structured resources.

Both services contained the same elements, focusing on young people's behavioural and emotional problems, family relationships and parenting. However, the balance was different, as families in contact with the specialist teams were likely to receive more direct work. Support workers worked with families for an average of 19 weeks, whereas social workers stayed in contact with families twice as long, on average. However, although the duration of their contact was shorter, support teams' contact was far more intensive. During the six-month follow-up period support workers had a mean of 33 hours face-to-face contact with families compared with 11 hours for social workers.

The goals of the largely task-focused work undertaken by support teams were, principally, helping parents to develop skills that were more effective in managing young people's behaviour, a reduction in problematic behaviour by young people and a reduction in parent–child conflict. Parents and young people were therefore helped to change their behaviours and, as we shall see, many found this valuable. There was little time, however, to address broader questions of motivation and need, underlying issues that might have longer-term consequences both for young people's well-being and behaviour.

For those young people who were using a mainstream social work service, the extent of social worker involvement was variable. In some cases social workers focused predominantly on obtaining services for the family from other agencies, such as family therapy or mental health services; some also tried to involve young people in local leisure activities, such as youth clubs or sports activities. A few social workers went further than this and worked directly with parents on parenting skills and communication, took young people out to talk to them about their difficulties, or mediated between parents and young people. However, a more limited role was more common and a greater proportion of their time was spent on the co-ordination of resources and liaison with other agencies.

Changes in child and family functioning

The six-month follow-up showed improvements for all young people in both groups. At this stage, in the sample as a whole, the mean number of problems reported had fallen from 9.73 to 7.62. On most of the specific problems reported at referral, outlined above in Table 5.1, between one third and two thirds of parents reported that matters had improved. Positive change was more likely to take place in behaviour within the home than outside it. In particular, nearly two thirds of parents who had previously complained of their child's violence towards them reported that this was now less of a problem. Nearly half of parents reported that parent–child conflict had decreased and that communication had improved, and nearly two thirds of those reported to be runaways at referral had ceased to run away. Young people tended to be even more positive than parents as, on all of these issues, a higher proportion of them reported improvement. However, there was little improvement in patterns of self harm, rates of exclusion from school, or offending behaviour.

Scores on measures of emotional and behavioural difficulties, family functioning, child well-being, severity of child difficulties and parental mental health all showed considerable improvement. For example on parents' ratings of children's emotional and behavioural difficulties on the SDQ, the proportion whose scores indicated high levels of need fell from 76 per cent to 55 per cent and the proportion in the category of 'low need' rose from 9 per cent to 25 per cent. Although one might expect some natural improvement over time for those scoring highly at referral, this is unlikely to account for the full extent of improvement that was reported, so it is certainly possible that the services provided did have a beneficial impact. Scores for family functioning (on the FAD scale) also showed significant improvement, indicating positive change in family problem solving, communication, behaviour control, affective involvement and responsiveness. Similarly, at referral 72 per cent of parents had scored above the threshold for the mental health problems measured by the GHQ (namely, depression and anxiety), whereas at follow-up only 38 per cent scored above this threshold.

Family views of their circumstances at follow-up reflected this general improvement, as 79 per cent of young people and 51 per cent of parents felt that the young person's situation had improved. Of course, we cannot be confident about the link between the interventions and positive outcomes for the young people since, for ethical and practical reasons, it was not possible for the study to include a comparison group receiving no service. This difficulty in arriving at clear-cut findings on the effectiveness of the specialist service is compounded by the complex multi-agency environment in which services for children are delivered and the impact of informal support from relatives and friends. These made it hard to tease out the effects of just one team's work, since changes in relation to one aspect of children's lives (for example, at school or in the family network), often triggered changes in other areas and positive changes were often mutually reinforcing. Young people and parents' motivation to change and their willingness to engage in work with support workers and social workers were also highly influential. Indeed, a particular strength of the support teams was their ability to engage young people who were not initially motivated. These were often young people with a history of chronic and severe difficulties.

However, despite the difficulty of teasing out the precise impact of a particular service, it is clear that many young people and parents did feel that the support teams had made a significant contribution to the positive changes that had occurred since referral. Young people tended to be more positive than their parents about the effectiveness of professional help, as shown in Table 5.2.

Table 5.2: Parents' and young people's views of professional help

How far professionals helped	Young people % (n=55)	Parents % (n=85)
Support workers 'helped a lot'	56	43
Social workers 'helped a lot'	39	24

Young people's and parents' accounts of how positive change had come about also indicated that many felt that support teams had had a substantial impact on child and family problems. For example, the mother of one girl aged 13 explained:

[The support worker] spent a lot of time with her explaining about boundaries and things she can do and can't do. He spent a lot of time with me just going over things, basically, and like helping to get my mind straight. I mean, it has improved considerably. I mean it's still going on now, but we know how to handle it. It's better, and the bits that still need working on, we know how to work on them as opposed to banging our heads against a brick wall.

However, despite differences in the nature, duration and intensity of the two types of service, there were no significant differences in the degree of improvement between young people in the two groups on any of the measures referred to above. This was perhaps not surprising, as numerous studies of intensive family preservation services in the US have also failed to find any major differences in outcomes between intensive and mainstream services. However, some of these studies did find that intensive services sometimes produced more positive changes in child or family functioning with particular subgroups, although the nature of these subgroups varies from study to study (for example, Bath and Haapala 1993; Feldman 1991). Consistent with this, a closer analysis of the data suggests that specialist teams were both more likely to be working with, and more successful with, a particular group, namely those young people whose problems initially appeared to be the most intractable.

Since a higher proportion of the young people referred to specialist teams had both chronic and severe difficulties, in comparison with those receiving mainstream services, it was likely to be harder for the specialist teams to achieve positive change. In other words, they might have been expected to be less successful than mainstream services rather than equally successful, since many of those using the specialist service had apparently more intractable problems. Yet there was no significant difference in the degree of change between the two groups on any of our standardized outcome measures *despite* the fact that the specialist teams were working with a higher proportion of young people with chronic and severe problems.

Placement

As we saw earlier, the principal aim of the support teams was to prevent unnecessary placement. Both support workers and social workers appeared determined to avoid this at all costs. One quarter of the young people were placed during the follow-up period but most placements were of short duration. Almost half of these were for less than four weeks and the majority were for less than three months.

Young people in authorities which did not have a support team service were twice as likely to be placed (50%) as those who were in contact with support workers (25%). Only 8 per cent of the sample as a whole were expected to remain looked after in the longer term, but again those who lived in authorities which did not have support teams were more likely to enter what was anticipated to be long-term care (29%) than those who received the support team service (6%).

Although it is probable that the timely and intensive response by support teams to families in crisis contributed to these outcomes, placement rates were also likely to be influenced by the policy and resource context in which the interventions took place. If resources are diverted from residential services to outreach work, as had occurred when most of the support teams were set up, then inevitably fewer young people will enter residential placements. Local policy directives to avoid placement wherever possible were also influential. These derived from concern about the high costs of placement as well as from pressure to meet performance indicators set by central government. The UK government's modernization programme for social services has set out a range of targets including, in the Quality Protects policy initiative, a requirement for local authorities to reduce the number of children who are looked after (Department of Health 1998b). This pressure to avoid accommodation at all costs, which has also been noted in other studies of social work with teenagers, occasionally led to situations where practice appeared to be resource-driven rather than needs-led, so that agency needs appeared to be prioritized over children's needs (Packman and Hall 1998; Triseliotis *et al.* 1995).

Professional concerns played an important part in decisions about placement too. Many workers displayed a degree of scepticism as to the value of placement and feared it would be damaging, so in most cases it was used as a last resort rather than as a positive, planned element of a family support service. There were also a few instances where children who had experienced severe emotional abuse and rejection over many years received only brief episodes of intervention, the principal aim of which was to resolve the current crisis without the need for placement rather than consider their longer-term needs. As others have also observed, a fixation with avoiding placement at all costs in the short term can lead to a failure to consider the longer-term welfare needs of children, as placement prevention is not invariably in a child's best interests (Littell and Schuerman 1999; Triseliotis *et al.* 1995; Ward *et al.* 2004; Whittaker and Maluccio 2002).

How did the interventions help?

Although the interventions often drew on structured programmes and resources, a key factor associated with more successful outcomes was to be found in the realm of interpersonal interaction between workers and families. It was the complex interaction between workers' considerable skills in building relationships with young people and young people's own histories, motivation and desire for change that lay at the heart of workers' success in engaging them. Positive change appeared most likely to occur when young people were engaged in the work in this way and, in most cases, where parents were also willing to consider alternative strategies. The specific methods used, such as solution-focused brief therapy, or programmes for enhancing parenting skills or anger management, encouraged a focus on concrete, achievable change that was helpful to families. However, their successful implementation depended on the uncertainties inherent in human motivation and on worker skills in building relationships and engaging families.

Fundamental social work skills in building therapeutic relationships with parents and children were therefore crucial, serving as a vehicle for delivering interventions in different areas of young people's lives. Where workers were successful in engaging young people and parents and were able to build on their motivation to change, interventions which addressed both child behaviour and parenting practices could set in motion a virtuous circle, whereby positive change by the parent reinforced positive change in the child, or vice versa, and such changes provided further positive reinforcement to both parent and child. Young people described the ways in which interventions had helped to improve parent–child relationships:

> She is ignoring me when I give backchat and it's making me wary not to give her backchat because she will just ignore me more... [The support worker] has made me and mum closer. Like, she gives me cuddles now and again. (Girl, aged 12)

The multi-faceted nature of the interventions was also important since risk factors often interact with and reinforce one another, so interventions which address difficulties in different domains of children's lives are likely to be more helpful to them (Bronfenbrenner 1979; Rutter, Giller and Hagell 1998). In cases which were more successful, workers intervened with both the individual child and the parent (and occasionally with the wider family), as well as mobilizing support from other agencies and helping the young people to develop relationships with peers and engage in positive leisure activities in their local communities.

Conclusion

Although specialist and mainstream services differed in many respects, there was no significant difference in changes in child and family functioning between the groups using the two different types of service. However, the specialist teams appeared to be working with a somewhat more difficult group, who were more likely to have long-term problems and severe emotional and behavioural difficulties. So although the degree of change was similar for the two groups, the support teams achieved this change with a group that included proportionately more young people with long-term and severe difficulties. Support teams also appeared to be more successful in preventing both short- and long-term placement, despite working with an apparently more 'difficult' group; it remains questionable, however, whether the principal focus of such services should be on preventing placement, which may on occasion be necessary to promote the young person's well-being.

The interaction of a multiplicity of factors, including family histories, motivation and the support provided by other agencies or by informal networks, may influence the outcomes that any type of social work service may achieve. What did not appear to influence outcomes to a significant extent, however, were the precise components of the service offered. If families were offered a service, were prepared to engage with workers and were motivated to change (or were encouraged by workers to become more motivated), then matters improved in many cases. Worker skills in engaging families and providing therapeutic help appeared to be more important than the particular techniques used. A multi-faceted approach that addressed difficulties in different aspects of children's lives also appeared to be particularly helpful. Families who were prepared to engage with workers made good use of either type of service, but support teams appeared to be especially successful in engaging young people who were not initially motivated.

Chapter 6

Catching Children as They Fall
The East Dunbartonshire Looked After Children Mental Health Project

Michael van Beinum, Andy Martin and Chris Bonnett

Children looked after by the state have long been recognized as being vulnerable and have a poor long-term outcome. Of particular concern has been their very high levels of mental health disorder. This chapter describes the development and evaluation of a specialist mental health service for young people looked after and accommodated in East Dunbartonshire, Scotland. Rather than work primarily with individual children in need, the project aimed to provide mental health expertise by developing the capacities of frontline residential care staff and their managers to think about and manage the complex psychological needs of young people in their care.

Introduction

Children who have been looked after and accommodated by local authorities are a special needs population, and for many their long-term future is poor. For instance, as Chapter 9 discusses in some detail, care leavers experience higher levels of unemployment, homelessness, disability, teenage parenthood and exclusion from education. Of particular concern is the mental health of those in residential care (Utting 1997); care leavers are also over-represented in adult psychiatric admissions, more likely to become addicted, to be depressed, to harm themselves and to commit suicide (Rushton and Minnis 2002).

The incidence of mental health problems amongst looked after and accommodated children has been shown to be significantly higher than in the general population of teenagers. For instance, McCann and colleagues found a point prevalence rate of 67 per cent for psychiatric disorders in teenagers living in residential units and foster care, compared with 15 per cent of adolescents who lived with their own families. A significant number of looked after children in this study were found to be suffering from severe but treatable psychiatric disorders that had gone undetected (McCann *et al.* 1996). These findings were corroborated by a recent national study of mental health disorders in children that found that 49 per cent of 11- to 15-year-old looked after children in England had a psychiatric disorder sufficiently severe to impair their social functioning, compared with 11 per cent of children living in private households. These rates went up to 67 per cent for children living in residential care (Meltzer *et al.* 2003). Notably, unusual psychiatric diagnoses, such as autistic spectrum disorders and eating disorders, were much more common in looked after children than in children living in private households.

There may be a number of reasons why children who are received into local authority care are more likely to develop serious mental health problems. Most will be vulnerable to such problems before they enter care, having experienced neglectful or chaotic parenting, traumatic early experiences, bereavement or serious illness in one or both parents. They are also more likely to have other risk factors for developing mental health problems, such as coming from low-income families and poor neighbourhoods, and living in overcrowded homes prior to being received into care (Bebbington and Miles 1989). Most will struggle with issues of separation and loss, and many will show signs of an attachment disorder. For many such children the experience of being looked after, especially in a group setting, may do little to moderate the effects of such early experiences and may contribute to later problems. A Scottish survey of the experiences of young people within the care system found high levels of distress, an absence of specialist mental health services and a clear sense that young people felt nobody was listening (Friday 1998). Furthermore, residential care staff who work closely with looked after young people displaying actual or embryonic mental health difficulties may feel undervalued, under-trained, marginalized and quite severely stressed themselves (Robinson *et al.* 1999). Lastly, looked after children often have poor access to medical help and to specialist mental health services. One study found that when looked after children were referred to mental health services they were less likely than other young people to attend their first appointment and more likely to default later on (Chetwynd and Robb 1999).

The shortcomings of residential childcare in Scotland and the dangers posed to children and young people growing up away from their families have been well recognized (Kent 1998; Skinner 1992). In response, social services have developed initiatives to prevent multiple placement breakdowns, encouraged a move from institutional to more domestic care settings and attempted to ensure safer care-giving environments and staff selection. In addition, a national review of child and adolescent mental health services in Britain highlighted the need for better coordinated, more accessible and more integrated services for young people, especially those at greatest risk of mental ill health in later life (National Health Advisory Service 1995). In particular, this report recommended that services should be made more accessible with a single point of entry; that identification of problems, assessment and intervention should happen earlier, and that staff who deal directly with young people should be better trained and supported and their work valued and legitimated.

Background to the development of a specialist service

In 1997 the local adolescent psychiatry service and senior social workers in East Dunbartonshire began to explore how they could work together to improve mental health care for looked after and accommodated children. East Dunbartonshire is a small unitary authority on the northern edge of the city of Glasgow, Scotland's largest city, with a population of around 116,000. It is a mixed suburban and rural community that, although its prosperity and health are above the Scottish average, contains significant pockets of deprivation. The Council looks after and accommodates a smaller proportion of children than all but three of the Scottish local authorities, between 35 and 40 at any one time. Less than a third of these children are placed in the Council's children's units, the majority being placed either in foster care or residential schools. The authority had been involved in the evaluation of Looking After Children in Scotland and the principles of care planning, review and assessment which underpinned this system, and subsequently chose to implement it. Looking After Children in Scotland focused on the outcomes experienced by looked after and accommodated young people, and linked these to their experience of day-to-day care. It asserted that if the detail of care could be improved, better planned and made more to resemble the care experienced by young people growing up at home within their families, then the outcomes for looked after and accommodated young people would be more likely to resemble those enjoyed by the general population (Ward 1995).

In 1997, East Dunbartonshire had one ten-bedded residential unit and a small number of foster families. The authority's Residential Child Care Strategy proposed the closure of this unit and the development of a group of four domestic houses accommodating no more than four children each, in an attempt to provide a better milieu to help children grow up in a healthy way. Within the ethos of Looking After Children, with its aim of improving outcomes for looked after children, senior social work managers argued that input from a specialist mental health service could provide an additional resource for social work staff, particularly frontline residential staff and care home managers. As a result, a dialogue was opened up with the local adolescent psychiatry service.

Initially members of the adolescent psychiatry team made themselves available once a month for an afternoon at the ten-bedded residential care unit. This time could be used, for instance, for face-to-face appointments with looked after and accommodated young people, with or without their carers, and for advice and consultancy to social workers and residential care staff wishing to discuss concerns about individual young people, including those not in residential care. Social work staff were in charge of this clinical time and the adolescent psychiatry team provided an input in whatever way was felt to be most useful. This ethical stance of mutual respect and trust has been an essential hallmark of the project, and contrasted with a situation where traditionally the relationship between Health and Social Services had been characterized by mutual distrust and suspicion. The (informal) expertise of frontline care staff, who knew the children better than any other professional, was particularly valued by the clinical team. Furthermore, the adolescent psychiatry team, usually regarded as 'experts' in the management of troubled teenagers, were able to legitimize a position that there would be many situations where nobody was an expert and solutions would have to be puzzled out together. Paraphrasing Levinas (1989), it was 'taking the other as point of departure', instead of oneself. This service quickly became an established and highly regarded resource to the whole local authority Children and Families Team. Its availability and impact were also welcomed by school guidance staff, educational psychologists and the Children's Panel.

In 1999 an opportunity arose to develop this service further when proposals were sought by the Scottish Executive for projects to be supported by a year of funding from the Mental Health Development Fund. On the back of established good working relationships, a substantial expansion of the service was proposed. This coincided with the closure of the local ten-bedded unit and the movement of staff and children, nearly all teenagers, to three four-bedded units staffed by 28 frontline care staff previously working in large children's homes. This presented opportunities for improvement in the day-to-day quality of care, but also posed significant challenges for staff used to much more institutional settings and the practices that grew from them.

The development of a specialist mental health service for looked after children

The remainder of this chapter will describe the design and development of a specialist mental health service, called the 'Open Door', and how this evolved in response to experience, available financial resources and the findings of an external evaluation.

By the start of 2000, a one-year grant of £143,000 had been received from the Mental Health Development Fund. A small, full-time team was established, consisting of a clinical psychologist, social worker, assistant psychologist and administrative assistance, supported by part-time input from a consultant adolescent psychiatrist.

A steering group was set up, with broad representation from the wider professional community, to oversee, structure and support the initiative. It had senior representatives from all the partners in the project, including social work, education and health, as well as representation from users, the MRC Social and Public Health Research unit at Glasgow University and the Scottish Executive. The steering group met at six-weekly intervals with the project team and proved to have a vital role both in protecting and sustaining the project while the local authority underwent major restructuring, and in helping to manage the transition to more secure funding after year one.

The senior social work manager and the consultant child and adolescent psychiatrist provided day-to-day management. The staff group were further supported by monthly external organizational consultancy.

In addition, as part of a reflexive and action research stance, external evaluation of the project was commissioned from an independent research organization.

The project aimed to make expert mental health help available to all young people who were looked after and accommodated, not just those identified as having a serious psychiatric difficulty. The central tenet of the joint initiative was that the skills, experience and insight of child mental health professionals had to be made available and translated into practical tools for frontline care staff and managers. The ethical stance of 'taking the other as point of departure' continued;

rather than starting with a fixed list of tasks, the team adapted the project to meet the needs of young people and the professionals charged with their care. At times this meant that unspoken prior assumptions about the project had to be challenged. For example, it had originally been anticipated that a substantial part of the work would entail individual sessions with young people. The children in residential care, however, quickly let it be known that 'we're no mental' and most were not interested in individual sessions with clinical staff. As a result, project staff instead worked predominantly with residential care staff and social workers. It was only towards the end of the first year that more children opted for individual work.

In the first year of its operation the project offered a wide range of services to young people, residential care staff, social workers and the educational and social work community. The team focused primarily on young people accommodated in the children's units rather than in foster families since they were seen as being in greatest need. The services included consultation to care staff and social workers about individual young people, consultation to staff teams about whole-unit issues, training seminars for frontline field and residential staff, assessment of individual young people and follow-up clinical work, and advice to looked after children reviews. In this way, as well as through frequent informal meetings, the project staff developed relationships with staff and young people at multiple levels.

Open Door offered a wide range of psychological approaches in working with seriously disturbed and needy children, including developmental and psychodynamic perspectives. By employing a variety of different perspectives, the team strove to encourage frontline care staff to think more reflectively about children, the significance of past experiences, their stage of development and the difficulties they posed to staff, in a social work culture that often expected instant action to solve problems.

To support this shift in perspective, two social workers and four residential carers went on a group-based intensive training course in psychoanalytic approaches to child development provided by a local child psychotherapy training centre. The objective was to equip each care home with at least one member of staff who could act as a resource to the rest of the staff group in this way of working. All participants brought ongoing problems from their work with young people to the course for discussion and supervision. Most residential care staff had never been on an academic training course before, but the training proved to be highly successful and much valued. The external evaluation indicated that the way staff related to the children in their care changed substantially following the course.

The project had to contend with an unpredictable and rapidly changing organizational context, including a major reorganization of the social services, the departure of key staff and a temporary reduction in funding. Changes in staff and funding from January 2000 are shown in Tables 6.1 and 6.2. When the Mental Health Development Fund grant ended in January 2001 the ongoing funding of the project was taken on jointly by the local authority and the health trust at a reduced level. This led to a reduction in staff and, as a result, the work of the team diminished significantly over the following year. Clinical work with young people and consultations about them continued but group consultations, teaching seminars and informal support were put on hold.

Table 6.1: Staffing levels for 2000–2002

	January 2000	July 2000	January 2001	July 2001	January 2002	July 2002
Clinical psychologist	1.0	1.0	0.5	0.5	0.5	1.0
Social worker	1.0	1.0	1.0	0.5 (vacant)	0.5	1.0 (0.5 vacant)
Assistant psychologist	0.8	0.8	–	–	–	–
Consultant psychiatrist	0.2	0.2	0.2	–	–	–
Secretary	1.0 (vacant)	1.0 (vacant)	0.5 (vacant)	0.5 (vacant)	0.5 (vacant)	0.5

Both health and social services, however, were by this point deeply committed to the joint project and to the priority of looked after and accommodated young people and their mental health needs. In the beginning of 2002 Greater Glasgow Health Board began to put into action a plan to develop mental health services for looked after and accommodated children across the whole of their catchment area, which covered six different local authorities, including East Dunbartonshire. The expanded service was to provide a broad-based mental health service for all looked after and accommodated children, from early infancy to 18 years of age. Open Door was combined with a similar project in East Glasgow for looked after children under 12 years of age (LACES). This latter project, started shortly after Open Door, had focused on providing a specialist mental health service for children who had been fostered and prided itself on supporting all those who had originated from East Glasgow, irrespective of their current address. In addition, in order to strengthen the service, the steering group was expanded to include representatives from the community paediatric service and the Big Step, a major Social Inclusion Partnership (SIP) based in Glasgow working in a range of ways to provide support, advice and assistance to young people leaving and having left care.

Table 6.2: Financial outlay (actual and planned)

	Health Board outlay	**Social Work outlay**
2001–2002	£40,000	Rent for office accommodation Social worker
2002–2003	£194,000	Rent for office accommodation Social worker
2003–2004	£329,000	Rent for office accommodation Social worker

By the middle of 2002 extra funding had been provided by the health trust and local authority and the health board had begun to recruit staff to expand the new, combined team. A full-time child and adolescent psychiatrist and a senior clinical psychologist were appointed and a further five clinical posts planned. The additional staff allowed the range of services to looked after and accommodated children in East Dunbartonshire to return to the levels provided at the end of the first year of the project.

Findings

There were two forms of evaluation: internal audit by the project staff and external evaluation from an independent research organization. Information from both was used to modify the service as it evolved.

Internal evaluation

The members of Open Door routinely collected monthly statistics describing their work, including keeping a record of all teaching seminars, consultations with social services staff (both about children and whole-unit issues causing concern), and direct clinical work with individual children. Some of the results are shown in Table 6.3.

Table 6.3: Activity levels for 2000–2002

	January–July 2000	July 2000 –January 2001	January–July 2001	July 2001–January 2002	January–July 2002
Consultations	83	184	94	45	32
Clinical contact	21	71	25	27	21

Direct clinical contact with individual children was only a small part of the overall work. As well as numerous consultation meetings, 13 teaching seminars were provided for unit staff and social work teams in the first year, on a range of topics such as the psychology of bereavement, attachment theory and understanding self harm in teenagers. In addition, a great deal of time, particularly in the first six months of the project, was spent by project staff in getting to know frontline care staff, social workers, managers, other members of the local authority and the young people themselves. This was largely done by Open Door staff making frequent informal visits to all the children's homes and being available to talk about the project and discuss how staff and children might wish to utilize the expertise available. Such informal contact was hard to quantify, but it was regarded as a vital part of the project's work that did much to allow frontline care staff to feel confident in managing the emotional needs of the children in their care.

Inevitably, activity in year two declined as a result of the temporary financial cutbacks and consequent staff shortages, but the reduced team worked hard to maintain the direct clinical contact with young people. This meant, however, that in year two informal visits to the residential units were curtailed and no teaching seminars took place.

External evaluation

External evaluation was an integral part of the design, both to demonstrate whether the project made a significant difference to the well-being of young people in care and, if so, to ensure its long-term viability. The philosophy of the project was to develop a learning culture. Therefore, rather than stand aloof and provide a report that was independent and objective in a positivistic sense, the evaluation was designed to allow findings to be fed back into the ongoing evolution of the project, thereby making it an integral part of the reflexive culture.

This meant that the research team, and particularly the senior researcher, played an important role in making people think about and reflect upon their work in the project. The calm and thoughtful manner in which the research was undertaken provided considerable support to key staff at times of difficulty. The high-profile evaluation also played a significant role in sustaining the project in the rapidly changing culture of a local authority undergoing radical reform.

The external evaluation took the form of individual semi-structured interviews with all those staff working with looked after and accommodated children (the project team, residential care workers, unit leaders, social workers, social work managers, teachers, educational psychologists, senior health service staff and Scotland's advocacy service for looked after children), as well as the children themselves. Interviews took place approximately eight months after the start of the project, and at approximately six-monthly intervals thereafter, and were conducted by a small research team that included members of Who Cares (Scotland), an advocacy service for looked after children. In addition, a feedback seminar was held towards the end of the first year for frontline care staff, teachers and educational psychologists, as well as senior staff from both health and social services, allowing staff to discuss their views about the project in depth. The research team submitted written reports after the first and second years (Jones 2003). The findings indicated that the project had been successful in a number of areas, but that some parts remained problematic.

After the first year residential care staff and social workers were enthusiastic, rated the project very highly and indicated that they had changed their stance towards the young people in their care. For instance, when a young person cut himself or herself it was now seen as indicating that he or she struggling to cope with overwhelming and distressing inner feelings, rather than an attempt at rubbishing the hard work of care staff. Staff said they felt more confident in their ability to support young people and help them work through difficulties. The easy access to mental health expertise and the informal working relationships with project staff were greatly valued by residential care staff and seen by them as an important reason for the success of the project. This positive evaluation continued at the end of the second year, but all staff expressed frustration with the reduction in services, and said they wished to return to the previous levels of service provision. In particular, residential staff wanted a return of the informal presence of the team in the units.

Young people said they felt the project had made little difference at the end of the first year, but by the end of the second year all but one of those interviewed said it *had* made a difference to their lives, in some cases a dramatic one.

Both social workers and the team soon felt that the original target group was too narrow. As a result, the project evolved rapidly to offer consultation and clinical sessions to children in foster care. By the end of the first year the service offered one-off consultations to social workers on any child under their care. The fact that the project became a service for all young people in care, not just those who had identified serious mental disorders, promoted the success of the project further. It became a right of young people received into care that responsible adults would utilize the best available expertise to think about their predicament.

Senior staff in both health and social work appeared to understand the project well and were broadly in favour of it, but joint working remained difficult. Given the major shake-up of social work services that took place over this period, this was perhaps not surprising. The management of the project, originally conceived as a joint process by health and social services, proved to be highly problematical. For instance, dedicated office space was a major headache, with the project being housed in temporary accommodation for the first two years; also, throughout this time administrative support consisted of a series of agency secretaries with long periods with no input at all. In the light of this finding, it was agreed by all partners that health would take the lead role in the future management of the service.

Teachers and educational psychologists felt they had not been given sufficient access to the project, particularly in the first nine months or so. They would have liked more help with looked after children who were having problems in educational settings.

Overall, the external evaluation concluded that the project had succeeded in establishing an innovative mental health service for looked after and accommodated children which appeared to make a real difference to their lives, effected a change in working practices of frontline care staff and social workers, and had substantially influenced the planning of both health and social services in Glasgow.

Evaluation reports are normally about fixing something on paper, standing outside of what was going on, and about objective reflection and debate. This contrasts with the daily reality of those working in the project, which was to engage, as best they could, with a confusing kaleidoscope of shifting social and psychological realities. Staff often felt a sense of being out of their depth, and having to sort out what to do next in situations that were ambiguous, rapidly changing and open to multiple interpretations. Evaluation here was a tool or a strategy to help people swim, not something that created the illusion of solid ground.

Evaluation in this project has been a form of action research (Toulmin and Gustavsen 1996), part of a strategy to change a situation that was recognized by all to be bad for young people in care. In this process, valuing and respecting looked after young people and the adults who tried to help them grow up in a healthy way have been as important as the rigorous analysis of outcomes. Evaluation raised a number of ethical dilemmas, exposing the role of the researcher and his or her values and the way he or she engages with the field. Who determines the questions and who will benefit? How does research feed into the complex political conflicts between the various parties, including young people, frontline care staff and senior managers? How can evaluation be conducted in a way that both addresses the social and psychological complexities of the field and adheres to high standards of trustworthiness and generalizability? The role of language and the meaning of words came to the fore, as participants struggled with what was, and was not, allowed to be thought, and even said, making evaluation part of the wider project's aim of development and consciousness-raising for both staff and young people.

Bahktin has drawn attention to how, in any dialogue between participants, 'every act of communication arises from a background of past ideological encounters and ideological struggles' (Sandywell 1998, p.197). Evaluation here was seen as participating in, and contributing to, an open and reflective set of conversations that allowed participants to become more aware of the ambiguities and complexities of their world and the ways in which they acted in and thought about this world. Such dialogues are never finished (Bahktin 1986) but always open to further possibilities, with every conversation a creative act exploring the world. This was a very different view of evaluation – and the work of a mental health team – from one that saw it as aiming to provide an authoritative and final answer, once and for all, to a defined problem.

Both internal and external evaluations concluded that change had occurred in the working practices of key staff. Being involved on a daily basis with mental health professionals and thinking about mental health issues appeared to help frontline staff to work through some of their own anxieties about working with needy and disturbed children. Residential care staff had to manage the broader anxiety born of the move from institutional methods of practice to smaller scale but also more intimate models, where it was more difficult for them to avoid working with disturbed and very needy children who often made the staff feel bad. The project team's sensitivity to such difficulties, as well as the intensive child psychotherapy training course for selected key staff, allowed staff to work with the dynamic between the distress of young people and the tensions set up inside individual staff members as a result of their work. Thus one tenet of the project was that by facilitating the psychological learning environment of the staff the healthy psychological development of troubled looked after children would be promoted. None of the frontline staff said that they saw the mental health service primarily or exclusively as being about the treatment or management of presenting problems, although they valued the practical insight and support that allowed them to manage young people's care on a daily basis. In this sense the project, represented by its staff group, acted as a transitional phenomenon that facilitated the personal and professional development of staff (Winnicott 1985).

All staff – residential care workers, teachers, field social workers, mental health professionals and others – saw the process as a longer-term intervention that would impact on the outcomes for young people in later life. The project helped to develop a sense of a community of professionals with a common purpose of caring for a defined population of looked after young people, fostered by shared thinking about them. However, this could be undermined by issues such as funding problems in year two and changes in key staff, leading to staff from participating organizations retreating, at times, into more bureaucratic and less joined up ways of operating. For instance, project staff began to feel that social work staff found it more difficult to take on board the results of child assessments, and project staff lacked the links to senior social work managers that could resolve such difficulties. A major challenge for the future, therefore, concerns the ability of very different organizational cultures – health services, education and social work – to work together for the benefit of children.

Initially young people were reluctant to become involved directly, fearing that they would be labelled as 'mad' if they did so. However, after the project's credentials were tested by one or two young people seeing members of staff for individual work over time, more were willing to be referred for individual work. This might explain the increased appreciation of Open Door after the end of the second year.

Overall, an approach that, rather than just providing an 'expert' psychiatric outpatient service, focused on developing the capacity of frontline care staff to think about and manage the psychological needs of looked after and accommodated children, appeared to have worked well. One measure of the effectiveness of the project was that no young person moved to another children's home during its lifetime. This was surprising, as previously, children had stayed an average of four months in a placement. In other words, one objective – to provide a stable home where long-term sustaining relationships could be established – was achieved. The critical question, however, remains to what extent interventions can improve the long-term outcomes for looked after young people, as they move on from local authority care into adulthood and independence. We need to know if, and how, such interventions can make a difference; prospective longitudinal cohort studies are urgently required.

Conclusion

The development of a dedicated mental health service for looked after and accommodated children in East Dunbartonshire, with its emphasis on promoting conditions where shared thought about complex and difficult children was facilitated in a community of professionals, together with a stress on evaluation, has begun to change the landscape of services for looked after children in East Dunbartonshire.

The development of a joint approach to the mental health needs of young people in residential care in East Dunbartonshire has been about a 'learning approach' to the way in which agencies – with their own priorities, cultures and practices – can come together to promote an integrated approach to the care of children in particularly difficult circumstances. This has allowed the participants to reflect on and talk about the complexities of feelings engendered by working with looked after and accommodated children as they are growing up. This has been vital, not just in terms of keeping the staff psychologically alive, but because it might also allow the children to imagine a different future for themselves. As a result, seeking ways of facilitating creativity has been a recurrent theme throughout the project, and the report given in this chapter is but a punctuation mark in an ongoing evolution. What has been central to the process, and shared from the outset by all the health and local authority players, is the conviction that, by intervening and healing young people as they pass through our system, we must be helping them towards better futures. We must catch children as they fall.

Acknowledgements

The authors would like to express their thanks and admiration to all those who made this project possible, and in particular to the frontline workers and young people themselves, the Scottish Office for funding this project, Greater Glasgow Health Board, East Dunbartonshire Social Services, the members of the project team Who Cares? (Scotland), Professor Patrick West at the MRC, Debbie Hindle at the Scottish Institute of Human Relations, and Lyn Jones and his research team at Scottish Health Feedback. They would also like to thank The Scottish Institute for Residential Child Care for permission to reproduce parts of this chapter that have been published in *The Scottish Journal of Residential Child Care* (van Beinum, Martin and Bonnett 2002).

Chapter 7

Promoting the Health and Well-being of Indigenous Minority Children in Canada and Australia

Richard Budgell, Mike Clare,
Jennifer Noonan and Lynn Robertson

This chapter examines the health and well-being of indigenous minority children in two different countries: Australia and Canada, and explores how the events of the past continue to shape government policies and initiatives today. It introduces two initiatives, Looking After Children in Western Australia, and Aboriginal Head Start in Canada, both of which are specifically designed to improve outcomes for these populations.

Historical context

Australia

The Commonwealth of Australia was not established until 1901. The jurisdiction now includes six states and two territories; responsibility to provide national security, employment, income support and immigration services remains with the federal government, which also continues to fund and influence a broad range of policies implemented by state governments. These include services from education, health, housing, justice, police, and statutory child and family welfare organizations.

Child and family welfare legislation varies across states and territories, all of which have different ways of defining needs and gathering data. Although services are generally fragmented, a few cross-departmental initiatives such as Families First in New South Wales and Strengthening Families in Victoria aim to offer a coordinated response to families in need. Aboriginal and Islander Child Care Agencies operate in most states and territories to provide services to indigenous children and families alongside government-funded child protection, family preservation and out-of-home care services, delivered by both statutory and non-government agencies (Australian Institute of Health and Welfare 2001).

Indigenous peoples have lived in Australia for at least 40,000 years. Before the British occupation in 1788 there were over 600 language groups amongst Aboriginal and Torres Strait Islander Australians. Each group had its own culture and outsiders were required to perform particular ceremonies and seek permission to cross territorial borders. Complex kinship arrangements prescribed patterns of family life including allowable marriage partners and child-rearing responsibilities. Aboriginal people were guided by the Dreaming, a system of religious beliefs that was the foundation of their belonging to the land. The traditional owners of the land were all colonized under the dominant assumption of *terra nullius* (empty land) – the legal position until 1991 when the Mabo Judgement of the High Court of Australia legally recognized the rights of those Aboriginal people who can prove continuous connection with their land.

The initial assumption of the colonists was that 'pure Aboriginal' people would die out as settlement impacted on more of the continent. Pastoralists and missionaries began the process of removing Aboriginal children from their parents, a practice that increased as the frontier widened in the nineteenth century. Voluntary and involuntary sexual relationships between white men and indigenous women led to increased numbers of mixed-race children. By the 1880s, each jurisdiction had appointed a Protector of Aboriginal People with powers to forcibly remove mixed-race children from their Aboriginal mothers at an early age in the belief that, being more 'animalistic', these parents would soon forget about their children.

Between the 1880s and the late 1960s thousands of indigenous children were removed from their parents. Many were adopted by non-indigenous couples into the white European culture, with the aim of assimilation. The status of Aboriginal people only changed when eventually they were given the right to vote in 1967. Inevitably this policy of separation and dislocation across generations has had a profound and enduring impact on most – if not all – indigenous families:

they experienced problems in physical, social, intellectual and emotional development manifested in learning problems, difficulties in forming social relationships, anti-social behaviour, lack of personal identity, emotional disorders and feelings of alienation. As adults they experienced breakdown of family relationships, high levels of unemployment, substance abuse, imprisonment, poor health and mental disorders. (Haebich 2001, p.415)

The adverse consequences of past policies continue to inform Aboriginal attitudes to 'the Welfare' and the use of adoption and residential care as placement options for children who cannot live with their parents. Reflecting on the historical legacy for Aboriginal children, their families and communities is essential in any review of policies designed to enhance well-being.

Canada

Policies and programmes for Aboriginal[1] children in today's Canada are developed against a similar backdrop of tragedy and error. Canada became a federated nation in 1867 and now consists of ten provinces and three territories. Responsibility for health and education is assigned to the provinces, while the federal government bears constitutional responsibility for 'Indians and lands reserved for Indians'. In practice, the federal government assumes a major fiscal responsibility for legally recognized First Nations people on reserves and provides a small number of programs or services for those living elsewhere. Inuit, who do not have reserves, came to be included under federal jurisdiction through a 1939 Supreme Court of Canada decision, but Métis are seen by the federal government as an exclusively provincial responsibility, although this is currently being challenged politically and in the courts. Relationships between Aboriginal organizations or governments, and provincial or territorial and federal governments, are strained more often than not, and many provinces assert that the federal government is not acknowledging its full responsibility towards Aboriginal people. In this context, that progress has been achieved is perhaps all the more remarkable.

As in Australia, Canada introduced a policy of separating Aboriginal children from their families and communities, through a system of residential boarding schools. These institutions operated from the mid-nineteenth century to the 1970s and were usually run by Protestant churches and Roman Catholic orders with financial support from the Canadian government (Indian Residential Schools Resolution Canada 2003).

The residential schools' mission was inherently assimilationist, designed to instil the acquisition of skills and cultural knowledge that would be of use to Aboriginal children in the 'white' world. The schools implicitly, and often explicitly, discouraged the retention of Aboriginal language, knowledge and cultural values. Many saw persistent physical and sexual abuse of the young in their care, which contributed to the future dysfunction of the victims and their families. At the time of writing, thousands of victims' legal claims are still being pursued.

After the waning of the residential school system during the mid-1970s, with the exception of the provision of education and child welfare services on First Nations reserves,[2] there was little focused attention by government on the needs of Aboriginal children until the 1990s. By then, there were enormous demographic, socio-economic and health pressures within the Aboriginal population. Nevertheless, the situation of Aboriginal peoples in Canada, while still deeply disadvantaged, may be better than that of Aboriginal people in Australia because of a higher degree of acknowledgment of their historical and constitutional place.

Current issues for Aboriginal groups

The indigenous population accounts for 2 per cent of the total population in Australia and 3.3 per cent in Canada. In both jurisdictions indigenous populations are significantly younger than non-Aboriginals, and show important disparities on a range of socio-economic and health indicators (Clare and Noonan 2002; Statistics Canada 2003).

Health

The state of Aboriginal health in Australia has been described as a 'national disaster'. Aboriginal people have higher rates of illness, disability and death than other Australians, and their life expectancy is 20 years below that of the wider population (Clare and Noonan 2002). For children and young people there are particular concerns. The rates of mortality and illness for indigenous children are higher than those for other Australians. Poor health in infancy can impact on later educational achievement: indigenous infants often have a significant exposure to otitis media in the first weeks of life, a condition which has been shown to increase the risk of problems with speech, language and literacy (Clare and Noonan 2002).

In Canada, the Aboriginal birth rate is about 1.5 per cent higher than that of the wider population. Mortality and illness rates for Aboriginal children are significantly higher than for other Canadians. Infant mortality rates are 8 per 1000 live births for First Nations people living on reserves, and 15 per 1000 for Inuit, compared with a rate of 5.3 per 1000 for Canadians as a whole (Canadian Institute for Health Information 2004). Life expectancy for First Nations people is between five and seven years lower than for other Canadians. Some diseases show much higher prevalence among Aboriginal people: diabetes, for example, is found three to five times more frequently (Probert and Poirier 2003).

In both Canada and Australia, suicide rates are significantly higher amongst the Aboriginal populations. They are about four times higher amongst Aboriginal boys aged 15–19 than amongst other Australians (Clare and Noonan 2002) and twice as high amongst First Nations people living on reserves as in the rest of Canada (Canadian Institute for Health Information 2004).

Education and employment

In 1994, a study found that 21 per cent of Aboriginal children in Australia aged 6 to 14 years were not attending an educational institution, and that despite making up 5 per cent of the school population, they constituted 30 per cent of all truants. Many Aboriginal students leave school at around the ages of 11 or 12 due to reasons such as family transience, absenteeism, peer groups which engage in crime and substance misuse, parental influences and early pregnancy (Clare and Noonan 2002). In 2001, 86 per cent of indigenous students stayed until Year 10 (age 15) compared with 94 per cent of all students. For those remaining until Year 12 (age 17) the retention rate was about half that of all students: 36 per cent compared with 73 per cent.

Canadian figures also show significant differences: in 2001, 6 per cent of Aboriginal people had university degrees, compared with 26 per cent of non-Aboriginal Canadians. The gap is smaller for those with college diplomas or certificates: 22 per cent compared with 25 per cent. Differences in educational attainment are reflected in income and employment rates. In 2000, the median Aboriginal income was CDN$13,593 compared with CDN$22,431 for non-Aboriginals; in 2001, 61 per cent of Aboriginal people aged between 25–54 were employed as compared with 80 per cent of non-Aboriginal people in the same age group (Statistics Canada 2003).

The high birth rate for indigenous Australians means that, within the next few years, the proportion of young Aboriginal people seeking to join the labour market will be almost three times as high (60%) as that of the total population (21%) (Australian Government 2004). Growth in jobs for indigenous Australians is unlikely to keep pace with the increased numbers of young people available for work. Hunter, Kinfu and Taylor (2003) claim that the economic situation for indigenous Australians is already deteriorating. They predict that the unemployment rate for indigenous Australians will increase from 26 per cent in 1996 to 32 per cent in 2006, while that for non-indigenous people will remain unchanged at 8 per cent.

Social exclusion

In both Canada and Australia, the disadvantages experienced by Aboriginal young people in the areas of health and education are also evident in other indicators of social exclusion. Aboriginal young people in Australia, for instance, are greatly over-represented in the juvenile justice system, particularly at its more punitive end. A study undertaken by Atkinson (1993) indicated that they were more than 24 times more likely to be imprisoned than non-Aboriginals.

Finally, there is a continued high rate of placement of indigenous children in care in Australian states and territories; the rate of 20 per 1000 is 7.8 times higher than that for non-indigenous children (Sultmann and Testro 2001). In Canada, approximately 40 per cent of the 76,000 children in out-of-home care are Aboriginal, although Aboriginal people form only 3 per cent of the Canadian population (Blackstock 2003). In 2001, 35 per cent of Aboriginal children living in large urban centres in Canada changed their residence at least once in a 12-month period (Norris 2003), indicative of the highly transient lives of many indigenous families.

Range of policies and programmes

Over the last 20 years there have been attempts to develop policies intended to improve outcomes for Aboriginal children and young people in both Canada and Australia. Such policies aim to avoid some of the tragic mistakes of the past, particularly by introducing programs that respect the culture of indigenous populations. The remainder of this chapter explores two such programs, one in Australia, and one in Canada, and sets them within the context of the policies that led to their introduction.

Australia

Since the early 1980s, the federal Department of Aboriginal Affairs in Australia has been involved in the development and implementation of the Aboriginal Child Placement Principle for those indigenous children who cannot live with their birth parents. Haebich (2001) summarizes its central premises:

> Aboriginal children were to remain with their families, removals were to be a last resort and children were not to be placed in white families or institutions. When removal was deemed essential, according to criteria determined by Aboriginal practices and values, then the children were to be placed with a member of their extended family or their own community in accordance with Aboriginal customary law, or with other Aboriginal families living in close proximity. (p.602)

However, Briskman (2001) asserts that, while these Principles have been enshrined in most Australian jurisdictions, their implementation falls short of the specified standards, one reason being that non-government agencies are under no compulsion to comply with them. The Child and Family Welfare Association of Australia (CAFWAA) (2002) estimated that 25 per cent of indigenous children in care are placed outside the Principles.

Important policy and practice developments and controversies in Australia have increased the pressure on under-resourced government agencies. The growing impermanence of the 'family' and the impact of drug and alcohol abuse by parents who are unable to care for their children have undermined policy moves towards 'family preservation' and 'reunification' programs aimed at reducing the numbers of children needing 'permanent long-term' placements. The CAFWAA report (2002) predicts that by 2010 the admission rate of indigenous children will have grown from almost 8 to 18 per thousand.

The growing number of state enquiries into child deaths and abuse in the system has contributed to the reduction in residential care – now approximately no more than 15 per cent of placements. Moreover, despite the commitment to placement stability, the use of adoption as a long-term placement option has virtually disappeared. These factors have all added to the current crisis in foster care and provided further incentives for moving towards kinship care. However there are further problems on the horizon; by 2010, 70 per cent of the total indigenous population will be under 30 years of age with profound implications for their ability to provide such placements (CAFWAA 2002).

Thus it seems likely that, despite the introduction of legislation aimed at supporting the Principles, disproportionate numbers of Aboriginal children in Australia will continue to come into the care system and be looked after outside their immediate kinship networks. Such children are likely to be doubly disadvantaged, both by the disproportionately poor outcomes commonly experienced by their population group, and by the detrimental consequences of the factors that led to placement; some will be further disadvantaged by their experiences in care. What compensatory measures are being put in place to try to improve their life chances?

IMPROVING OUTCOMES FOR CHILDREN IN CARE

First, there are encouraging signs that the need to improve the quality of care for children in out-of-home placements is increasingly recognized. Debate in this area has been promoted by recent publications which have presented a detailed review of national and international literature on the role and risks of foster care, considered the problematic issue of standards in foster care and leaving care (Barber and Gilbertson 2001) and presented a framework of principles and goals for an improved foster care service (Carter 2002). A further publication has identified placement trends for out-of-home care and demonstrated the growing reliance on family-based care (Sultmann and Testro 2001). The debate is further informed by reviews of both the educational achievement of children in care across states and territories (CREATE Foundation 2002) and the research and practice in two important specialist services: kinship care and foster care (Mason *et al.* 2002; McHugh 2002).

A further cluster of publications has addressed the fragmentation of policy and practice in Australia (CAFWAA 2002), and made the case for an integrated Commonwealth and state government policy process with leadership from the federal minister with responsibility for children and families.

Perhaps most importantly, there are emerging signs that the federal government and CAFWAA (the lead organization for non-government provider agencies) are recognizing that a key responsibility is to operationalize 'good enough standards' for the care of vulnerable children and to manage the collection and dissemination of evidence of state and territory governments' performance against those standards. One method of doing so has been to pilot, and in some areas to implement, the Looking After Children materials in a number of states and territories. Licences to pilot this program have been taken out in four Australian states; this chapter explores specifically the experience in Western Australia, where there has been a particular focus on the use of the materials with Aboriginal children.

THE LOOKING AFTER CHILDREN PROGRAM

Looking After Children: Good Parenting, Good Outcomes is a recording system developed in the UK to provide a means of evaluating outcomes for children placed in out-of-home care (Parker *et al.* 1991; Ward 1995). The program is intended to improve the parenting experience of children looked after by the state by introducing ideas about outcome into everyday social work practice. The materials were developed within a framework of information gathering, assessment, planning and review and were intended to help social workers and carers set an agenda for work with children and young people (Ward 1995).

At the heart of the system are the Assessment and Action Records, a series of assessment tools that focus on the child or young person's developmental needs across the seven key dimensions of health, education, identity, social and family relationships, emotional and behavioural development, social presentation and self-care skills. The Records set standards for the quality of day-to-day care to be expected when children are placed away from home, and ask questions which monitor how far they receive those parental inputs necessary to promote good outcomes. When used over time the Assessment and Action Records should enable agencies to assess children's progress in each of the seven dimensions.

Since 1993, when the first attempts were made to introduce agency managers, practitioners and carers in Western Australia to the Looking After Children materials (Clare and Peerless 1996), there has been considerable consultation with Aboriginal colleagues in both government and non-government agencies. Doubts were initially expressed about the cultural appropriateness and the intrusive assumptions of the practice tools; there was also concern about the 'ownership' of the information about indigenous families. Some of these issues were reiterated in a further consultation exercise that sought the views of staff in two non-government Aboriginal child and family welfare agencies in 2002. Comments by workers from the agencies indicated which adjustments would be necessary to address specific items included on the Assessment and Action Records: 'Some questions do not suit remote communities (eg cooker guards) but translators are needed to localize', or that the approach might need to be modified:

> Nyungar…parents tend to protect and speak for their children for a longer time span than non-Aboriginal parents – it would be offensive to pose questions to a 10–13 year old especially regarding cannabis use or other drugs, sex and pregnancy – this would have to be handled sensitively.

> Question and answer format is not an Aboriginal thing – too many questions – need to have a yarn and write it up later.

However, this does not mean that the system or materials are irrelevant. In the UK, the materials were piloted with a community group of families from a range of occupational and ethnic groups, and different family structures. The evidence suggested that few considered the content of the Records to be inappropriate (Moyers and Mason 1995). Instead, approaches need to be developed which best meet the need of the community and the content adapted accordingly.

Moreover some of the comments introduce questions about social work practice that have also been raised in the United Kingdom (Ward 1995) and are not therefore specific to the indigenous population of Australia. Undertaking assessments of this nature requires a relationship between the young person and carer, another point raised by both communities:

> The chances of getting answers are entirely dependent on the previously established relationships – unlikely to exist in current circumstances.

There were also several positive comments:

> They [Looking After Children materials] are everything you would wish for in providing a framework to ensure optimum care – or inquiry into standards of care – for the child.

> No problem in principle – need to be careful who asks the questions.

In 1998 a decision was made to implement the Assessment and Action Records for all non-indigenous wards of the state in care in Western Australia; this was subsequently extended to include all children in care (wards and non-wards). The project eventually included the administrative records developed to support the processes of information gathering, planning and review, and the complete system was implemented in October 2001.

Looking After Children has a firm research basis and focuses on child development. Another strength is the explicit recognition of the responsibilities of 'government as parent'. Without such a national policy initiative and standard data collection, there is a lack of an organizing structure for establishing and monitoring standards and outcomes. Time will show whether implementation will succeed in the face of the current workload demands on case managers and their practice supervisors, and the resource implications for the foster care and residential care systems.

Canada

Looking After Children has been widely implemented in contemporary Canada and again issues concerning its relevance and adaptability for indigenous children have been explored (Kufeldt *et al.* 2000). However this is only one of a range of programs that have the potential to improve outcomes for indigenous children. A variety of approaches are in use, with the common characteristic that the delivery agents are Aboriginal organizations, typically with funding from the federal government. Most of the programs being delivered on First Nations reserves are culturally and community specific for Aboriginal people. Some, such as child welfare and family services, are equivalents to existing programs for other Canadians; some are Aboriginally targeted programs on- or off-reserve; and some are delivered as part of larger national initiatives directed at a wider group of socially or economically vulnerable populations.

The spark for the creation of new children's programs was Canada's participation in the United Nations-sponsored World Summit for Children in 1990, which produced the Convention on the Rights of the Child. In response, the Canadian government established a policy initiative called 'Brighter Futures', which included a range of programs directed at children aged 0–6 (Government of Canada 1991). Two of these programs had a significant impact on Aboriginal children: Brighter Futures On-Reserve, and the Community Action Program for Children (CAPC). Although only the former was specifically directed at First Nations and Inuit communities, a significant proportion of children and families participating in CAPC are also Aboriginal, recruited through specific targeting. A negotiator recalls that: 'when you looked at populations most at risk, most of them were from an Aboriginal culture' (Walker 2003). In the case of CAPC, the proportion of projects targeting Aboriginal people is as high as 63 per cent in some provinces.

Contemporaneous with the development of these new programs was a policy change led by the federal Department of Indian Affairs to support the creation of child and family services on the reserves, designed, controlled and managed by First Nations people. These would be comparable to those existing off-reserve managed by provincial governments or provincially funded agencies (McDonald *et al.* 2000). By 1998, 91 such agencies with a full range of services were operating in 359 First Nations (McDonald *et al.* 2000).

ABORIGINAL HEAD START

A second generation of Aboriginal children's programs emerged in the mid-1990s; amongst these were the Canada Pre-natal Nutrition Program (CPNP) (see Chapter 11) and the Aboriginal Head Start (AHS).

Aboriginal Head Start is an early childhood development program focused on children aged 0–6 years and their families, with an emphasis on three- to five-year-olds. Child development centres managed by Aboriginal community organizations provide direct service to children between the ages of three and five in structured half-day pre-schools that involve parents in the management of the site (Health Canada 2000b). The design is based on research about the effectiveness of quality early childhood education and care. The service was initially modelled on the Head Start program in the US, with which it shares five of its six components: education, health promotion, nutrition, parental involvement and social supports. Unlike the significantly larger US program directed at low-income families of any cultural background, AHS is the only national early intervention program of its type in Canada, with no equivalent or larger program in place for other Canadians.

Aboriginal Head Start's most distinctive program component is Aboriginal culture and language, the explicit inclusion of which is a marked departure from earlier projects. The program is in line with approaches being discussed by international organizations such as UNICEF, which notes that early childhood development initiatives 'might well provide a pathway to reducing poor learning capacity and low self esteem of the kind that negatively reinforces notions of cultural inferiority and second-class citizenship' (UNICEF 1997, p.22). Aboriginal people were directly involved in the definition and implementation of the program; the inclusion of Aboriginal culture and language as an integral component has resulted in a highly positive reception by the Aboriginal community. A local project coordinator in Yukon Territory reports:

> The children learned to sing five traditional songs, in Han language – their native language. We would attend birthday lunches for Elders once a month and sing the five traditional songs for them. As well, they would sing Happy Birthday to them in Han. They also sang at the Head Start graduation in 2001. As more people heard them sing around the community, we found ourselves getting invited to a lot of different community events and singing for different functions such as meetings and dinners. (Health Canada 2002a, p.13)

In 2001, 97 per cent of AHS sites were teaching daily in an Aboriginal language, although the primary language in use in most sites is English or French (Health Canada 2002a, p.10).

Aboriginal Head Start's assumptions about how to develop a culturally appropriate yet high quality program are as yet unproven. At the time of writing, an impact evaluation being conducted on its urban and northern sites has still to provide data. What is known, however, is that the program has been successful in creating many Aboriginal early childhood development centres where none existed before. There are 114 sites in urban and northern communities serving 3500 children, approximately 7 per cent of all those in the three- to five-year-old target group (Health Canada 2002a) and, in addition, sites on approximately 225 reserves, serving over 6000 children, approximately 16 per cent of all those targeted (Health Canada 2000a; Indian and Northern Affairs Canada 2000). Discussions with program participants reveal that:

> community members place importance on the AHS project's role in Aboriginal community building and development of advocacy in participants on issues such as Aboriginal language. Aboriginal community members [want] to see programs like AHS strengthen and rally, instead of divide their communities. (Budgell and Robertson 2003, p.126)

What next for indigenous policy and practice

Australia

Given the evidence of the poor health and well-being of indigenous children in Australian states and territories, an effective and integrated set of intervention policies is required which operates on different strategic levels and employs a variety of methods. There is profound multi-generational trauma to address, with the need for restoration of tribal lands to their original owners, an apology from the federal government to continue the stalled process of reconciliation and the education of all citizens and professionals working with Aboriginal children, families and communities to develop a multi-level systematic approach leading to self-determination and self-management.

Any move towards systems integration will require federal government leadership to implement a national research agenda across Australian states and territories. The Council for Australian Governments is now commissioning regular reports against key indicators of indigenous disadvantage (CREATE 2002). All states and territories have also agreed to the development of a National Indigenous Child Safety and Family Well-being Strategy and Action Plan. The CAFWAA Report (2002) supports a national Aboriginal and Torres Strait Islander family policy developed by indigenous organizations. The Commonwealth, states and territories are all committed to reducing the number of indigenous children in care and expanding family support and early intervention programmes.

However, much still remains to be done to overcome systemic inertia and arrive at achievable policy objectives, high standards of service delivery and a process for evaluating outcomes. Without an accepted political definition of minimum standards in child and family welfare, state agencies are vulnerable to operating in an environment of inadequate resources, reactive decision-making and denial of responsibilities. The Community Services Commission inquiry into the circumstances of Aboriginal children and young people in care found, for instance, that:

> The current culture of 'hands-off' when it comes to Aboriginal children and young people and their families translates in practice to a reluctance, particularly for departmental workers, to provide oversight once a child is settled in a family or culturally appropriate placement. (Community Services Commission 2001)

The Looking After Children tools, if adopted across the jurisdictions, could become the internationally recognized framework for these national service standards (Wise 2003). Another advance would be to further engage the Aboriginal community in designing and delivering services appropriate to their needs, following the Canadian model described in this chapter.

Canada

In Canada, discussion continues about methods and approaches for effective programs for Aboriginal children. On First Nations reserves, where the federal government is typically the only funder, the challenge is to coordinate and integrate programming approaches to meet community needs, while providing a high standard of accountability for funding.

Off-reserve, there are further challenges in coordinating and integrating approaches which include programs funded by or provided by other levels of government – provincial, territorial, municipal – linking, for example, federal Aboriginal early childhood programs to the provincially funded school system. Developing this kind of systemic connection has become increasingly important in the light of the high mobility of Aboriginal people. The goal should be to ensure that well-coordinated, appropriate and well-run services are available to Aboriginal children in need, regardless of where they live or which level of government provides the funding. The involvement and empowerment of Aboriginal parents is especially critical, to overcome a history of colonial paternalism, in which their responsibility was negated.

This array of Aboriginal children's programming appears fragmented, but given the complexity of jurisdictions in Canada, that is hardly surprising.

Attempts at coordination are also relatively new. Canadian government expenditure on Aboriginal children continues to show growth, which indicates some priority being given to the issue: Aboriginal Head Start and other early childhood development programs received an increase in government funding in 2002 (Health Canada 2002b). Nevertheless, the full extent of need is far from being met.

Aboriginal people themselves will and should continue to insist on being involved in defining program approaches. Appropriate methods of delivery may become more and more complex, as the lives of Aboriginal people increasingly become intermingled with the rest of the Canadian population in urban centres. In 2001, 49 per cent of the Aboriginal population lived in urban centres, half of them in Canada's ten largest cities; only 31 per cent now live on reserves (Statistics Canada 2003). Whether this decreasing isolation and increasing urbanization will eventually eliminate the large socio-economic and health disparities between Aboriginal people and other Canadians remains to be seen.

In 1966, a report on the situation of Aboriginal people in Canada observed: 'Public knowledge [about Aboriginal people] does not even match public misconception. Not enough is known of the problems to create a call for their solution' (Hawthorn 1967, p.13). It could be argued that the understanding of the Aboriginal populations in Canada and Australia continues to be superficial and prone to stereotypes. The high growth rate could foster greater intercultural comprehension simply because of greater Aboriginal visibility and predominance or it could lead to the entrenchment of racially segregated urban ghettos and incarceration of ever higher numbers of Aboriginal children through the criminal justice or the care systems – prospects few would relish. Policy decisions will affect which of the two scenarios ensues. In any event, the futures of many Aboriginal children, as members of one more ethnic minority in multicultural Canada and Australia, will be very different from the lives of their ancestors.

Notes

1   The term 'Aboriginal' is widely used in Canada to refer to all three national indigenous groups: First Nations people (still sometimes called 'Indians'); Inuit (formerly referred to as 'Eskimos'); and Métis (people of mixed Aboriginal and European ancestry). The Canadian Constitution Act, 1982 recognizes 'Indian, Inuit and Métis peoples' within the definition of Aboriginal peoples.

2   Reserves are 'land set aside by the federal government for the use and occupancy of an Indian group or band' and are under federal constitutional jurisdiction (Indian and Northern Affairs Canada 2000). Six hundred reserves exist across Canada.

Chapter 8

'Better than Being at Home'

Disabled Children's Views about School

Clare Connors and Kirsten Stalker

This chapter presents findings from a two-year study funded by the Scottish Executive exploring disabled children's understandings and experiences of disability and impairment. First, the chapter outlines the social relational model of disability, which provided a theoretical framework for the study, and the research methods used. The main focus is on the experiences of 26 children at school, looking at their overall views about school, the impact of impairment and the barriers they faced – physical and attitudinal, including bullying. Overall, the children emerge as enthusiastic pupils, good friends and active participants in school life. Finally, some policy and practice implications are highlighted.

Introduction

A large body of research has reported the strains and stresses experienced by parents looking after disabled children and many studies have documented families' unmet needs. A considerable literature is devoted to identifying how parents 'cope' with looking after a disabled child and 'what works' (or not) in terms of formal services. The vast majority of this work is based on parents' and/or professionals' views: relatively few studies have tried to find out disabled children's own views about their everyday lives, the support they receive and what they think could be done differently, or better. Disabled children are not alone in frequently being excluded from consultation about their views, and this chapter is complemented by Chapter 9, which considers how another frequently neglected group, children who have been placed in care or accommodation, rate their experiences.

Current child care legislation in the UK – the Children Act 1989 in England, the Children (Scotland) Act 1995 and the Northern Ireland Children's Order 1995 – identifies disabled children as 'children in need'. Local authorities have a duty to assess the needs of individual children and to offer certain support services. In Scotland, for example, such services must be designed 'to minimize the effect on any disabled child of his disability [sic]' and give them 'the opportunity to lead lives which are as normal as possible' (Children (Scotland) Act 1995, 23 (1)). However, several years after the passing of these Acts, comparatively little is known about children's views of the impact of disability, or what they see as a 'normal' life.

This was the starting point for a two-year study, funded by the Scottish Executive, at the Social Work Research Centre in the University of Stirling. The main aims of the research were to explore disabled children's understandings of disability, to examine how they negotiate the experience of disability in their everyday lives and to explore their perceptions of professionals and experiences of using services. See Connors and Stalker (2003) for a full account.

In analysing the data, the authors drew on Carol Thomas' (1999) social relational model of disability. This chapter begins by briefly outlining that theoretical framework, and how the researchers sought the children's views. This was important because, despite their statutory duties in this area, policymakers and practitioners do not always consult disabled young people, often on the grounds that 'they can't communicate' or 'won't understand' (Morris 1998).

The main part of the current chapter focuses on what the children had to say about their experiences at school, which, not surprisingly, played a central role in their lives. Indeed they had a good deal more to say about education, in the form of school, than they had about health or social work services – a finding in itself no doubt! Differences and similarities with parents' accounts are noted. The concluding section draws out the main implications for policy and practice in terms of developing effective and supportive educational environments for disabled children.

The social relational model of disability

Most readers will probably be familiar with the social model of disability (Barnes 1991; Oliver 1990) which distinguishes between *impairment*, the loss or limitation of physical, sensory or intellectual functioning, and *disability*, meaning the material and social barriers which exclude people with impairments from mainstream life. This analysis, given a political voice by the disabled people's movement, has had a huge positive impact in tackling discrimination. At the same time, it has been argued that the social model fails to address both the range and diversity of disabled people's personal experiences and the impact of living with impairment on a daily basis (French 1993; Morris 1992). Thomas (1999) addresses these points by arguing that disability is rooted in an unequal social relationship, the effects of which can be manifested as barriers restricting people's lives. She draws a distinction between barriers to *doing*, which constrain activity, such as inaccessible transport or buildings, and barriers to *being*, which result from what she calls psycho-emotional disablism. This term refers to the hostile, negative or unhelpful attitudes and/or behaviour sometimes shown to disabled people, such as being stared or laughed at, called names or patronized. Thomas also acknowledges the day-to-day implications of living with impairment, which she calls impairment effects. These might include the pain, discomfort or fatigue that accompany certain conditions, or the inability to perform an activity due to physical limitation. These are not related to disability per se, although they may become conduits for disability if, for example, an individual is discriminated against on the grounds of impairment.

Thomas developed this framework for understanding disability while exploring the experiences of disabled women: however, it fitted well with data collected during this study of children's lives.

Seeking children's views

'Guided conversations' were held with 26 disabled children, aged 7 to 15, each of whom the research team met on three or four occasions. Semi-structured interviews were held with 24 siblings and 38 parents. Families were recruited through schools and voluntary organizations. These agencies were asked to pass on a letter to parents informing them about the research and inviting them to take part. Those who gave a positive response were then sent separate information leaflets and consent forms for parents, siblings and disabled children.

The research team was fortunate in having two disabled girls (aged 11 and 12), recruited through a voluntary organization, to act as 'study advisers'. They provided very useful feedback on draft interview schedules, leading to various changes and amendments in the materials. Piloting with five families confirmed the view that a semi-structured interview schedule worked best with the younger children – and those with learning disabilities – while those aged 11 to 15 responded well to a looser topic guide (covering the same subjects). A number of activities and visual aids were introduced in the interviews with the younger children, to help facilitate communication, sustain interest and make them more 'fun' (see Stalker and Connors 2003).

Four young people communicated in either British Sign Language or Makaton (a signing system used by people with learning disabilities, accompanied by speech). One of the authors is fluent in both and she video recorded and transcribed these interviews. One child used Facilitated Communication, which involves a facilitator holding the disabled person's hand and being guided to letters on an alphabet board, gradually (or sometimes rapidly) making up words and sentences. In this case, the child's mother acted as facilitator on our behalf. Two children used gesture and movement to communicate. Here the issue was not so much about communication style as cognitive ability. Had time permitted, we could have used observation and perhaps eventually non-verbal communication to explore their feelings and preferences. Unfortunately, time did not permit and it was decided to interview their parents instead. The data thus gathered were not treated as 'proxy' responses for the children, but as the parents' own views.

Sample characteristics

The 26 children included 15 boys and 11 girls, reflecting the higher incidence of impairment among males than females (Meltzer, Smyth and Robus 1989). They were aged between seven and fifteen, although half were either nine or ten. There was only one child of mixed race, reflecting the low level of black and minority ethnic communities in most parts of Scotland. The children had a range of impairments. Fifteen had learning disabilities, ranging in nature from mild to profound. Some had additional diagnoses, including autism, Attention Deficit Hyperactivity Syndrome and Soto's Syndrome. Two had complex support needs, that is, a profound learning disability along with sensory and physical impairments. Six had a primary diagnosis relating to physical impairment, such as cerebral palsy or cystic fibrosis, the latter being a life-limiting condition. The remaining five children had a visual or hearing impairment. Reflecting this wide variation, the children were attending a range of schools – twelve were in special (segregated) settings, five in 'integrated' units (units for disabled children within mainstream schools) and nine were in fully inclusive mainstream schools. The inclusive settings were mostly primary schools: all but one of the older children were in special schools by the end of the fieldwork period.

Children's experiences at school

Overall views about school

Most of the children gave largely positive accounts of their school life; indeed, some were downright enthusiastic: 'It's brilliant; being at school is better than being at home. I enjoy most things in school' (boy, aged 9). Most children were able to identify particular aspects of, and activities within, school that they enjoyed, although in some cases their enthusiasm was linked to the fact that they were often bored at home. Some were not allowed to go out alone; some were unable to access places that other children frequented, such as fast food outlets or shopping centres; those attending schools outside their local area often lacked friends in their neighbourhood. Indeed, one or two children said they spent most of their time at home watching television or videos in their bedroom. Thus school provided welcome opportunities for activity, participation, friendship and some independence from home and family.

However, a few children were either ambivalent about school or clearly unhappy. This was either related to difficulty completing work or dissatisfaction with their current school placement, a point that is discussed further below.

During a 'word choice' exercise, children were given a sheet of paper containing 12 adjectives and asked to select all those which described 'what they were like' at school. The word chosen most often was 'helpful', followed by 'keen', 'happy', 'jokey', 'friendly' and 'sporty'. One girl said she was often asked to take messages to other classes, a responsibility that she was clearly proud of; she also liked helping other pupils, especially the younger ones. Indeed, most of the children perceived themselves as giving help as much as receiving it, being good friends to other pupils, good fun to be with and having an active role to play at different levels of school life. These are important points, since they differ from the more stereotyped view of disabled children as passive, helpless or isolated.

Some children described themselves as 'bored', 'fed up' and/or 'sad' at school. On the whole, such feelings were linked to specific recent incidents, such as falling out with a friend or not being allowed to do something they wanted to. At the same time it appeared that a few children spent most of their time at school feeling bored: it simply did not engage their interest.

Impairment effects

Overall there was little evidence of impairment effects interfering with children's ability to benefit from school life. The two children who had mixed feelings about school said they had difficulty completing their work: this was due to a lack of manual dexterity in one case, and to literacy issues in the other. Throughout the study, most of the children showed a pragmatic attitude to their impairments; when asked if there was anything in their life they would like to change, only two referred to their impairment, saying they would like to be able to walk. At another point, one boy, aged nine, said 'That's it; I'm in a wheelchair so just get on with it. Just get on with what you're doing.' This practical attitude may explain the few references to impairment effects in the children's accounts. It may also be related to parents' and in some cases schools' efforts to mitigate or reduce the impact of impairment in children's lives. As discussed below, however, there were instances when impairment was allowed to become a conduit for disability.

Barriers to doing

Four types of barriers to doing can be identified from the children's accounts of school life, all of which restricted their activities at times – transport, the built environment, the impact of attending schools outside their local neighbourhood and, in one case, lack of support for communication.

No problems were reported in travelling to and from school for lessons, but a few children had found that transport was not available for after-school activities, which are an important part of young people's social life, especially if they face difficulties attending social events at home. One 14-year-old boy wanted to attend a youth club at school but there was no transport to take him there. His local authority suggested he stayed in school from the end of lessons at 3pm until the club began at 7pm. Not surprisingly, he did not relish the idea of hanging around in school for four hours after his friends had left, nor did he want to go to the club wearing his school uniform.

Another boy who had attended a mainstream primary could not go on to the local high school with his friends because it was inaccessible to wheelchair users. He then had the choice of another mainstream school where he would not know anyone, or special school. He opted for the latter because he was worried about being bullied in the mainstream school. However, he found that academic expectations were low in the special school, and he was taking fewer standard grade exams than he would have done in mainstream. Another boy, who did remain in mainstream secondary with his friends, nevertheless came up against barriers on a daily basis. His parents' account suggests that although the school appeared welcoming, it failed to prioritize meeting his access and equipment needs.

Attending schools outwith their local community had implications for young people's friendships. First, it was hard for them to meet up with their school-mates in the evenings and at weekends. Special schools usually have large catchment areas so pupils may live far apart. One girl, aged 13, commented: 'I get a good education and people are looking out for me and all that. My friends, that's the difficult part…I don't see them a lot.' Second, it was difficult for the children to make friends in their local neighbourhood. Not only were they absent during the daytime, they may also have been seen as 'different' if they went to school in a 'special' taxi or bus.

The parents of the child who used Facilitated Communication told us that the boy's school did not accept this method of communication as valid, at least in his case, and declined to try it at school. The boy, aged nine, had written the following letter to his head teacher: 'I am feeling very frustrated and annoyed as a result of attitudes to Facilitated Communication. I feel able to avail myself on a level of education far beyond what your school is providing me at the moment. I believe I need an education more suited to my needs.'

Barriers to being

The young people recounted a range of incidents at school that might be said to result in 'barriers to being'. These can be grouped into two themes – the management of difference (by adults) and bullying (by other children).

How difference should be managed may be formalized within school policies but from the children's perspective it was manifested in the way an individual staff member responded to a particular set of circumstances. Inclusion polices worked well for some children. They talked about having additional help with learning, attending one-to-one or small group tuition and seeing a variety of specialist staff. The young people's descriptions of such support, as part of everyday school life with no sense that it made them 'different', suggest that the introduction of additional equipment or specialist staff was sensitively handled and well embedded in school routines (a point also made by Shaw 1998). However, some children did not mind being seen as different if this was presented in a positive manner – or on their terms perhaps. The mother of a nine-year-old boy recounted a story from his head teacher: 'During assembly, the children had been asked: "Does anybody in here think they are special?" and he put his hand up and said "I am because I have cerebral palsy" and he went up to the front…and spoke about his disability to everybody.' On the other hand, the data suggest that some schools had inclusion polices which were not well thought out, and rested on a fairly superficial understanding of the concept. One head teacher declined to give parents information about this study because she thought its focus on disabled children was incompatible with the school's inclusion policy, suggesting that 'inclusion' was perceived as assimilation. One mother recounted an incident at her son's school that illustrates a failure to take account of difference at a practical level. This 14-year-old was a wheelchair user and would normally use a lift. However, lifts were 'out of bounds' during fire alarms and no alternative arrangements had been made to evacuate wheelchair users:

> He was telling me the other day how they did the fire alarm and everybody was screaming out in the playground. Richard was still in the school and everybody was outside. He was saying 'Mum, I was really, really worried about what happens if there's a real fire'. No one came to his assistance at all.

Another parent reported that his son had been excluded from school trips, despite being keen to go. This child had cerebral palsy and used a walking frame; he moved much more slowly than his peers. The school's action in excluding him meant he was both barred from participating in an activity (a barrier to doing) and made to feel hurt and of lesser worth than the other children (a barrier to being).

A further example of ineffective inclusion policies centred on the role and activities of special needs assistants (SNAs), whose job is to facilitate the inclusion of disabled children in mainstream schools through practical, one-to-one support. Some of the young people described their SNAs as very helpful. Others were less satisfied. For example, one of the younger girls was annoyed that, during playtimes, her helper took her to the younger children's playground, away from her friends. Other parents also reported difficulties arising from the inappropriate actions of SNAs, for example, taking an eight-year-old child into the nursery class for lunch, because the SNA was friendly with the nursery staff. Another SNA was, in the family's opinion, overly attached to their son, constantly ringing his parents when he was in hospital.

Among the children placed in integrated units, only one said that his typical day involved some time spent in the main school. The others spent the entire day in the unit and thus, in effect, in a segregated setting. None of the children complained about this. Rather, they spoke positively about their teachers, and two reported close friendships with fellow pupils. Their parents, however, were less satisfied with the amount and quality of inclusion on offer, feeling their children would benefit from mixing with those in mainstream classes.

The management of difference took another form within special schools. Some children were glad to be at a special school that catered for pupils with their particular impairment. One boy, aged 14, said: 'The only reason I like going to my school is because of my wheelchair.' Another boy, aged nine, had this exchange with the interviewer:

Interviewer: You want to go to a school where there are lots of deaf children?

Child: Yes…where there's signing, where everyone signs, all the teachers, all the children.

Interviewer: Why is that better than going to a school with hearing children?

Child: Hearing children – no one signs. I don't understand them and they don't understand me.

Children attending special schools talked more openly and spontaneously about impairment than the other young people. In many ways this might appear to be 'a good thing', particularly given the indications that some schools, in their desire to treat everyone the same, may have given a subliminal message that impairment was a subject best avoided. However, one girl explained how pupils were referred to as 'wheelchairs' or 'walkers' and even said 'I'm happy being a cerebral palsy'. Despite expressing acceptance of, or contentment with, her impairment, the experience of hearing herself referred to in this way over a period of time seems unlikely to have fostered a well-rounded self image. An older boy of 14, a wheelchair user at the same school, was asked what he thought of this terminology. He replied: 'Sad, because we're just the same. We just can't walk, that's all the difference.'

Seven children reported having been bullied at school. Both the children's and their parents' accounts strongly indicate that this bullying was related to impairment – there was no suggestion that other factors were involved. Bullying took place in all school settings and included name calling, excluding or not talking to the child, extracting money and, on occasion, physical violence. In some cases, these were isolated incidents and children had taken steps to 'see off' the bullies, by reporting them to parents or teachers. While some schools took action quickly, others apparently did not and parents had to raise the matter several times. One older girl decided against approaching her teachers but, with support from her mother, faced up to the bullies who, she said, did not bother her again.

Comparisons with parents' views

As indicated above, children's accounts sometimes coincided with their parents' and sometimes differed. Parents' views of SNAs were very similar to the young people's, albeit illustrated through different examples. The parents of both boys who were unhappy with their current school voiced similar concerns and were taking steps to secure a different placement.

Overall the children painted a more positive picture of school than did their parents. The latter tended to worry about how their children were 'coping', whereas most of the young people, as we have seen, portrayed themselves as enjoying friendships, helping out the teachers and playing an active part in various aspects of school life. This difference may be partly explained by the fact that some children had more to do – and more friends – at school than at home. In some cases, school may have provided greater opportunities to acquire skills and express talents than were available at home.

The other noticeable difference between the two sets of accounts was that several parents talked at length about the difficulties they had experienced securing a placement in the school of their choice. In some cases they had wanted their child to go to special school while the local authority had recommended a mainstream placement. In other cases, it was the opposite way round. Parents also recounted the 'battles' they had waged securing the 'right' support for their child once in a particular setting. For the most part, the young people did not refer to these matters. They were not actively involved in such discussions and, particularly in the case of the younger children, may not have known about them.

Conclusions

The methods used in this study confirm that communicating with disabled children is usually no different from communicating with any other young people. In most cases, special skills and techniques are not needed: it is more important that the researcher – or practitioner – approaches the child as a child first, as a child with an impairment, second. The findings also revealed that while children agreed with their parents on some things, they had different perceptions about others. Therefore using parents as proxy respondents is not advisable.

Overall, the children presented a positive picture of school life. Most were happy (although there were notable exceptions) and had a strong sense of achievement relating to academic work or sporting activities. The young people enjoyed the sense of control and independence they had at school. They generally spoke well of teachers, although a few were unhappy with special needs assistants who obstructed rather than promoted contact with their peers. Parents were much more critical than children of the education system and of some education staff.

Impairment effects did not feature much in children's accounts of school. This may be linked to their largely pragmatic attitude. They did experience and report various barriers to doing, some of which could result in barriers to being. How difference was managed was crucial to the children's psycho-emotional well-being and is an aspect of school life which should receive more attention. The children's accounts tended to focus on their 'sameness' to others, but at times they had felt hurt, rejected and of lesser value when they were made to feel different in a negative way. Bullying of course had a similar effect. Other commentators have noted that insufficient attention is paid to disabled children's emotional needs (Hollins and Sinason 2000). At the same time, however, it would be wrong to portray the children in this study as passive victims: some were proactive in dealing with the incidents that bothered them, such as those who 'saw off' the bullies, or told their parents about poor practice among SNAs.

This study was not intended to be an evaluation of, nor a comparison between, different types of school setting. Therefore it would not be appropriate to draw conclusions nor make recommendations about their relative merits. The aim was to hear children's views: the findings show they had good and bad things to say about all three types of school settings and certain policy and practice implications can be drawn from their accounts, and those of their parents.

First, the findings highlight the importance of inclusion being embedded in every aspect of school policy. It should not be a 'stand alone' item which has little impact on day-to-day practice or overall ethos. There seemed to be a degree of misunderstanding about inclusion in some schools. It is not about minimizing difference, avoiding discussion of impairment and a refusal to 'single out' disabled children. Rather, energy should focus on educating all children to accept and understand difference. Pupils have a key role to play in making inclusion effective. In the absence of opportunities to learn about and discuss difference, intolerance and bullying are more likely to thrive. Mainstream schools need to accommodate difference in a positive way by providing the right kind of support to meet individual need. Simply placing a child in a mainstream school and hoping he or she will 'fit in' is not enough. Indeed the findings show that poorly thought out polices can lead to exclusionary practice. When choosing a mainstream school for their child, parents can look out for features such as

- clear statements about equality, diversity and inclusion in the School Handbook
- examples of physical aids and adaptations in the school, such as wide doorways, ramps, chair lifts and handrails
- accessibility of teaching areas, toilets, eating and recreation areas to all pupils (Scottish Consortium for Learning Disability undated, p.2)

It was evident from children's and parents' accounts that most pupils in integrated units were in effect segregated from the rest of the school. This issue has been identified elsewhere (Shaw 1998), indicating a pressing need for change.

While pupils attending special schools were more open about discussing impairment – apparently a healthy attitude – the impersonal way some children were defined seems likely to have had a deleterious impact on their self esteem. The practice of referring to children within school in terms of impairment group is based on a medical model that is at odds with recent developments in social theories about disability. This finding, along with many others reported above, suggests that education staff at all levels need training in disability awareness and inclusion, preferably delivered by organizations of disabled people.

Our findings about bullying are also echoed in previous studies. They call into question the effectiveness of current anti-bullying strategies, indicating an urgent need for review. Some schools in Britain have introduced peer mediation schemes, whereby certain pupils are trained to mediate between the perpetrators and victims of bullying. Such schemes can reduce bullying in the playground by two thirds, and children as young as eight can act as mediators.

Having friends was very important to these children, as to most young people, but some faced difficulties maintaining friendships outside school hours. Disabled youngsters need better support and opportunities to develop the kind of social lives they want and which are taken for granted by many non-disabled children. This could be addressed through better transport provision, more after-school clubs and mainstream agencies, such as those offering sports or arts activities, becoming much more inclusive.

Finally, it should be added that recent legislation is intended to address some of the issues identified in the study. The Special Educational Needs and Disability Act 2001 (SENDA) (implemented September 2002) extended the provisions of the UK Disability Discrimination Act (1995) to education. Some sections of SENDA apply to Scotland, England and Wales, while others, including those covering special education needs, relate to England and Wales only. However, where this is the case, similar duties have been introduced to Scotland through the Education (Disability Strategies and Pupils' Records) Act (see Riddell 2001 for a fuller discussion). Thus, schools in England, Wales and Scotland now have to make 'reasonable adjustments' to all their policies, procedures and services to ensure disabled children are not discriminated against unfairly. For example, it would no longer be acceptable to exclude a disabled child from a school trip solely on the grounds of impaired mobility. The legislation requires all local authorities to adopt proactive strategies to improve disabled children's access to the physical environment, the curriculum and information. Progress in implementing this legislation needs to be closely monitored.

Acknowledgements

The authors are grateful to the children and families who took part in the study, to Danielle Atai and Gemma Houldscoft who acted as study advisors and to Margaret Burt who conducted some of the interviews. Thanks also to colleagues at Stirling University for advice and practical support.

Chapter 9

The Voice of Young People

Reflections on the Care Experience and the Process of Leaving Care

Kathleen Kufeldt and Mike Stein

This chapter explores young people's transitions from care from UK and Canadian research studies. The findings highlight the accelerated and compressed transitions of care leavers in contrast to normative transitions. Three groups are identified, those who *move on*, those who *survive*, and those who become *victims*. The Canadian research found that a majority of young adults believed that coming into care was the best solution for them. Young men thought they were less ready for independence than young women and readiness was associated with stability in care. Reflections on care describe good memories, turning points and helpful people. The chapter concludes by sounding a cautionary note about family preservation, recognizing the importance of education and the positive role played by foster carers in preparing young people for adulthood.

Introduction

This chapter presents the reflections of young adults, and those approaching adulthood, on the experience of growing up in care and leaving care. These reflections emerge from complementary studies in the different jurisdictions of the United Kingdom and Canada.

First, there is an exploration of young people's transitions from care, including their early experience of independence when aged between 16 and 20, drawing upon the results of research studies carried out in the UK between 1980 and 2002. Second, the findings from a Canadian study, derived from the experiences of young adults aged between 23 and 31, who had been in care, are presented. The first part of the chapter focuses primarily on the transition stage whereas the second part provides insights into longer-term outcomes and their relationship to the care experience.

Transitions from care

It gets lonely, it's only when you leave care you know you've been dumped. (Care leaver, 1986)

Leaving were like a rush job, I felt that they didn't want me. (Care leaver, 1995)

It's being away from my mum, I'm only 16 and still a bairn and get a bit weepy at times. (Care leaver, 2002)

From the early 1970s, a body of small-scale surveys and qualitative research revealed how poorly equipped young people leaving care were to cope with life after care – practically, emotionally and educationally – and made connections with their subsequent experiences of loneliness, isolation, poor mental health, unemployment, poverty, drift and homelessness (Stein 1997).

In addition to confirming their poor life chances after leaving care, more recent research has attempted to compare the experience of care leavers with other young people through the use of comparison samples and secondary sources. The main message from these studies is that in comparison to their peers in the general population, most young people leaving care have to cope with the challenges and responsibilities of major changes in their lives at a far younger age. In short, many have compressed and accelerated transitions to adulthood (Stein 2002).

The experiences of young people leaving care contrast with the findings of the Joseph Rowntree Foundation programme of youth research in the UK and similar studies in Canada which identified the extended transitions of the majority of young people who stay on in education and remain dependent, to varying degrees, upon their families until their mid twenties (Human Resources Development Canada 2001; Joseph Rowntree Foundation 2002).

Their experiences also contrast with the 'polarized' second group identified by the Joseph Rowntree Foundation research, the 'fast track' transitions of those young people who leave school at 16 or 17. Although these young people enter the labour market at a similar age, they generally do so whilst still living in the family home. More direct comparisons may be made with teenage parents – although, again, there are likely to be significant qualitative differences between young parents who have supportive families and those living in care, who may be estranged from them. And in comparison with both non-disabled care leavers and other non-care young people, young disabled care leavers are likely to have more delayed and abrupt transitions, due to poor planning and restricted housing and employment opportunities (Rabiee, Priestley and Knowles 2001).

Canadian research has also identified the risks of homelessness – over half of young people on the streets have been in care – of early parenthood, of being drawn into deviant ways of surviving, and leaving care early (Kufeldt and Burrows 1994; Kufeldt *et al.* 1992; Martin 1998). In the UK a majority of young people leave care at just 16 and 17 years of age (Biehal *et al.* 1995; Dixon and Stein 2002; Stein and Carey 1986). This represents a serious barrier to promoting positive outcomes for the following three reasons (also discussed in Stein forthcoming).

First, during the last 20 years patterns of transition into adulthood have been changing. This period has witnessed: a major decline in the youth labour market based on manufacturing and apprenticeship training; the extension of youth training, further and higher education; and the reduction in entitlements to universal welfare benefits for young people. These changes have resulted in young people being more dependent on their families for emotional, financial and practical support, often into their early twenties (Joseph Rowntree Foundation 2002). In today's 'risk' society, parents, grandparents and other relatives are increasingly occupying a central role at different life stages. Yet young care leavers, who are the most likely to lack the range and depth of help given by families, are expected to cope at a far younger age than young people living with their birth families.

Second, psychological research – focal theory[1] – suggests that most young people cope with the major changes in their lives, during their journey to adulthood, by dealing with them over a period of time, resolving one issue then moving onto another. The theory has been tested by empirical research carried out in New Zealand, Scotland and the United States. This demonstrated that young people who have to cope with the greatest number of life changes in the least time had far poorer outcomes including fewer educational qualifications and lower self esteem (Coleman and Hendry 1999). Yet the accelerated and compressed transitions of care leavers deny them the psychological opportunity to focus, to deal with changes over time.

Third, and closely linked to point two, the process of social transition has traditionally included three distinct but related stages: leaving or disengagement; transition itself; and integration into a new or different social state. However, due to the changes outlined above – especially in relation to education, employment and housing – for many young people the overall process is becoming more extended, connected and permeable. For example, further education takes place over a longer period of time, young people frequently return home after higher education, and there has been a growth in temporary and short-term employment markets.

The second stage, transition itself, is critical to this changing process, preparing young people for the 'risk' society. Having an opportunity to 'space out' provides a time for freedom, exploration, reflection, risk taking and identity search. This is a stage that is critical to the promotion of resilience both through opportunities to re-frame adversities so that the beneficial as well as the damaging effects are recognized; and exposure to challenging situations which provide opportunities to develop both problem-solving abilities and emotional coping skills – key resilience-promoting factors identified in the international literature (Higgins 1994; Newman and Blackburn 2002; Stein forthcoming). For a majority of young people today, this is gained through the experience of further and higher education. Yet, many care leavers, as a consequence of their pre-care and care experiences, are unable to take advantage of educational opportunities. Instead there is often the expectation of instant adulthood on leaving care, a conflating of the three distinct stages of social transition into the final stage, often when young people reach just 15 years of age: 'It's a big thing at 16 to step out on your own…a big task…it's scary at first' (Care leaver, 1995).

Transitions in the context of care careers

How does the experience of life after leaving care help or hinder young people? UK research studies completed since the 1980s suggest that the answer is linked to whether the person falls into one of three groups: the *moving on* group, the *survivors* group, or the *victims* group (Biehal *et al.* 1995; Dixon and Stein 2002; Stein and Carey 1986; Stein forthcoming).

Moving on

> She just makes my life…and I enjoy the responsibility and I am glad I am a parent. (Young mum, Care leaver, 1995)

> I feel more of a person now that I'm on my own and I ain't got to go and ask permission from social services for this and that and the other. I feel like myself now, more normal. (Care leaver, 1995)

> I think I am special because I tried and finished college. (Care leaver, 2002)

The first group, those *moving on*, were likely to have had stability and continuity in their lives, including a secure attachment relationship, to have made sense of their family relationships so they could psychologically move on from them, and to have achieved some educational success before leaving care. Their preparation had been gradual, they left care later and their moving was likely to have been planned. Being more normal – developing a post-care normalizing identity – through, for example, participating in further or higher education, having a job they liked – but not any job – or being a parent themselves, played a significant part.

These young people have welcomed the challenge of independent living and gaining more control over their lives – often contrasting this with the restrictions imposed whilst living in care, including the lack of opportunities to make or participate in decisions which affected their lives. In general, their resilience has been enhanced by their experiences after care and they have been able to make good use of help they have been offered, including that from former carers (Schofield 2001; Sinclair *et al.* 2003; Stein forthcoming).

Surviving

> No social worker's done any of this for me, got me into any of the youth work or college… This was all done off my own back. (Care leaver, 1986)

> I've become more independent, more tough, I know more about the world. (Care leaver, 1990)

> As I've grown older I've found it out for myself… I've brought myself up really. (Care leaver, 1995)

The second group, the *survivors*, had experienced more instability, movement and disruption whilst living in care than the *moving on* group. They were also likely to leave care younger, with few or no qualifications, and often following a breakdown in foster care or a rushed job, a sudden exit from their children's home. They were likely to experience further movement and problems after leaving care, including periods of homelessness, low-paid casual or short-term unfulfilling work and unemployment. They were also likely to experience problems in their personal and professional relationships through patterns of detachment and dependency.

Many in this group saw themselves as 'more tough', as having done things 'off my own back' and as survivors since leaving care. They believed that the many problems they had faced, and often were still coping with, had made them more grown up and self reliant – although their view of themselves as independent was often contradicted by the reality of high degrees of agency dependency for assistance with accommodation, money and personal support.

Research from both sides of the Atlantic demonstrates that surviving was enhanced by the personal and professional support received after leaving care. Specialist leaving care workers, key workers, as well as mentors – the latter identified in the international literature as a resilience-promoting factor (Newman and Blackburn 2002) – and different family members, or some combination of formal and informal support networks, could help them overcome their very poor starting points at the time of leaving care and thus promote their resilience (Biehal *et al.* 1995; Kufeldt and Burrows 1994; Stein forthcoming).

Being a victim

> I was in a bed-sit on my own, I couldn't handle it, being on my own, being lonely, no family behind me, no friends. I was stopping at home, being bored, I got into financial difficulties and was evicted. (Care leaver, 1990)

> I am 16 and have no friends… I always feel unsafe and very lonely… I have no confidence. (Care leaver, 2002)

The third group was the most disadvantaged. They had the most damaging pre-care family experiences and, in the main, care was unable to help them overcome their past difficulties. Their lives in care were likely to include many placement moves – the largest number of moves in the different research studies – and related disruption to their lives, especially to their personal relationships – they were the least likely to have a redeeming relationship with a family member or carer – and they were the least likely to succeed in education. They were likely to leave care younger, following a placement breakdown. At the time of leaving care their life chances were very poor indeed.

After leaving care they were likely to be unemployed, become homeless and have great difficulties in maintaining their accommodation. They were also highly likely to be lonely, isolated and have mental health problems. Aftercare support was unlikely to be able to help them overcome their very poor starting positions and they also lacked or alienated personal support. But it was very important to these young people that somebody was there for them (Biehal *et al.* 1995).

Adult reflections on the experience of care

So far this chapter has explored the experiences of young people at the time of leaving care, including their early experiences of independence. The reflections of Canadian care leavers, now aged between 23 and 31, echo and affirm the main themes arising from the UK research findings. Most Canadian care leavers showed signs of loneliness and rootlessness; their economic circumstances were far poorer than similar cohorts in the general population; they also lagged behind with respect to attainment of the normal developmental tasks of young adulthood, particularly educationally (Kufeldt 2003). The majority had to struggle to meet basic needs, and to cope with the emotional struggles of multiple losses, a dearth of positive family supports and breaks in continuity. As in the UK studies, there were examples of all three of the transition groups, *moving on*, *surviving*, and being *victims*.

The Canadian survey explored variables related to the tasks of adulthood (Havighurst 1972; Whitbourne and Weinstock 1979), the basic dimensions of healthy child development (Parker *et al.* 1991; Ward 1995), and outcomes of the care experience identified in the literature (Biehal *et al.* 1995; Wedeven *et al.* 1997). A questionnaire was completed by adults who had left care in the years 1987, 1991 and 1995. The average ages of the three groups were 31, 27 and 23 respectively. The final sample size was 87 (return rate 53%).

An overview of the analysis of selected quantitative variables has been published elsewhere (Kufeldt *et al.* 2003). In this chapter, two particular questions are the focus: these are 'was being taken into care the correct decision?' and 'how ready were young people for independence when leaving care?' Reflections of the respondents regarding their experiences within care are also presented.

Was being taken into care the correct decision?

One of the most crucial decisions that a social worker has to make is whether to place a child or young person in care. Not only is this pivotal for the child and family, but also removing a child from home flies in the face of cultural beliefs concerning family values. The latter issue has been reinforced in Canada in the last 25 years because of legislative and policy changes favouring family preservation. The data demonstrated statistically significant effects of these changes. Seventy-eight per cent of the oldest age group entered care before the age of seven (57% before age two). This is in contrast to the youngest group of whom 27 per cent were in care before age seven, with only 3 per cent entering care before age two (p <0.0001, see Table 9.1).

Table 9.1: Age when entering care

| Age at entry into care | Percentage of respondents currently aged: | | | Percentage of all respondents (n=84) |
	22–26 (n=38)	27–30 (n=27)	31–35 (n=19)	
<2 years	3	15	57	19
2–6	24	15	21	20
7–12	39	52	11	37
13 +	34	18	11	24
Totals	100	100	100	100

Cross tabulation of variables indicated differences in educational attainment between the three groups: a much higher percentage of those between 22 and 26 (43%) failed to graduate from high school before leaving care as compared with the other two groups (21% of 27–30 and 5% of 31–35). This is most likely related to the fact that the youngest cohort, entering care at later ages, were left in dysfunctional circumstances too long and their education suffered (Kufeldt *et al.* 2003). This assumption is reinforced by the responses to the question: 'was coming into care the best decision at the time it happened?'

Seventy-two of the eighty-seven respondents answered this question. Seventy-one per cent felt that coming into care was the best possible solution for them. Some said that they should have come into care earlier. This is similar to the findings of an earlier study (Kufeldt, Armstrong and Dorosh 1989): when children aged 9 to 16 and currently in care were asked the same question, 85 per cent (n=73) answered in the affirmative. In short, taking children into care is not necessarily a bad thing, nor should it be seen as a last resort. This is a point that has also been made by Biehal, see Chapter 5, and Skuse and Ward (2003).

How ready were they for independence?

A signifier of adulthood status is the degree to which young people are prepared for living independently of their family of origin. As indicated above, this is normally a gradual transition, with the option of returning home, or having ongoing support from the family – but for care leavers it is more accelerated and compressed. To ascertain this degree of preparation, a number of questions were put to the study participants. Their responses are presented in Table 9.2, with totals given in percentages.

Table 9.2: Readiness for independence

	Yes		Partly		No/not sure		Total	
	n	%	n	%	n	%	n	%
Did you feel ready for independence?	41	47	27	31	19	22	87	100
Did you have the necessary money?	21	25	26	30	39	45	86*	100
Were you able to take care of your basic needs (e.g. cooking, laundry, etc)?	58	67	18	21	11	12	87	100
Did you know how to access a doctor?	71	82	9	10	7	8	87	100
Did you know how to access a dentist?	70	81	7	8	10	11	87	100
Did you know how to apply for a job?	57	65	11	13	19	22	87	100
Did you know how to apply for assistance if needed?	57	65	13	15	17	20	87	100
Did you have a suitable place to live? **	66	76	9	10	12	14	87	100
Did you have someone to call if you ran into difficulties?	60	70	6	7	20	23	86*	100

* One person chose not to answer these questions

** More females than males reported that they had a place to live when they left care (83% versus 60%, $p < 0.05$)

There were interesting gender differences in perceptions of readiness for independence. Males with less than high school education did not feel ready – a realistic perception. Conversely, females who were less well educated were more likely to declare themselves ready. This was partly related to the achievement of early parenthood. More than two thirds (68%) of the women who had children reported that they were ready for independence. Women were more likely to report that they either had enough money or partially enough money for independence; they were also more likely to have a place to live after they left care.

As in the UK studies, readiness was related to stability and the continuity of care this often provided. The fewer moves experienced, the more prepared respondents felt for independence. Fifty-one per cent of the people who had only one or two moves reported that they were ready for independence in contrast to only 22 per cent of those with six or more. Over a third of those with a stable care experience felt that they could have received more practical experience and skills training before leaving care, such as money management and practical help with employment, but more than a quarter suggested that they could not think of anything they *needed* to help the transition. The majority of this group were female (82%), between 22 and 26 years old. Most (71%) were earning below the poverty line yet felt they had enough to live on. While in care, 96 per cent had contact with their family and all currently have family contacts. Seventy-seven per cent knew why they were in care and 86 per cent felt that entering care was the best solution for them.

It was from this last group that young people were most likely to *move on* from care. They were more likely to have experienced stability, and achieved an adult status such as parenthood, a satisfying career, be settled in accommodation and have positive contact with their birth family.

Reflections on growing up in care

When you think back on your foster care experience, what was best about it?

> They became my real family with whom I am still in contact with a lot. They are my mom/dad/brothers/sisters. (Male, aged 33)

> At Christmas – I got presents. This was a first for me. My mom didn't buy us stuff for Christmas – saying we didn't deserve toys because we were bad girls. (Female, aged 32)

> My foster mother wrote me a poem on my wedding day. (Male, aged 33)

Other good memories were being removed from an abusive situation, learning skills, meeting other people and contact with birth family. But, sadly, 14 per cent had no positive memories: 'Nothing. It was a nightmare in hell.' (Female, aged 29)

What could have been done better or differently?

> I hardly ever saw a social worker. I never received counciling [counselling], I should have been better informed on what was going to happen to me, I should have had a choise [choice]. I spent my life on hold. (Female, aged 31)

> Really resented the fact about being shuffled about from home to home. Really feel being placed in a group home would have been better. (Male, aged 33)

Some people had nothing to report or did not know what could have been done differently. Some were quite negative while others wished they had been provided with better services and preparation for independence.

What, if any, were the turning points in your life?

It was expected that leaving care would be seen as a pivotal point in these young adults' lives. In fact this was identified by only 11 per cent and these were most likely to be the oldest group. On the other hand, 14 per cent said that entering or re-entering care, or going to a good placement, was their turning point. More than a quarter of respondents mentioned getting married or starting a family. Some turning points were as disparate as going to jail or finding religion.

Who was the person most helpful to you while in care?

The most frequent answers were a foster parent (over 43%), followed by a social worker (35%), and friends (19%). The youngest age group were more likely than the others to have found that their social worker was most helpful.

Do you have any contact now with any of these people who were helpful to you while in care?

The theme of discontinuity continued into adult life. Thirty-six per cent had contact with their foster family, but 23 per cent had no contact with anyone from their time in care: 'Every young person leaving care should have that opportunity to reconnect' (Female, aged 24).

If you could tell children coming into the foster care agency anything right now, what would you tell them?

The most typical response was that children should give foster care a chance:

> It is there to help you. (Female, aged 23)

> Don't blow it, it could turn out to be the best thing for ya, all you have to do is try it, give it a chance. (Female, aged 31)

A few, most of whom entered care because they had experienced abuse, would advise children to have someone to talk to or go to if they need help. Other advice included 'continue your education', 'try to stay with your family or extended family', and 'know your rights'. The implications of some advice were disturbing: 'Make sure the case worker knows or does a complete investigation [of foster homes]. I mean complete not just oh they seem like nice people' (Female, aged 33).

Would you say that your time in foster care influenced your later life?

Sixty per cent felt that foster care had a positive influence:

> Yes, because they taught me to love myself and others. If I was to have any children, they taught me how to treat my children (Young female, aged 26).

But 28 per cent felt it had a negative effect:

> The early portion has left me emotionally, mentally and I believe physically scarred. Thank God for psychotherapy. (Male, aged 33)

As in the UK studies, there were examples of victims and survivors. Two young women who responded were *victims*. Both said no one was helpful while they were in care. They were unemployed and living below the poverty line, though they graduated from high school and one had some post-secondary training. While they both had children they reported that they currently have no friends in their life. They had either a clear or some understanding of why they were in care and both felt that they were at least partially ready for independence.

'Tell them sex with an adult is wrong' (Male, aged 28). The man who made this observation was a clear example of a *survivor*. He had endured years of sexual abuse by a therapist while in care, had committed offences and served a prison term, but was now settled with a supportive wife and children and determined to overcome the earlier damaging experiences.

Conclusion

The research findings discussed in this chapter as well as explorations of current practice through the Looking After Children initiatives in Canada (Flynn *et al.* 2003; Kufeldt *et al.* 2000) and the UK (Ward 1995) suggest that much needs to be changed if we are to reduce the number of *survivors* and *victims* and enable young people leaving care to *move on* to success.

Four aspects of practice stand out. These are the need to re-think family preservation, the potential of foster care to compensate young people, the importance of education, and the overarching issue of promoting a sense of identity and self worth.

Family preservation, support and care

Family preservation, including what often embraces family support in the UK, is an important ideal to promote. The majority of children reported for neglect come from what Nelson described as non-wilful or circumstantial neglect (Nelson 1973). More recent studies (e.g. Cameron 2003 and Prilleltensky, Nelson and Peirson 2001) continue to reinforce her message and offer ways in which the goal of family preservation can be achieved.

Nevertheless removal from family is clearly necessary for a significant number of children. Some of the Canadian young people said that they should have come into care earlier; there were also better educational outcomes for those where intervention occurred earlier. In this, and in other UK and Canadian studies, some children have been returned home, only to regress and re-enter after further abuse (Sinclair *et al.* 2003). The ideal of family preservation should not be practised at the expense of a child's need for protection. Sinclair and colleagues (2003) and Clarke and Clarke (2003) affirm the restorative value of foster care and adoptive care. Many of those young people who 'moved on' were those who were able psychologically to make sense of their family relationships and for some this meant being able to leave them behind and form new relationships.

The importance of education

Research studies completed on young people leaving care since the beginning of the 1970s consistently reveal high levels of truancy and school exclusion as well as low levels of attainment and participation beyond the minimum school leaving age (Jackson 2001; Kufeldt *et al.* 2003; Social Exclusion Unit 2003). This needs to change. Many of the Canadian adults, against great odds, had improved their educational status after leaving care. However, an often mentioned regret in both the UK and Canada was poor school performance. When taking over the guardianship of children the state has a responsibility to support and encourage children's educational aspirations and potential in the same way that a good responsible parent would.

Promoting self worth

Those in transition demonstrated the major struggles they face. Adults who had been in care expressed, in general, satisfaction with their lot in life; many were positive about the substitute care received by individual foster parents and workers. However, expressed satisfaction about living in poverty or in less than ideal living conditions suggests that they have lower expectations of their entitlements than their more fortunate peers (see also Skuse and Ward 2003). This, as well as other indicators, suggests that much needs to be done to promote a sense of worth and self esteem in young people needing care. Protection from harm and provision of good physical care in themselves are good but not sufficient to ensure healthy personal development. Participants in the UK and Canadian studies reinforced what we know about survival and resilience. Knowledge is expanding about what promotes resilience (Rubin 1996; Stein forthcoming); this knowledge should contribute to improved transitions and better outcomes for future cohorts of young people.

Fostering care and adulthood

One of the factors influencing the emphasis on family preservation has been past failures of the foster and residential care system. More recent studies reflect on the value of foster care. On both sides of the Atlantic (Kufeldt *et al.* 2003; Sinclair *et al.* 2003) recent studies have highlighted the contribution made by foster carers to good outcomes for young people: giving affection; providing stability and compensatory attachments; and involvement with schooling. And for some young people these dimensions, combined with gradual transitions and ongoing support, will provide a strong foundation for their journey to adulthood. However, the contrast between normative transitions in modern society and those experienced by many young people leaving care is disturbing. In promoting positive outcomes there needs to be more recognition of the nature and timing of young people's transitions from care. This includes giving them the emotional and practical support they will need well into their twenties, providing them with the psychological space to cope with changes over time, as well as recognizing the different stages of transitions.

Note

1   Focal theory or the focal model of adolescence is based on empirical research showing that adolescents psychologically cope with major changes in their lives by dealing with one issue at a time, or as they come into focus (Coleman and and Hendry 1999). Too many care leavers during their journey to adulthood have to cope with major changes in their lives at a far younger age than other young people and in a far shorter time – they are denied the psychological opportunity to focus.

Part III

Promoting the Well-being of Vulnerable Families

Chapter 10

Themes from a UK Research Initiative on Supporting Parents

David Quinton

Supporting Parents was a major UK government-funded research initiative intended to discover the informal and formal supports parents need to help them look after their children effectively. The parents' own views on this were a key element in the thirteen studies funded under the initiative, together with analyses of the services they received and the degree of cooperation or inter-agency working between them. The studies were both general and special population-based and ranged from large-scale surveys to detailed investigations of special parenting issues. This chapter summarizes the cross-cutting findings that are common to all or many of the projects.

Introduction

While interventions explored in the previous chapters are aimed directly at promoting the well-being of children, factors in their parents' capacity, the wider family and the environment may also need to be addressed if they are to achieve a successful standard of well-being. Chapters in this part of the book explore a number of support services aimed at promoting the well-being of parents – the second side of the Assessment triangle.

Background and history

This chapter summarizes the key cross-cutting themes from the Department of Health-funded research initiative *Supporting Parents: Messages from Research*

(Quinton 2004).[1] This is the latest in the Department of Health series on Messages from Research. For many years these non-technical overviews have been produced in order to make the findings from research programmes and initiatives useful to policymakers, service providers and practitioners. The most recent overviews have dealt with child protection, residential care and adoption. This programmatic approach to research and the emphasis on drawing the findings together in an accessible way is unique in the British context and, as far as we know, in the international arena as well.

The idea behind this initiative was to look at how parents generally might be helped to look after their children and to move away from a research emphasis on more marked family and parenting problems. One important consequence of this change in thinking was to shift the discussion away from one in which services are seen as *interventions*, to one in which they are seen as part of a range of *supports* that parents can draw on to help them look after their children in their own way.

The first study in the programme began in the autumn of 1996 and the last one reported in the autumn of 2002. The period between these dates was marked in the UK by a great deal of activity in policy and practice around parenting and parenting support. These policy changes have ranged from those affecting parenting and parents' resources generally, such as tax credits for poorer families or changes in benefits, to initiatives intended to change parents' and children's behaviour, such as parenting orders or parent training, to specific policies and guidance around helping and supporting parents with specific problems, such as children's disabilities.

Many of the studies fed into the reshaping of policy. The fourteen studies are briefly described in Table 10.1. The table gives the formal names of the projects and also the ways in which they are referred to in the text. Not all studies are referenced because this chapter concentrates on the service implications of the research, not on the issues of support of other kinds, although these are touched on. The institutions to which the researchers were attached are those at the time the grants were made. Many have since moved on and upwards to other universities or research units.

Table 10.1: Projects in the initiative

Title	Details
Parenting in Poor Environments Referred to as the Poor Environments study (Ghate and Hazel 2002)	A representative national interview survey of 1754 parents, randomly sampled from geographical areas objectively defined as providing 'poor parenting environments'. The areas represented were drawn from the top 30 per cent of the national distribution of disadvantaged areas. This survey was followed by a qualitative study of 40 parents in especially disadvantaged circumstances.
A Study of Step-parents and Step-children Referred to as the Step-family study (M. Smith 2003)	A representative community sample of *new* step-families in London was identified through a large-scale screening exercise. Ten thousand questionnaires were returned and 434 families fitting the research criteria were found. Half of these – nearly 200 – took part in the study, in which the parent, step-parent and up to two children within the age range were interviewed separately at home.
A Study of Normal Injuries Referred to as the Injuries study (Smith, Boddy, Hall, Morse, Pitt and Reid unpublished)	A randomly selected community sample of nearly 700 families with children aged from birth to eight years was selected from inner and outer London and non-metropolitan areas. Parents completed a detailed 'incident diary' covering nine days recording all the incidents when the child appeared to have hurt him or herself and any resulting injuries. Mothers were then interviewed about the family, parenting, supervision and safety practices, and the child's history of more serious injuries.
Parents' Strategies with Children with Behavioural Difficulties Referred to as the New Forest study (Thompson, Raynor, Cornah, Stevenson and Sonuga-Barke 2002)	The study was based on an earlier sample of 1047 children on whom data were obtained around their third birthday. A sub-group of 560 was contacted again at the time of their eighth birthday and parents filled in questionnaires on their behaviour. Four groups were defined: those without behaviour problems at either age (320), those with behaviour problems at both ages (53), those who showed behaviour problems at three but not at eight years (85) and those who did not show behavioural problems at three but did so at eight (102). Parents were interviewed on the ways they parented and how they dealt with problems.

Continued on next page

Table 10.1 continued

Title	Details
Supporting Parents on Kids' Education Referred to as Supporting Parents on Kids Education project (SPOKES) (Scott and Sylva 2002)	A study of an innovative community-based intervention to support parents of five- to six-year-olds in managing their children's difficulties in behaviour and learning. Children with problems identified by questionnaires were randomly assigned to the intervention or to a basic advice service. The programme covered three school terms and helped parents with behaviour problems and reading. The sessions were conducted in primary schools.
Supporting Foster Placements Referred to as the Supporting Fostering study (Sinclair, Wilson and Gibbs 2000)	A study of 476 foster placements at two points in time, roughly a year apart. The information came from postal questionnaires to carers, social workers and family placement social workers; 151 older children in these placements responded to a brief questionnaire asking about their experience of fostering and what they wanted from it. There were also 24 detailed case studies, intended to check and illuminate the conclusions from the statistical analysis of the questionnaires.
The Fostering Task with Adolescents Referred to as the Fostered Adolescents study (Farmer, Moyers and Lipscombe 2004)	This study looked at the relationship between foster carers' skills and placement stability after one year for 68 young people aged 11–17 in placements intended to be medium- to long-term. Carers, young people and social workers were interviewed at three months into the placement and again nine months later.
Supporting Parents Caring for a Technology-Dependent Child Referred to as the Technology-dependent study (Kirk and Glendinning 1999)	A qualitative study that explored parents' experiences of caring for a technology-dependent child at home. Twenty-four families were interviewed, including three who were seen before and after hospital discharge. Families were purposively selected so that the sample included differences in technologies, lengths of time that children had been at home and domiciliary nursing support services. Thirty-eight professionals were interviewed in depth about their experiences and views.
South Asian Families with a Child with Severe Disabilities Referred to as the Asian Families study (Hatton, Akram, Shah, Robertson and Emerson 2004)	This study gave a comprehensive picture of the lives of UK South Asian families with a child with severe disabilities. The project involved structured interviews with 136 parents, sampled across five local authority areas and semi-structured interviews at two time points with 26 parents to provide qualitative information on the lives of families. All interviews were conducted in the first language of the participant.

Table 10.1 continued

Title	Details
Parenting and Disability: The Role of Formal and Informal Networks Referred to as the Disabled Parents study (Olsen and Clarke 2003)	Eighty families were interviewed, including 12 in a sub-study of the impact of the onset of or major changes in disabilities. Parents had a wide range of physical and mental health impairments. They were recruited mainly through voluntary sector groups, and a few through GP surgeries. The study opens a window on the 'normative' experience of disabled parents.
Pregnancy and Parenthood: The Views and Experiences of Young People in Public Care Referred to as the Pregnant Teenagers or the Teenagers study (Corlyon and McGuire 1999)	This study was carried out over a three-year period. Data were collected (a) from local authority officers, social workers, carers, pregnant young women and young mothers who were being or had recently been looked after by a local authority, and (b) from groups of 14- to 15-year-olds, half of whom were looked after, predominantly in residential care, and half of whom were not.
The Parenting Role of Imprisoned Fathers Referred to as the Imprisoned Fathers or the Prisons study (Boswell and Wedge 2001)	The study interviewed 181 men from 25 geographically spread prison establishments that had either parenting/fatherhood courses, children's/family visits schemes, or neither of these. These included six Young Offender Institutions. The researchers also interviewed 127 partners or other principal carers of inmates' children. Interviews investigated the father's role whilst in prison, the value of fatherhood courses or visiting schemes, links between prison and community agencies and families, and impacts on the children.
Parents who Reject One of their Children Referred to as the Rejecting or Emotionally Abusing Parents study (Rushton and Dance in press)	Children singled out for rejection by birth parents have particularly poor adjustment and difficulty forming attachments. This study explored issues of identification, intervention and social services response in three studies: a survey of 107 health visitors; interviews with 53 mental health professionals in CAMHS services; and a case-file study of children referred because of possible emotional abuse in two London authorities.
Family Centres, Services and Networks Referred to as the Family Centres study (Tunstill, Hughes and Aldgate in press)	The study used quantitative and qualitative methods to look at family centres as a gateway to services and coordinators of family support. The data provides a fascinating picture of the organization, provision and networking of family centres between 1998 and 2001. There was a postal survey of over 400 family centres in England; semi-structured interviews with managers of 40 family centres; structured interviews with 100+ family centre users and postal questionnaires to over 60 professionals with links with family centres.

Definitions and issues

Entitlement and effects

Before summarizing the findings it is helpful to draw an important distinction between conclusions drawn on the basis of *entitlement* (or *rights* in an everyday sense) and those made on the basis of *effects*. The main thrust of the initiative was towards the latter. The idea was to discover ways of supporting parenting that 'made a difference' by promoting better parenting. Policy is rightly directed towards making this kind of a difference in demonstrable ways.

However, much of what the studies have to say does not depend on showing that giving help improves parenting. Listening to parents' concerns; taking their views seriously; treating them as partners in solving problems with their children; giving them useful information; paying attention to the realities of their lives rather than the agendas of particular services; all these things, which are reflected in the findings from many of the studies, are a matter of the right and proper way to treat people. We do not need a demonstration that these behaviours promote better parenting in order to change our approach to service delivery to take them into account.

What is support?

'Support' is a very general term. It is easy to respond to a problem by saying that we should 'put in more support', without being at all clear what we mean or what we want to achieve. The word itself implies something that is helpful, so we can be fooled into thinking we are doing some good simply by giving something we label 'support'. But, this can range from saying 'never mind' to providing a very specific service. The danger in using 'support' as an umbrella term is that it can become devalued as an idea.

Support involves both a giver and a receiver. Their views on what is needed may not be the same. Support is sometimes not there when we want it, or is not what we want or is inappropriate or intrusive. We may blame what goes wrong on a lack of support even if this is not justified. We may claim that we did something without the help of others, even if this is not so. If we offer support we may be rebuffed. We may even include under 'support' some action counter to the views of the person we are trying to help. We may even decide that something needs to be done against one person's wishes in order to support another.

Support for parenting is complex to assess, to get right and to deliver because of the balance between the neglect of family problems and intrusion into family life, not to mention ideas of what satisfactory parenting is, how and when this needs support and who should decide that. Understanding 'support' includes understanding how being given support makes people feel. Put the other way round, it makes nonsense of the everyday meaning of 'support' to call services and interventions 'supports' if they do not fulfil the normal notion of 'supportive behaviour'.

What is parenting?

If we want to support something we should be clear about what we think it is. Three key points about parenting should be made. First, in modern industrial societies it includes a formidable range of tasks and responsibilities. It is made much easier by resources and social supports that can be drawn on when needed. For this reason, for example, single parents are at a disadvantage as are couples who cannot work together harmoniously.

Second, it is essential to take an ecological perspective on support. What this emphasizes is that 'parenting' – what parents actually *do* with and for their children – arises from a very wide variety of influences. Some of these derive from parents' own characteristics, others from their experiences of being parented, and others from their current mental and physical health. The translation of these individual differences into 'parenting problems' is strongly influenced by the circumstances in which they are trying to look after their children currently. The influences do not just go in one direction. Our own behaviour influences our relationships as well as the other way round. It follows from this that the best ways of supporting parenting may be far from obvious.

Third, formal services themselves should be seen as *part* of the ecology of parenting, not just as something trying to influence it. If this is not done we may tackle one problem – say adult mental health difficulties – without tackling related ones, such as poverty or the children's behaviour. Because of this the intervention may be ineffective.

Finally, these general considerations apply to a wide range of circumstances. At one extreme are the parents of the technology-dependent children, whose lives are taken over by the needs of their children, to the extent that the boundaries between parenting and nursing become blurred, where their homes often become extensions of the clinic, and where parenting becomes professionalized. At the other extreme are the emotionally abusing or rejecting parents who seem not to want to care for one of their children at all, or to blame him or her for all the family's ills.

Findings

Support from family and friends

SUPPORT BEGINS AT HOME

It was clear from many studies that relationships at home were a critical part of parents' support. This was true both for positive effects of support and the harm done by its absence or even more, by discord and hostility between parents.

The foster carers in both of the fostering studies put their partners first amongst those who helped them; the Asian parents leant on each other for comfort and decision making; the technology-dependent parents had to work in a highly coordinated way; and the imprisoned fathers relied on the tenacity of their partners in maintaining contact with their children. This in-house support involved children as well. This was an important source of help for the disabled parents, the Asian families and the fosterers of adolescents.

BALANCE AND INDEPENDENCE

Family and friends can anticipate and adapt to needs in a very flexible and responsive way. We think about what is on each other's minds or is making life difficult at the moment. But there also needs to be a sense of give and take and that support is reasonably balanced. Accepting support can lead to a fear of loss of independence. Parents in the Poor Environments study who felt most in need of help were the most apprehensive about accepting support from family and friends. They feared that asking for help showed that they could not cope, so that accepting help would weaken the independence of the family and open the door to interference.

FAMILY AND FRIENDS AS A SOURCE OF STRESS

Families and friends are not necessarily supportive. Indeed, family and friends were especially a source of stress for the parents with the most problems. The pregnant looked after teenagers had poor relationships with their own mothers, who tended to look to them for support rather than giving it. The imprisoned fathers – whilst loyally visited by their wives and partners – seemed very short of family support in other ways. The emotionally abusing parents also had very poor relationships with their own families and little support from anyone within their social circle. Even in the fostering studies a third or more of carers experienced criticism from family, friends and neighbours.

The disabled parents and the parents in the Asian families not only experienced the limitations on support that arose because of their special needs, they often faced incomprehension or hostility from their families because they did not understand the problems, or even blamed them for them.

Community groups and users' groups

There is no room here to deal in any detail with the findings on community groups, like toddlers' groups and toy libraries, or with specialist and users' support groups, such as groups for foster carers of parents of disabled children, but a few key points can be made.

Parents in the Poor Environments study used community groups on a 'take it or leave it' basis, depending on how well they fitted with their current needs. Use was not related to any measures of need except for children's special health problems. Strikingly, use was *less* common amongst those who saw themselves as most in need and more common amongst those with relatively higher family incomes. Community groups increased the flexibility of support available to parents, but it seemed that parents needed sufficient energy and resources if they were to add these to the supports they used.

Users' groups were valued by the foster carers for emotional support and advice. Over 70 per cent of carers in both fostering studies had personal contact with other carers, such contact often arising through the organized groups. Support groups were less positively thought of by other parents. Cultural and language barriers affected the use of support groups by the Asian parents with disabled children. Only 19 per cent belonged to a support group and these generally did not find them helpful.

The situation with regard to formal support for prisoners and their families was depressing. Forty-two per cent of adults, 30 per cent of young offenders and 64 per cent of all partners had no contact with any voluntary or statutory agencies and none mentioned self-help groups.

The relationship between informal and formal supports

There was little evidence that support from family and friends and support from services complemented or made up for lacks in each other. Indeed, a common finding was that parents who got support from one source tended to get more from the other. Thus in the Poor Environments study there were relatively high and relatively low consumers overall. The Asian parents were more aware of services if they had better informal and semi-formal support. Those who spoke

English got more services. In the foster care studies getting on well with social workers went along with more input from them, with better connections with other services and with higher use of foster carers' support groups.

LOOKING FOR EMOTIONAL SUPPORT

Nevertheless families were likely to look to formal services for emotional as well as practical support. Heavy users of services in the Poor Environments study did this, as did the parents of technology-dependent children, the Asian parents, and depressed parents in the New Forest study. Sometimes the need for emotional support turned into dependency, a concern noted by the social workers looking after the pregnant teenagers and some family centre staff.

Parents' views of services

PARENTS' OVERALL REACTIONS TO SERVICES

We tend to hear most about parents' criticisms of services, but it is important to summarize their positive views as well.

The parents in the Poor Environments study were usually positive about the help they received. Indeed, those who were frequent users of services often felt less ambivalent about turning to services than to their families and friends, as did the parents in the New Forest study, who saw health visitors as having an important and valued role in giving information and emotional support. Over half the carers in the Supporting Fostering study and over 70 per cent in the Fostering Adolescents study thought their link worker gave them good support. On the whole carers got on well with their social workers and made allowances for their shortcomings.

Parents attending the family centres said they got more from the centres than they anticipated. It was quick and easy to get a response to a problem and they valued the fact that the centre knew them. They also liked the atmosphere, the warmth and friendliness of staff and the fact that they could just drop in. Indeed, they wanted more of the same services, not different ones.

The Asian parents were less positive. They said that it took too long to get services organized for their children (87%); that they did not know what services were available (82%) and that they had to fight to get them (75%).

The pregnant looked after teenagers were especially negative. Only 4 per cent included social workers amongst the people they could trust. Most had a long litany of complaints about them, that they: did not listen; did not listen to their opinions; did not give honest accounts and explanations; could not be trusted; were difficult or impossible to contact; did not stand up for them; were unreliable; and sat in judgment on them. They liked their after care workers much better because they dealt with practicalities, gave emotional support and were free of the hard decisions about the mother and baby.

WHAT PARENTS WANTED SERVICES TO BE LIKE

What parents wanted was very consistent across the studies. The parents in the Poor Environments study liked services that were practical and professional, took their views on their needs seriously, listened to them, and were emotionally supportive as well as practically helpful. In short, parents wanted services to treat them like adults and to see them as partners in solving their problems.

The carers in the Supporting Fostering study were also quite clear. They wanted their social workers to be there for them, respectful of their views, considerate, warm, approving and ready to listen, and practical. This meant sorting out finance and transport, arranging professional services, working with the birth family, working with the child, enabling the carer to work with the child, and supporting the carer. For the adolescents' foster carers the key element was availability and responsiveness, especially shown in returning phone calls.

The question of responsiveness was especially important for the parents of the technology-dependent children, something they only got if they were lucky enough to have key workers. The use of mobile phones was particularly important. Key workers gave emotional as well as practical support and helped the parents organize and argue for services and supplies.

PARENTS IN CONTROL

An abiding message from all the parents was that they wanted to feel in control when they had parenting problems. Regardless of whether they were drawing on the help of family and friends or using the expertise of specialist services they did not want their parenting decisions to be taken out of their hands. It is important for all those providing support to understand how strong this feeling is, even in circumstances where parenting is clearly problematic, as with the rejecting parents.

The need for control was reflected in a more negative way in the step-parents' wariness of formal services, whilst they were still establishing their families; or in the pregnant teenagers' rejection of social work 'interference' in their parenting; or in some of the imprisoned fathers' resistance to the idea of support. It was, perhaps, strongest in the denials of a substantial proportion of the emotionally abusing/rejecting parents – who were well known to social services – that anything was wrong.

Support was too easily determined by service agendas, for example Asian parents felt they had little control over service supports or were 'slotted in' often inappropriately or unreliably, or that support offered did not have the expertise to cope with the child.

PARENTS AS EXPERTS

It is important for services to treat parents as experts on their own families and to take their views seriously. Experience may in the end prove otherwise – for example, when rejecting parents want to locate all their family problems in one child – but it is the right place to begin. For example, the parents of the technology-dependent children began as novices in specialized care but became the people who delivered specialist procedures and the best judges of the children's needs.

PARENTS AS PART OF THE 'TEAM AROUND THE CHILD'

Services need to see their role as *enabling* not *providing* care. For example, foster carers felt that social workers wanted them to be 'professional' but were unwilling to treat them as part of a 'team around the child'. If social services expect carers to be 'professional' they should treat them like professionals. Fewer than half of the carers in the Fostering Adolescents study felt that they were part of the team.

Key features of support
SUPPORT AS A RELATIONSHIP

The parents in the Poor Environments study wanted services to be efficient and expert but also to be respectful and to take their views seriously. As Ghate and Hazel (2002) assert, 'relationships are at the heart of support'. Respectfulness is the way in which services can deal with the power imbalance inherent in the relationship. Parents cannot give something back to the service, but a sense of equality can come through treating them as partners in problem solving. Support should not make parents feel vulnerable, small or obligated; without these features it is, simply, not 'supportive'.

Attention to this balance is more critical the greater and more complex the needs, but becomes harder to keep in mind if services concentrate on their technical expertise, as they did with the technology-dependent parents, or on their formal responsibilities, as happened most dramatically in the relationship between prison authorities, prisoners and their families.

SUPPORT AS A PROCESS

It was clear that support is not just a question of giving help in a piecemeal way. It is more effective if support is seen as a process. If relationships are good from the start, parents feel better about the help they are getting and are more likely to stay engaged with the service.

For example, for the Asian parents the process started with how, when, where and what they were told about their child's disability. Telling the parents in a supportive way helped them accept it; acceptance made it easier to get understanding from kin and friends; this helped parents to become more aware of and confident about services. But services themselves needed actively to provide good language support and develop a collaborative relationship with the parents. This reinforced collaboration and helped identify unmet family needs.

The Supporting Parents on Kids Education (SPOKES) project worked hard to get things off to a good start with very careful approaches to parents; adapted the parenting programme in a way that would appeal to parents; visited the home to learn about pressures that might affect school attendance; and used schools as a non-threatening venue for the work.

COOPERATION BETWEEN SERVICES

Inter-agency working is a focus of policy but the studies did not provide many good examples of this. The more common picture was of services protecting their boundaries and professional identity in order to conserve resources or deal with funding problems. For example, the needs of the disabled parents *as parents* were not taken into account in planning. For the technology-dependent parents, arranging short-term care and obtaining equipment was often difficult because of disputes between hospital trusts, community trusts and GPs over who should pay. In the Rejection study coordination between services was poor. Health visitors and social workers did not have positive views of each other. Social workers found Child and Adolescent Mental Health Services (CAMHS) unhelpful and made very few referrals to adult mental health services. There was a picture of services protecting themselves by setting high thresholds for their intervention or circumscribing the limits of their responsibility.

INFORMATION

The issue of information crops up in many studies. Good information is key to helping parents solve problems. Information sharing between agencies is a good reflection of the quality of their cooperation and the extent to which they are providing coordinated services tailored to families' needs on the basis of comprehensive assessments.

Parents wanted information in order to understand their problems and to work out ways of solving them, either on their own or with the help of services. The carers in the Fostered Adolescents and Supporting Fostering studies needed information on the young people's lives and problems before the placement was made. The young people wanted to know something about the people who were going to look after them. Lack of both kinds of information predicted poorer outcomes.

The parents in the Poor Environments study wanted videos and leaflets. Providing information on services was an important function of family centres. The Asian parents wanted information on their child's disability in their own language and in terms they could understand. They wanted this not just when they heard about the disability but also as their experience of parenting developed and the children's needs changed.

Parents often knew little about services that might be available to them. This was particularly so for the prisoners and their partners who identified little beyond social services and probation and never mentioned support groups.

The exchange of information between services was often notable by its absence. In the Rejecting Parents study social services case files seldom had copies of the social workers' formulation of problems or letters back from other services giving an opinion or course of action. Referral letters to CAMHS often contained no assessment of the problem.

Delivering support

Most studies concluded that family needs should be addressed 'holistically', not piecemeal. By this they meant that services should not concentrate on their narrow area of expertise and ignore the broader context of parents' problems. Parenting problems often went along with social disadvantage, poor mental health, difficulties in intimate relationships and sometimes with disabilities in the parents or children as well. Parenting problems are often a consequence of these overlapping difficulties and it makes little sense to deal with one whilst ignoring the others.

Where coordination was good it too often depended on a particularly energetic consultant here or a particularly effective social worker there. There was seldom a built in mechanism for assessment and coordination. Even for the technology-dependent children, post-discharge multi-disciplinary meetings to plan care and agree funding were rare.

ASSESSMENT OF NEEDS

The holistic assessment of needs is top of the list of ways to improve coordination and delivery of services, but it was rare. Thus, although the mental health of the Asian parents was poor, they did not use mental health services. None of the disability studies showed services consistently paying attention to support around parenting *itself*, or giving help with parenting approaches or relationships. Systematic assessments of parenting by health visitors or social workers were lacking for the rejecting parents. Indeed, health visitors did not see this as part of their role. Social workers concentrated on the reported incident. Only about 3 per cent of emotionally abused children received a full developmental assessment on referral and there was no evidence that this had ever been done in the past.

The new Integrated Children's System provides a model for systematic assessments, but without a willingness of services to cooperate in agreeing the assessments of need and coordinating the delivering the appropriate services, the assessments on their own will not be sufficient.

LINK AND KEY WORKERS

Support does not just arrive, it has to be sought and organized as well. Parents were the usual coordinators of support and services, but there are many occasions where the task becomes too complicated and onerous and when someone with professional leverage is needed to identify and battle for support. Link or key workers were easily the most favoured method of coordinating services to meet needs holistically. The list of those who were positive about them is long: parents in all three disability studies; foster carers in the Supporting Fostering and Fostering Teenagers projects; and the pregnant looked after teenagers, who liked the practical role taken by after-care workers.

The foster carers rated link and key workers highly because they did what the carers wanted social workers to do: they respected their views, were considerate, warm, approving, ready to listen and practical, were available and returned calls. In short, they were 'there for them'. The foster carers of the adolescents used their link workers for day-to-day support as well as for organizing and arguing for services. Indeed, link workers came top of these carers' lists of those who were both available and useful. Services for the technology-dependent children were delivered best when a key worker helped deal with the complexities of getting supplies and support. Again these workers were available through their mobile phones, a highly valued means of contact.

In short, link workers were able to combine the flexibility and relationship qualities of family and friends with professional knowledge and expertise and a greater power to argue for services. Of course, this was not always the case. Some link workers were not effective in their jobs. Moreover, outside social services, the use of link workers was still unusual. There seems no doubt, however, that this role provides a demonstrably effective way of supporting parents.

Families who are hard to work with

Three studies dealt with support for parents who have complex and suspicious relationships with services – and often with their own families and friends as well: the looked after pregnant teenagers; the imprisoned fathers; and the emotionally abusing or rejecting parents. All three groups of parents were socially disadvantaged; their personal relationships were often negative and fragile; and their relationships with family and friends often weak and unsupportive. They were often, indeed, difficult families to help, even with the best of intentions. The pregnant teenagers thought they knew how to parent and did not want social workers helping them; the imprisoned fathers often thought they were close to the ideal of what a parent should be, and sometimes wanted to keep help at arm's length; the rejecting parents frequently denied the incidents which led to their recent referral and were hard to engage in interventions designed to help their parenting.

Service responses reflected this negativity. Social services had no policies for dealing with the pregnant teenagers and their over-dependency or demandingness. The prisons generally failed to meet the requirements to facilitate and strengthen prisoners' family ties. Social service responses to the rejecting parents were incident-, not needs-based, even though the families were well known to services. Developmental assessments of the children were a rarity. Families were passed from health visitors to social services and sometimes from social services to mental health services, but no service had a very high opinion of another and referrals often led to no clear action. Even the family centres, which frequently tried to work with parents with complex problems, were aware that they needed to limit the length of their interventions and to resist becoming the parents' main source of support.

Support in the community

Many studies advocated delivering support on a non-stigmatizing basis through, for example, family centres. The advantages were that services would be better linked and it might be possible to engage parents who are unlikely to use social services, CAMHS clinics or other bodies who they fear are 'spying' on them. However, there was a constant pressure on family centres to deal with the most complex families, a move that can easily make using them stigmatizing.

There was no clear evidence that such approaches would be more successful in engaging parents. However, social workers and health visitors working with the rejecting parents were most positive about the responses and the help they got from community-based parenting programmes; the parents attending the family centres liked their atmosphere and style; the SPOKES project went out of its way to set itself up as a community project and to avoid the dangers of seeming 'official'. Engaging parents in planning the programme was successful as was the effort at understanding their lives and agendas. We do not know how well this approach will bring in parents who are suspicious of services. Nevertheless, the current UK policy push to increase the number of community-based holistic services receives much support from the studies in this initiative.

Conclusions

At the beginning of this chapter a distinction was drawn between how parents should be treated ('entitlements' or 'rights') and whether support of particular kinds is effective in helping them with their problems. It is worth emphasizing this distinction again. The studies clearly showed how parents saw support and what they wanted from it. These are very clear messages for services. Taking serious note of these views is not only a matter of entitlements, it is also likely that doing so will make it easier to engage even those with the most complex parenting problems in services intended to help them.

It seems reasonable to assume that services that make parenting less stressful will have an effect on what parents do with and for their children and that, in the majority of cases, they can be given the information and encouragement to work out their problems in their own way. Nearly all parents want to do this, but many have more complex problems that need specialist input. Specialist services should work to help parents solve their problems and not just tell them what to do. The complexities of inter-agency workings and the battles between agencies over professional boundaries and funding are not matters that ought to complicate the parenting task.

On the other hand, the studies suggest that we are far from the point at which needs are assessed holistically and in partnership. The objectives of 'support' are still often poorly defined and its effectiveness untested. These studies show that parents can be helped directly with their parenting, but also that what influences what is a very complex matter. This suggests that research to promote 'evidence-based services' should do so through studies such as those described in many chapters of this book, that test the effectiveness of different interventions. On top of all this we need to keep social disadvantage clearly in our sights. So many of the studies show the overlap between parenting problems and poverty and disadvantage. This needs to be addressed both as a matter of 'rights' and as a key to positive 'effects'.

Note

1   This programme of research was coordinated by Dr Carolyn Davies of the Children's Social Care Research and Development Division of the Department of Health and the academic coordinator, Professor David Quinton from the School for Policy Studies at Bristol University, who compiled this overview.

Chapter 11

The Canada Pre-natal Nutrition Program and Breaking the Cycle

A Nation's Response to Programming for its Most Vulnerable Citizens

Judy Watson and Margaret Leslie

The Canada Pre-natal Nutrition Program (CPNP) provides pre-natal education, counseling, food supplements and post-partum support to 40,000 pregnant women across Canada each year who are at risk for poor health outcomes.

This chapter defines the critical success factors of the CPNP and further examines the evolution of one of its targeted local programs, Breaking the Cycle, for women living in Toronto who experience substance use problems.

Introduction

The United Nations' 1990 Summit for Children encouraged the world's governments to prepare national plans of action that would provide every child in the world with a better future (Health Canada 1997). This call to action envisioned a reduction in the number of children suffering from the effects of poverty and malnutrition, and in the number of women suffering from complications related to childbirth.

In Canada, federal, provincial/territorial and local governments were increasingly concerned about the needs of vulnerable women and children (Health Canada 2001). The federal government launched a comprehensive initiative of four programs, designed to meet the needs of a particular segment of the at-risk population, each having distinct, overlapping objectives and approaches to reduce the number of women and children who have, in the past, fallen between the cracks of social programming.

One of these, the Canada Pre-Natal Nutrition Program (CPNP) is a national, community-based health promotion intervention, directed towards those women most likely to have unhealthy babies due to poor maternal health and nutrition. Its overall aim is to improve the health of both infant and mother.

The involvement of federal and provincial/territorial governments and local organizations enables the CPNP to reach many women in Canada who are at risk, including those in small prairie towns, remote First Nations communities and downtown neighbourhoods. Across Canada, more than one third of pregnant teenagers who carry to term participate in CPNP projects; participation is close to 100 per cent in some communities (Barrington Research Group Inc. 2002a). While CPNP funding and projects are often matched with complementary programs, CPNP projects are the sole providers of appropriate support in many remote communities of Canada.

Ongoing national, regional and project-level evaluations and monitoring have made an important contribution to the continued success and tailoring of the CPNP since its inception in 1994. The multi-faceted approach has consistently identified program design characteristics central to ensuring that the CPNP continues to meet its goals and the needs of vulnerable women. A decade later, the CPNP is proving its worth as a viable and sustainable national program, as a model of collaboration among different levels of government and community organizations, and equally as a flexible, community-based program of interventions that offers a wide range of opportunities at a critical time in the lives of women at risk.

The first part of this chapter offers insight into how these factors work in combination against the backdrop of an increasingly multi-cultural target population spread across 13 provincial/territorial jurisdictions and in diverse communities. The second section describes Breaking the Cycle, a program in Toronto providing services to women experiencing substance abuse.

The Canada Pre-natal Nutrition Program (CPNP)

The CPNP is designed to serve pregnant women facing conditions of risk, including: those who live in poverty, who abuse alcohol or drugs, teens, those living in violent situations, on- and off-reserve Aboriginal women, those living in isolation or with limited access to services, new immigrants, and those diagnosed with gestational diabetes (Barrington Research Group Inc. 2002b and Health Canada 1998). Of CPNP participants in 2000–01:

- 45.5% were not living with a partner
- 33.6% were aged 19 and under upon entry to the program
- 21.6% were of Aboriginal descent
- 23.3% were immigrants, an increase from 9.8 per cent in 1996–7
- 56.4% had a household income less than C$1000 per month and 21.2 per cent had less than 10 years of education. (Barrington Research Group Inc. 2002a)

Its goals include improving health during pregnancy, increasing the number of babies born with healthy birth weights, promoting breastfeeding, and increasing access to services (Health Canada 2000c).

The CPNP is jointly managed by the federal government and the provincial/territorial governments. Representatives of the federal department of health and provincial/territorial health and social service agencies work together with representatives of community organizations – themselves sponsors or partners of CPNP projects – on Joint Management Committees (JMCs), responsible for determining how best to meet local needs in each province or territory (Barrington Research Group Inc. 2002b).

There are currently 350 projects operating in over 2,400 communities across Canada (excluding First Nations and Inuit communities) (Barrington Research Group Inc. 2002a). In partnership with community organizations (i.e. food banks, school boards, religious groups) the programs offer such services as pre-natal nutrition counseling, food supplements, collective kitchens, peer counseling, breastfeeding education and post-partum support (Health Canada 1997).

The number and levels of government organizations involved, the range of community organizations, and the cultural diversity and related needs of participants called for a finely tuned combination of structure and flexibility to be built in to the CPNP from its inception. Similarly, the sheer number and diversity of programs demanded a multiple matrix approach to evaluation and monitoring.

At the national level, the CPNP has been adapted to fit existing federal government structures. The program is delivered through two separate arms of the federal Department of Health: the First Nations and Inuit Health component,[1] which serves pregnant women in First Nations and Inuit communities, and Population and Public Health Branch, serving all other Canadian women living off reserve. This division is compatible with the funding structures and arrangements for other health programs aimed at First Nations and Inuit communities through Health Canada.

In the First Nations and Inuit component of the CPNP, training at both the local and regional levels has been a real priority. More than 500 community health providers received training during 2000–2001 in such key areas as breast-feeding, general nutrition and fetal alcohol syndrome.

Ingredients for success

Within the CPNP projects are designed to break the negative cycles of substance abuse, poverty, teen pregnancy, poor nutrition, unhealthy weights and low self esteem. By providing interventions during the pre-natal period – a critical time in women's lives – the CPNP provides the opportunity for pregnant women to improve their own circumstances, as well as those of their children.

Evaluation and monitoring of the CPNP provide a wealth of information on the program's performance in terms of development, performance in achieving goals and objectives, and the outcomes and impacts on individual participants.

Evaluation results demonstrate factors and qualities that make a clear contribution to the overall success of the CPNP, including:

- firm guiding principles and essential program elements which provide a strong, national foundation
- sustained federal funding which covers staffing costs, providing stability and allowing for longer-term planning
- collaborative governance across federal, provincial/territorial governments, and local organizations
- local flexibility offering the freedom to select effective interventions
- a multiple matrix approach to evaluation and monitoring.

Guiding principles and essential program elements

The CPNP is built on a strong foundation of guiding principles. These provide the 'spirit' of how the CPNP projects are run and articulate the underlying philosophy. Project staff across the country credit the guiding principles as the key to successful program management, capacity building, participant involvement and reaching those most at risk (Health Canada 2001). Key guiding principles include:

- putting mothers and babies first in program planning, development and delivery
- strengthening and supporting families
- equity and accessibility for participants
- partnerships with other services in the community
- community-based decision making flexibility in programming.

The essential program elements help to articulate the letter of the CPNP by defining the services and supports offered to women at risk. The unique approaches to delivering services and collaborating with a wide range of community partners build on the key elements of the program. Far from pinning projects to a rigid formula, the elements ensure that all women receive a range of pre-natal support. Flexibility in emphasis and delivery becomes a reality once the following basics are determined:

- food and pre-natal vitamin/mineral supplements, dietary assessment and nutrition counselling on food and good eating
- promotion of breastfeeding, mother–baby bonding, healthy baby feeding and birth planning
- participation of pregnant and new mothers in the planning and delivery of the program
- education about food preparation, shopping on a budget, parenting, baby feeding
- preparation for labour and delivery
- support and counselling on lifestyle issues such as stress, tobacco, alcohol, drugs, family violence
- social supports including counselling, education and other help from professionals, lay family workers or peers through home visits, drop-in centres and group sessions
- support for sufficient and nutritious food through community activities such as collective kitchens, community gardens and food buying clubs
- linking and referral to other resources, community programs or services.

These tools provide solid and consistent direction to help communities determine needs, set goals, establish program direction, evaluate and improve their projects. At the national level, the principles and program elements ensure projects can be evaluated consistently, regardless of their differences. Adherence to the principles and elements is an important factor in determining whether a project qualifies for initial or renewed funding.

Sustained federal funding

Acknowledging that effective early childhood development is a long-term commitment, the federal government has provided the CPNP with incremental, predictable and sustained funding since its inception (Canadian Intergovernmental Conference Secretariat 2000). The CPNP provides approximately 40 per cent of funded projects with adequate or nearly adequate resources to satisfy their annual budgets. Another 34 per cent have up to half of their budgets met through CPNP funding (Health Canada 1998). The total CPNP budget for 2002 was $31 million (Health Canada 2001).

National evaluation results demonstrate that adequate core funding is key to the effectiveness of community-based programs. Projects that have sufficient resources tend to be successful at all levels, including achievement of goals and objectives, effective management of human resources, building and sustaining partnerships, participant involvement, community capacity building and effective program development and service delivery (Health Canada 2001).

Collaborative governance

The programs are managed jointly by the federal government and the provincial/territorial governments through provincially based Joint Management Committees (JMCs), which determine how best to address provincial/territorial priorities and allocate CPNP funds. As a result, there are significant differences between the provinces and territories with respect to size, sponsorship and geographic distribution of projects (Health Canada 2001).

Community flexibility and partnerships

As one of the six guiding principles of the CPNP, flexibility was identified most often in the formal project renewal process as being vital to program success (Health Canada 2001). Flexibility enables projects to meet local needs through interventions that work for the community and participants, while still adhering to guiding principles and essential program elements.

The CPNP enters into an average of 32 community partnerships per project. These provide clients with more comprehensive services, and increase awareness and access in both directions. Most commonly, partnerships are with health professionals (80% of projects), not-for-profit groups (76% of projects) individuals, schools, other government agencies and businesses (40–50% of projects) and, less frequently, with substance abuse agencies, friendship and drop-in centres, service clubs and smoking cessation programs (20–40%) (Health Canada 1998 and Barrington Research Group Inc. 2002a).

The diversity of approaches, models, partnerships and settings through which CPNP projects are delivered is testament to the creativity, resourcefulness and varying needs and opportunities available across Canada.

Evaluation and monitoring – a multi-faceted approach

Evaluation processes were developed to fit a program that is national in scope but contains substantial local decision making and flexibility in delivery. All projects, regardless of their delivery model, setting or clientele, can be monitored and evaluated against a single set of goals, objectives and outcome indicators. This layered approach to evaluation includes:

National and regional evaluations which examine project activities and impact with respect to the national framework and regional priorities. Measuring achievements and demographics provides important management and planning information. Annual evaluation questionnaires covering 28 issues are completed by each of the program's 350 projects. A second, participant-focused questionnaire requires all projects to answer a core set of questions and select additional items from a prepared menu. This maintains the flexibility so important to the CPNP – from project design right through to evaluation.

Project Renewal is a periodic and formal review of all CPNP projects to ensure they are well managed, financially accountable, reflect the Guiding Principles and continue to meet their funded objectives. Projects are individually assessed when existing agreements expire and applications are made for further funding. The process provides Health Canada with an opportunity to learn from the innovative work of projects and to share lessons learned both with other projects and regions inside the program and with other social programs, federal and provincial/territorial departments. This is now a permanent component of the accountability structure of the CPNP (Health Canada 2001).

Individual project monitoring and evaluation by the regional offices of Health Canada ensure that projects are well managed and financially accountable. In addition, many projects conduct their own local evaluations, using results to improve program and service delivery (Health Canada 2001).

Evaluation results are used to make improvements to the CPNP at the national level, and to allow project staff to learn from their counterparts in other parts of the country. Formal evaluation reports are complemented by user-friendly publications that present results in a way that is useful to project staff and participants.

Canada Pre-natal Nutrition Program results

The evaluations show that approximately 40,000 women are served each year through CPNP projects (excluding those operating in First Nations and Inuit communities) (Barrington Research Group Inc. 2002a). Geared toward the 10 per cent who are at risk for poor health outcomes (see box below), the CPNP targets women who are disadvantaged in terms of income, education, age, and behaviours such as substance abuse or physical abuse, that put both the health of themselves and their babies at risk. Participants include those who are unlikely to participate in or have access to pre-natal support.

The 10 per cent factor

The CPNP uses a composite index approach through which a 'reasonable estimate' of at risk pregnancies is made. This takes into account the prevalence of:

- *poverty* – women in the lowest socio-economic group are four times more likely to have pregnancy related complications that require hospitalization (Mustard *et al.* 1995)
- *tobacco use* – one half of female smokers aged 18–24 years smoke during pregnancy
- *age* – 47 in 1000 teenagers become pregnant each year
- *Aboriginal link* – infant mortality is triple the national rate
- *alcohol use* – three in 1000 children in industrialized countries (likely more in some Aboriginal communities) are affected by Fetal Alcohol Syndrome
- *depression* – 15 per cent of new mothers experience significant post-partum depression.

Two key indicators are used to determine whether the CPNP has a positive impact on participants. Evaluation results show that breastfeeding initiation rates – believed to be low among disadvantaged women – are virtually the same among CPNP participants as for the general population (78% compared with 79%). Similarly, though not definitive, the rate of low birth weight pregnancies for CPNP participants (6.9%) compares favourably with that for the general population (5.8%) (Barrington Research Group Inc. 2002b; Statistics Canada 2002). In fact, CPNP results suggest that, leaving aside those in the highest risk category, the rate of low birth weight pregnancies decreases among participants as exposure to CPNP services increases. Women who participate in many CPNP activities and take advantage of multiple service offerings are less likely to have low birth weight babies than participants who have less involvement.

In addition to meeting its own goals and reaching its target audience, CPNP has demonstrated some positive spin-off impacts. The national evaluation of 2000–2001 reported the creation of 471 new activities or services as a direct result of CPNP projects (Barrington Research Group Inc. 2002a). Building skills in the community, establishing the infrastructure for social programs, and creating awareness of need are all long-term investments that have led to the creation of a variety of services, including parent support groups, clothing and baby equipment banks, community kitchens and breastfeeding support groups.

Research demonstrates that the best predictor of high-risk children avoiding abuse and neglect is the degree to which their mothers are enmeshed in a supportive social network (Child and Family Canada 2001). Projects funded by the CPNP continually report that the program is enabling the empowerment of women, fostering their participation in community affairs and creating social networks.

The Canada Pre-natal Nutrition Program in action: Breaking the Cycle

One of the programs that receives sustained funding from Health Canada, including the CPNP, is Breaking the Cycle (BTC). Located in downtown Toronto, BTC delivers an early intervention program to women experiencing substance use problems. The program serves women who are pregnant or parenting at least one child under the age of six years, and who are experiencing problems and want help with their substance use or recovery.

Breaking the Cycle integrates a number of interventions which address issues such as drug or alcohol addiction, health and medical concerns, mental health, parenting and child care as well as children's early intervention, developmental and child welfare services. The program also provides material support such as food, transportation and clothing. Programs are delivered using a combination of individual and group counselling approaches. The Breaking the Cycle Pregnancy Outreach Program is the pre-natal component of the program funded by the CPNP.

Collaborative governance

A partnership of agencies delivers Breaking the Cycle: Mothercraft, Jean Tweed Centre, Children's Aid Society of Toronto, Catholic Children's Aid Society, Toronto Public Health, Hospital for Sick Children – Motherisk Program and St. Joseph's Health Centre. Each agency brings expertise in one of the core services delivered at BTC; for example, Mothercraft provides parenting and child development expertise, the Jean Tweed Centre provides addiction treatment expertise, the children's aid societies bring child welfare knowledge, and the hospitals and health department provide leadership in the area of health/medical services.

Partners make a formal commitment through a signed service agreement, provide direct service support to participants, clinical consultation to BTC staff and participate in the collaborative governance of the program through the BTC Steering Committee.

Guiding principles

Building on CPNP Guiding Principles, Breaking the Cycle provides a 'seamless system of services', adapted to families' needs, as opposed to forcing families to adapt to agency processes. Core services are offered from a single, community-based site, reducing participants' problems with transportation, distance, financial resources and fragmentation of services. Services are offered in a warm, supportive atmosphere where families can safely disclose their health worries and parenting concerns. Partnering with a range of organizations creates a synergy, allowing each agency to deliver better service than when they work independently.

The single access model is more successful than originally anticipated. Clients, staff and BTC partners view the one-stop service delivery approach and the use of a harm reduction model as major contributing factors to the success of BTC, to engage women and provide them with the services they need.

> Addicts sometimes have a hard time getting their act together and controlling their lives. BTC is a one-stop shop. A lot of places will help you with one thing, but you have to go across town to get something else you need. Here, they deal with you, your children, parenting, and emotions all under one roof. (A BTC mother in Moore, Pepler and Motz 1998, p.79)

Obstacles or problems can come up suddenly, and having all these services means you can get them dealt with right away…when you're an addict, you sometimes lose your coping skills. Having these things right here at BTC makes it easier to get stuff done. (A BTC mother in Moore *et al.* 1998, pp.78–9)

The program focuses on prevention through early identification by implementing a three-part strategy that involves awareness, education and outreach. Engaging women in the earliest stages of their pregnancy helps reduce the biological, psychosocial and cumulative risks to the fetus, provide health, treatment and pre-natal care, and help women actively plan for themselves and their children.

To improve participants' parenting skills and prevent child abuse, BTC provides childbearing women with information about the risks of alcohol and drug use and promotes its reduction during pregnancy. The program encourages optimum planning for the birth, supports mothers' efforts to develop a foundation for a positive attachment relationship and creates opportunities for maternal self sufficiency (Moore *et al.* 1998).

Flexible programming

Each year, between 4000 and 6000 newborns in Toronto are exposed to crack cocaine during the last trimester of pregnancy (Forman *et al.* 1994). Hicks (1997) identified a strong incidence of homelessness and lack of access to health and treatment centres among pregnant women using substances. At the time, only 22 per cent of participants engaged in Breaking the Cycle during pregnancy. In response to these findings, the need to create a unique, flexible program was recognized in order to reach this newly identified sub-population.

Breaking the Cycle created the Pregnancy Outreach Program, with objectives to:

- consult other networks and agencies and build an integrated, responsive community referral network
- provide education and training to other agencies
- decrease participants' isolation and marginalization
- increase participants' knowledge of community resources
- promote the use of primary health care, pre-natal care, medically managed withdrawal programs, and methadone programs

- increase maternal involvement in planning for herself and her expected infant

- establish a mobile outreach link to and from BTC and the community

- study and research effective techniques to engage this population.

The main activities of the outreach program are: street outreach, liaison with homeless shelters, hostels and drop-in centres, providing information and resources, providing milk and food coupons, transportation to appointments and, where appropriate, referrals to other services.

Program evaluation

Since 1995, over 200 families have participated in ongoing evaluations of this program. The results gathered inform ongoing program development and measure service efficacy.

Local level monitoring demonstrates the value of early identification of participants' needs for comprehensive support from multiple agencies. The vast majority of these women use substances in the context of multiple, high risk factors including: poverty, homelessness, transient or unsafe housing, domestic violence, a family history of substance use, a history of physical, sexual or emotional abuse, multiple previous pregnancies with child welfare and custody experiences, mental health problems, and previous addiction treatment. Their isolation from supportive health and treatment services during pregnancy exacerbates the risk for poor fetal and maternal outcomes, and results in inadequate planning and preparation for parenting (Leslie 2002).

The introduction of a proactive, street-based outreach component has proved successful in engaging women, increasing the number of participants by 60 per cent. Engagement of women in services at earlier stages in their pregnancies has led to significant benefits in fetal and maternal outcomes (Pepler *et al.* 2003), including:

- fewer pre-natal risk factors

- reduced pre-natal substance exposure

- higher birth weight

- fewer birth complications

- better post-natal health

- reduced length of hospital stay

- decreased mother–infant separations.

The program's success is demonstrated by the fact that the majority of referrals are made by the women themselves and by their high degree of compliance and acceptance of referrals to other health and treatment providers in the community (Leslie 2002).

Evaluations show the program's ability to provide accessible services to one of the most vulnerable, marginalized and isolated sub-populations in Toronto: homeless, pregnant women using substances. Forty per cent of the women accessing BTC are pregnant at intake, and of these, almost 40 per cent are engaged in their first trimester (Leslie 2002).

More than 60 per cent of Breaking the Cycle mothers have other children they have not been able to parent because of their substance use problems. At admission to BTC, mothers indicate they do not know if they parent appropriately. Many mothers report they have grown up in dysfunctional family situations, experienced poor relationships with family members, sexual or physical abuse by family members or partners, and have used substances from an early age. After participating in BTC programming, these mothers report increased parenting knowledge and improvements in attitude, behaviour and mother–infant feelings of attachment.

Mothers report less use of inappropriate discipline, increased number of mother–child activities, and increased positive feelings about parenting since attending BTC.

> I can't imagine I would have the same skills and the same relationship that I have with my child if I hadn't come here. When I first came here I said, I just want to know how to deal with this little person that I produced, because I haven't got a clue. I just want to know what makes her work and what makes her tick. I also wanted to make sure that she doesn't grow up to be like me because that would kill me. I'm an addict, so she's got a really heavy chance to become an addict. BTC taught me a lot about how to deal with my child... (A BTC mother in Pepler *et al.* 2003, p.67)

Maternal use of substances during pregnancy can increase the risk of negative outcomes for both the mother and the fetus. Children born to BTC mothers who were using substances during their pregnancy, or who were exposed to a substance-using environment, were expected to experience developmental delays. Evidence to support this hypothesis remains unconfirmed but it is promising that BTC children developed substantially during the evaluation period (Pepler *et al.* 2003). 'The children are the main focus here – that's how they help us break the cycle' (A BTC mother in Moore *et al.* 1998, p.78).

Breaking the Cycle builds community capacity by addressing the needs of vulnerable families with concerns of substance use. The program has become increasingly involved in knowledge transfer and managing national and regional level projects addressing Fetal Alcohol Syndrome (FAS). BTC's success has led to requests for training locally, nationally and internationally; staff engage in training and consultation activities to support other communities developing projects for pregnant and parenting women using substances, based on the BTC model (Pepler *et al.* 2003).

Continuing development of partnerships with the justice and housing sectors is an ongoing priority for BTC. External partnerships are being formed with researchers interested in furthering understanding of this high-risk population. BTC continues to raise public awareness and disseminate information concerning issues of substance abuse for women, children and their families.

The Canada Pre-natal Nutrition Program as a platform for expanding well-being

Each year, the Canada Pre-Natal Nutrition Program successfully provides pre-natal nutrition and support to over 40,000 women. National evaluation results indicate that 91 per cent of participants made use of more than two CPNP services. Since the program's beginnings:

- 77% participants reported receiving food supplements
- 62% participants reported receiving breastfeeding support.

Staff reported providing nutritional counselling to almost all (98%) participants. More than eight out of ten (82%) received a dietary assessment. With such a track record, where to next?

The participatory and multi-faceted approach to evaluation of the CPNP is that it allows policy makers and program planners to view 'success' from many different angles. Lessons learned at the project level, especially what works well with various target groups, are invaluable when planning for the future. Partners use the knowledge learned to broaden their organizations' mandates and develop more comprehensive programs.

Some of the lessons learned will be integrated into the next level of CPNP development – investment in participants as peer leaders and mentors. Projects from across the country report on the power of peers in delivering the CPNP. Future plans include contributing to the literature documenting the effectiveness of peer interventions in attracting and sustaining participation of at-risk women. Investing further in qualitative assessments of CPNP projects will allow experience to be shared across projects, allow knowledge transfer and inform work with other audiences and on other health and social issues. Future plans also include the development of a methodology to describe the emergent program delivery typologies, an increase in project-level capacity to use evaluation results for continuous program improvement and an increase in dialogues to increase understanding of the strategic potential of community-based programming for emerging government priorities. It is also hoped to create opportunities to contribute to the training and development of health professionals and lay or peer community workers; and finally, to continue to serve at-risk pregnant women, in the face of such social and economic challenges as poverty and dramatic increases in immigration.

A longer-term plan is to follow CPNP participants into the future, ideally comparing health outcomes of their babies with those of women at risk who are not served by the CPNP.

Achieving health for all is a complex and relentless task. The reward in the CPNP is in engaging with participants as partners to achieve stronger families and communities.

Note

1   Unless otherwise indicated, all project and participant numbers, and dollar amounts exclude the First Nations and Inuit component. More information about First Nations and Inuit programs is available at www.hc-sc.gc.ca/fnihb-dgspni/fnihb/index.htm.

Chapter 12

Promoting the Well-being of Children and Families
What is Best Practice?

Geoffrey Nelson

This chapter focuses on strategies for the promotion of well-being and the prevention of negative outcomes for children and families. Using an ecological perspective to understand children's well-being, a conceptual framework for promotion and prevention programs is introduced that consists of four dimensions: (1) the promotion–prevention–early intervention continuum, (2) focusing the intervention, (3) length and intensity, and (4) value-based partnerships for intervention. In line with the emphasis on 'evidence-based practice', research pertinent to each of these dimensions is reviewed. Finally, the Highfield Community Enrichment Project (Better Beginnings, Better Futures) is presented as a Canadian program that exemplifies many of these best practice dimensions. This program is described and evidence regarding its short-term impacts on children, families/parents and the community is summarized. The chapter concludes with a recommendation about where the field of prevention and promotion for children and families should be headed.

Introduction

The purpose of this chapter is twofold: to provide a conceptual framework for best practices for the promotion of child and family well-being and the prevention of problems in living, and to describe a policy research demonstration project in Ontario, Canada, the Highfield Community Enrichment Project

(Better Beginnings, Better Futures) (Nelson *et al.* 2004) that embodies best practice principles. This project complements other programs explored in this book. It addresses issues similar to those of the UK Parenting Initiative described by Quinton in Chapter 10; it also has relevance to the themes explored in the community initiatives discussed by Bouchard (Chapter 15) and Friedman and colleagues (Chapter 16). However, its unique feature is its focus on how a disadvantaged population can generate change themselves.

Promoting child and family well-being

In this section, four key dimensions of a conceptual framework for best practices in the promotion of child and family well-being are identified:

- distinguishing promotion, prevention and early intervention
- focusing the intervention
- the length and intensity of the intervention
- value-based partnerships for intervention.

Promotion, prevention and early intervention

The Institute of Medicine (IOM 1994) in the US has developed a typology that has been useful in distinguishing different levels of prevention. First, universal interventions and focus on the promotion of well-being (Cicchetti *et al.* 2000; Cowen 2000) are targeted to a whole population that has not been identified on the basis of individual risk or the manifestation of problems. Second, selective or 'high-risk' preventive interventions are targeted to individuals or subgroups who are at risk of developing problems by virtue of their exposure to risk factors. Third, indicated interventions are targeted at individuals who have been detected as already having a problem, but in its early stages. Thus, universal and selective approaches are preventative in nature, whereas indicated approaches constitute early intervention. A similar typology is also used in the UK to distinguish between universal, targeted and specialist interventions (Department for Education and Skills 2003a). MacLeod and Nelson (2000) conducted a meta-analytic review of 56 controlled evaluations of programs designed to promote family well-being and prevent child maltreatment. The team were able to compare the effectiveness of universal and selective interventions (home visitation, multi-component and social support/mutual aid programs) and indicated interventions (intensive family preservation, multi-component, social support/mutual aid and parent training programs) on a number of different outcome indicators (e.g. removal of children from the family, maltreatment).

One important finding from this review was that the effect sizes[1] (ESs) for family/parent outcomes were larger at follow-up intervals (ES = 0.50) than post intervention (ES = 0.38) for the universal and selective interventions, while the ESs for the indicated interventions showed the opposite pattern; larger at post intervention (ES = 0.54) than at follow-up (ES = 0.43). This suggests that the gains made from prevention are not only sustained, but enhanced over time, while the gains of after-the-fact interventions diminish over time.

Focusing the intervention

Pre-school/school interventions

Pre-school education programs provide direct educational activities for young children to promote their cognitive development (Ramey and Landesman Ramey 1998). These are typically selective in nature and were initially implemented and evaluated during the 1960s in poor, urban communities in the US under the auspices of Head Start. Research has shown that the early Head Start programs had positive impacts on children's cognitive development, although the magnitude of cognitive gains diminished with the passage of time (Lazar and Darlington 1982).

Family/parent interventions

A Canadian national review of child welfare interventions known as the Family Wellness Project (Prilleltensky, Nelson and Peirson 2001) identified a wide range of family/parent interventions designed to promote family well-being (Nelson, Laurendeau and Chamberland 2001). Home visitation and parent training programs, for example, have been implemented primarily at the selective level with at-risk families. Intensive family preservation services (IFPS), which provide support to keep families together and functioning better following confirmed reports of child maltreatment, are an example of the indicated approach.

In the previously mentioned meta-analysis of the 56 family support programs, MacLeod and Nelson (2000) found positive impacts for all of the above-mentioned types of programs on different indicators of family well-being. The average weighted ES in the meta-analysis was 0.41, indicating that 66 per cent of those in the intervention groups reported better family outcomes than those in the control/comparison groups. However, in a subsequent meta-analysis of the 34 pre-school intervention programs that had a follow-up when the child was in elementary school (kindergarten to grade 8), Nelson, Westhues and MacLeod (2003) found that while family/parent interventions have impacts on indicators of family well-being and children's social-emotional functioning, they do not affect children's cognitive development.

Pre-school/school and family/parent multi-component interventions

Pre-school education programs are focused on enhancing children's cognitive development and family/parent interventions are targeted to enhance family/ parent functioning; since both types of programs appear to achieve these goals, there has been a conscious shift away from programs with a single focus to multi-component programs that provide both pre-school/school and family/ parent components. Not only do the latter achieve impacts on several outcome domains (Nelson *et al.* 2003), but they may also lead to stronger outcomes. In the meta-analysis of family support programs, the highest overall ES (0.58) was found for universal or selective multi-component programs (MacLeod and Nelson 2000).

Community interventions

Many of the selective pre-school and family interventions reviewed have been implemented in communities that are beset with poverty, violence and crime. Community development projects, including economic development and the creation of affordable housing, act as revitalizing programs (Eisen 1994), building on the strengths of the community and its members. While community-driven interventions can improve capacity and partnerships as demonstrated in Chapter 15 (see also Beauvais and Jenson 2003), there is little evidence to suggest that community-level changes have positive ripple effects on the well-being of children and families. However, an analysis of the work described by Friedman and colleagues in Chapter 16 may eventually refute this argument.

Social interventions

Chapter 2 has shown how socio-economic inequalities and poverty are strongly related to a variety of problems experienced by children and families. Moreover, there has been a 'feminization of poverty', with increasing numbers of women and children falling below low-income cut-off lines (Peirson, Laurendeau and Chamberland 2001). Barlow and Campbell (1995) have argued that increased poverty and socio-economic inequality are direct outcomes of neo-liberal policies of globalization. These policies, which are based on the values of individualism and competition and the assumption 'that markets are the best and most efficient allocation of resources in production and distribution' (Coburn 2000, p.138), are designed to promote the interests of multinational corporations and a nation's most wealthy citizens. Such policies, which have been aggressively promoted in the US, UK and Canada, have created tremendous pressure to dismantle the welfare state.

To address poverty, economic inequality and gender inequality, there must be an alternative social movement that fights to maintain the welfare state and to reduce the inequalities that result from unchecked market forces. Thus, social intervention addresses the root causes of child, family and community problems by striving to create social policies for more just and equitable societies (Febbraro 1994). In a comprehensive review of social policies to promote the well-being of children and families for the Family Wellness Project, Peters *et al.* (2001) show how many countries in western and northern Europe have implemented tax and transfer policies that effectively reduce economic inequality, as well as other universal policies that provide benefits to families (e.g. parental and extended childcare leave policies, day care). Chapters 2 and 3 of this book discuss the effectiveness of the UK New Labour government's policies in some of these areas.

Length and intensity of the intervention

In the meta-analytic review of 34 pre-school intervention programs discussed above, Nelson and colleagues (2003) recently tested the hypothesis that intervention length and intensity is positively related to child and family outcomes. They found that the ESs on child and family outcomes for programs that lasted more than 1 year (high in length, ES = 0.31) and had more than 300 sessions for children (high in intensity, ES = 0.40) were two to three times larger than for those programs that lasted less than 1 year (low in length, ES = 0.11) and had fewer than 300 sessions for children (low in intensity, ES = 0.16). It is not surprising that length and intensity are moderators of program efficacy, but it is interesting that it is the length and intensity of the intervention for the children rather than the parents that appears to be most important.

Value-based partnerships for intervention

While a sound conceptual framework for promotion/prevention programs is important, one must also have a framework for engaging community members in their development, implementation and evaluation. Traditionally, prevention programs are conceived and implemented by professional 'experts' with little to no consultation with the people whom they aim to serve. Such an approach may unintentionally perpetuate the power imbalances between disadvantaged people and professionals.

More recently, some promotion/prevention programs, such as Better Beginnings, Better Futures (described in the next section), 1, 2, 3 GO! (see Chapter 15), and Communities that Care (Utting, Rose and Pugh 2001), have become more community driven, with residents in low-income communities actively participating in the planning and implementation of prevention programs in their communities. Budgell and colleagues (Chapter 7) also show how such principles are fundamental to the design and implementation of services for Aboriginal populations.

Nelson and colleagues (2000) developed a framework for partnerships in prevention programs that emphasizes the values of health promotion, compassion, inclusion, power sharing and social justice, which underpin a process of negotiation and a melding of the strengths and knowledge of community members and professionals. Such value-based partnerships create a process that is inclusive, participatory and empowering for community residents and result in a program that is neither exclusively professionally driven nor exclusively community driven, but rather one that is partnership driven and represents a creative synthesis based on the collaboration of many different stake-holders. The remainder of this chapter offers an example that illustrates the best practice dimensions identified above.

Better Beginnings, Better Futures

Better Beginnings, Better Futures is a 25-year longitudinal policy research demonstration project funded by the government of Ontario (Peters *et al.* 2000). The project was designed to achieve three objectives:

- to prevent serious social, emotional, behavioural, physical and cognitive problems in young children
- to promote the development of children in all these areas, and
- to enhance the family and community environments in which children are raised.

Situated in eight low-income communities, Better Beginnings is a multi-site, universal intervention that focuses on children either from the pre-natal period to age four (younger cohort) or from ages four to eight (older cohort). From their inception, Better Beginnings projects were expected to:

- develop high quality and comprehensive programs that focused on multiple levels (e.g. pre-school/school, family, community)

- create partnerships and integrate existing services in the community

- meaningfully involve community residents in the planning, implementation and management of programs, and

- provide four years of programming and community development during the demonstration phase (Rae-Grant and Russell 1989).

The Highfield Community Enrichment Project

The Highfield Community Enrichment Project is one of the eight Better Beginnings sites (Nelson *et al.* in press; Pancer *et al.* 2003). It is located in the northwest corner of Toronto and is housed in portables on the grounds of Highfield Junior School, which serves students from junior kindergarten (age four) to grade five (age ten). The project is an older cohort site. Highfield is a densely populated, low-income community (in 1995, the average family income was $36,000 compared with the provincial average of $60,000). With nearly 60 per cent of the area's population born outside Canada (mostly from India and the Caribbean) and over 40 different languages spoken by children in the school, the Highfield community is characterized by considerable cultural and ethno-racial diversity.

The program model

Highfield provides programming in three areas: pre-school/school; family/parent; and community. Among the pre-school/school programs are the Lions-Quest Skills for Growing program, a social skills program implemented by all classroom teachers from grades one to five, and a health and nutrition program. Enrichment workers and parent volunteers also provide assistance with academic, social and language skill building in the classrooms. The enrichment workers were designed to lower the student–teacher ratio, and these staff worked with the children in the focal research cohort (described in a subsequent section) through the four-year demonstration period.

Family/parent programs are based in the Family Resource Centre, which is located on the school grounds. This provides a drop-in four mornings a week for families with children from birth to four years of age. The project also runs playgroups and a toy lending library. The enrichment workers both do home visitation and spend time in the classroom, providing a valuable link between home and school. Community programs include a wide range of celebrations (e.g. community breakfasts) and ethno-cultural events (e.g. Black History Month), before- and after-school programs for children, recreational programs, leadership training for adults, and volunteer recognition, including an annual dinner and awards ceremony for volunteers.

Management of the project and partnerships with residents

The project is managed by an 'executive team', whose membership has included at least four residents (one of whom acts as chair), the principal of Highfield Junior School, and one or two representatives of community agencies. Each of the three program areas has a committee that oversees its work. The membership of each committee includes project staff, residents and service providers. Residents form a significant proportion of the membership of all these committees; the majority of the staff live in the Highfield community; and community residents volunteer in a wide variety of roles in the project and the school (Nelson *et al.* 2004). Residents have a strong voice in all aspects of the project.

Program evaluation

All of the Better Beginnings research is coordinated by a central unit and managed at each site by a research team and a research committee. As with other Better Beginnings sites, the evaluation of the Highfield Community Enrichment Project is divided into two major areas of activity: the (primarily quantitative) evaluation of project outcomes; and the (primarily qualitative) project development and program model research. Common protocols are used for both the quantitative and qualitative research to enable cross-site comparisons.

Quantitative outcome evaluation

Two types of quasi-experimental research design were used to assess the impacts of the project: a baseline-focal cohort design and a longitudinal comparison site design. The baseline-focal cohort design involved administering baseline measures relating to child, family/parent and community functioning to the families of 56 eight-year-old children in 1992–3, before the Better Beginnings programs were in operation. Five years later, the same measures were administered to the families of 81 eight-year-old children (the 'focal cohort') who had had the benefit of programming from the time they were in Junior Kindergarten until the time they were in Grade Two. Data were collected from children, teachers and parents.

The longitudinal comparison site design involved comparing children and parents from the Highfield focal cohort with those from a nearby matched comparison community which did not receive Better Beginnings programming. This design involved annual assessments of children and families. Information was collected on a wide range of outcomes, including children's emotional and behaviour problems, pro-social behaviour, cognitive development and academic achievement, and parents' parenting behaviour, social support, and perceptions of their families, their children's school, and their neighbourhoods. The number of children and parents from the project group who were assessed ranged from 52 to 89 over the five years of measurement, and the number from the comparison community ranged from 59 to 118.

Qualitative research

Qualitative methods (Patton 2002) were employed to document the ways in which the project developed in each of the Better Beginnings communities. Information was collected from two sources:

1. An extensive set of semi-verbatim field notes and analytic comments that the project's site researchers made during key meetings of Highfield's executive team and of the major sub-committees, as well as from program documents such as newsletters and quarterly reports.

2. Interviews (both individual and group) with residents, staff, community partners and others.

Short-term evaluation findings

IMPACTS ON THE CHILDREN

Parents and teachers completed reports on children using the Ontario Child Health Study revised checklist (Boyle *et al.* 1993) and the Social Skills Rating Scale measure (Gresham and Elliott 1990). With the exception of teacher ratings for the baseline-focal cohort design, the ESs for the impacts of the Highfield project on both children's behaviour problems and pro-social behaviour (e.g., decreased overanxious and oppositional behaviour, increased cooperation and assertiveness) were in the 0.40 to 0.50 range.[2] A variety of academic and achievement test measures were also administered to the children, but none of these showed any significant effects for participation in the Highfield project.

A number of Highfield residents spoke of the positive impacts the program had on their children. They indicated that their children had benefited indirectly through their participation, as well as directly through their involvement in Highfield programs: 'I have seen my son grow and achieve new challenges and skills' (Parent interview).

IMPACTS ON THE FAMILIES/PARENTS

Parents completed self-report measures of parenting (Johnston and Mash 1989; National Longitudinal Survey of Children and Youth [NLSCY] 1994, 1996, 1998) and other measures of family and parent social and emotional functioning. There was a large ES (0.76) for parenting in the longitudinal design, indicating that parents in the Highfield project improved their parenting skills much more than those in the comparison community. Also, the Highfield project had a significant impact on the measures of family and parent social and emotional functioning (ESs in the 0.40 range for both designs). Furthermore, an analysis of Children's Aid Society (CAS) records showed a significant decrease in the percentage of total CAS cases and children in care coming from the Highfield community since the project started in 1992.

Interviews demonstrate the many different positive impacts on individual residents who participated in this project. Increased self confidence and self esteem were most frequently mentioned:

> People like [the project manager] have made me feel quite tall. I didn't just give, I received in return. I've really gotten a lot out of it. I came with a certain amount of confidence, it has grown, matured. . . Without encouragement, it wouldn't have happened. (Field notes)

Increased knowledge and skills was another positive outcome. In some cases, these led to paid employment with the project or elsewhere:

> I have become a healthier, stronger parent and all-around much better person. I have had the confidence and skills needed to apply for and receive a part-time position with the project. (Field notes)

A third positive impact was enhanced social contact and support. The project had served to reduce social isolation and to help residents develop new relationships with others: 'Before this program, I used to just sit [and stare] at the wall' (Parent interview).

A fourth positive impact was the leadership and advocacy skills that some parents learned: 'So they're learning about the community and how it works and how to advocate on their own…who to contact and what to contact them for and all that' (Staff interview).

Residents also mentioned a few negative impacts of participation, including burnout, time away from children, and dissatisfaction of male marital partners: 'A lot of husbands don't want their wives [participating], they want them at home...we've had people tell us that. "He wants me home."' (Parent interview).

IMPACTS ON THE SCHOOL AND THE COMMUNITY

Parents completed self-report measures of sense of community cohesion (Buckner 1988), satisfaction with the child's school and their relationship with the child's teacher (NLSCY 1994, 1996, 1998), and satisfaction with their own housing and their neighbourhood (Institute for Social Research 1977, 1979, 1981). In both designs, there were no significant impacts of the project on the sense of community cohesion measure. However, there were significant impacts from both designs on both school and neighbourhood ratings (ESs ranged from 0.31 to 0.57) with Better Beginnings parents reporting higher scores on these measures than parents in the comparison site.

The qualitative data also indicate impacts on the school. When one walks in the door, one can see parent volunteers throughout the school, in classrooms, in the kitchen preparing the children's snack for the nutrition program, or in the community lounge, which is for the exclusive use of community residents and the project.

> The school has really opened up its doors to the community because of Better Beginnings being around. The school would have been more secluded from the community... Now it's wide open and it's more used and I think people in the community are feeling now more pulled into the school. It's not off limits. It's a space they can share and access. The school is more accessible to parents and residents... The school is nothing like it used to be prior to Better Beginnings. (Field notes)

Participants also reported improved relations among different cultural and ethno-racial groups in the community: 'I've never seen and been associated with so many people from so many other cultures. It's like one big happy family' (Parent interview).

Finally, the project has been the springboard for the development of a number of community events, activities, resources and partnerships with other service providers.

Conclusion

This chapter has outlined four dimensions of best practice for interventions to promote child and family well-being and prevent problems in living. These have been illustrated with research from the Highfield project, a program that exemplifies them. Research on this project has shown that prevention programs which are focused at several different ecological levels (pre-school/school, family/parent, community), that provide lengthy and intensive intervention, and that work in partnership with low-income community residents can achieve many positive impacts on children, families and the community. Programs like this show that the field of prevention and promotion for children has come a long way since its early days of short-term, single-focus projects designed by professionals with little or no input from parents and community members.

Of the three 'older cohort' sites that participated in the Better Beginnings research, the Highfield project had the best outcomes in the short term (Peters *et al.* 2000). The research team believe that the main reason is that it provides the most intensive intervention for children. Some of the project resources, such as the provision of educational assistants, were concentrated on children in the focal research cohort at Highfield throughout the four years of intervention. In contrast, at the other two sites, resources and programs focused on all children in the identified age range (four to eight), not just those in the research cohort. The 'older cohort' site that showed the least favourable outcomes devoted few resources directly to children and did not have many school-based programs.

The Highfield story is inspirational; both the process and the outcomes have been quite positive. While we could end here, it is perhaps more useful to conclude with some more sobering and challenging observations and questions. First of all, projects like Highfield Better Beginnings are the exception, not the norm. That is, most low-income communities in Ontario and Canada more closely resemble the comparison site.

Second, it is quite remarkable that during the time period in which the Highfield project achieved its positive outcomes, the Highfield community experienced declining income. While the average family income for the province rose from about $57,000 to $60,000 from 1990 to 1995, the average family income for Highfield residents dropped substantially from $44,000 to $36,000. In other words, the economic conditions of the community actually worsened over the demonstration period. While positive changes in children, families and the community were the focus of the project, the economic conditions for low-income communities were being targeted for cutbacks by a neo-conservative government.

A third and related issue is the participation of low-income women as volunteers. Although many of these women described their experiences with the project as personally empowering and satisfying, it is important to ask whether they are being empowered or exploited (Febbraro 1994). The Highfield project, and others like it, depend heavily on women to volunteer their time. During the demonstration phase of the project, the percentage of unemployed women in the Highfield community rose from 12.6 per cent to 17.5 per cent (the provincial average for women increased less, from 8.4 per cent to 9.6 per cent).

We cannot continue to ignore government cutbacks that increase economic and gender inequalities because they have enormous implications for the promotion of child and family well-being. The author's prescription for the future is for increased social intervention to reduce structural inequalities as another strategy for promoting child and family well-being. We need to advocate vigorously for initiatives like Better Beginnings so that the benefits can be enjoyed by many more children and families. It is also important and necessary to engage more in social intervention by advocating for social policies that benefit low-income families, and to take a hard look at issues of pay and gender equity in projects like this, lest we perpetuate low-income (and immigrant) women's disadvantaged position in society.

Notes

1   Effect sizes are computed by subtracting the mean of the control/comparison group from the mean of the intervention group and dividing by the pooled standard deviation. Effect sizes are also adjusted for sample size. An effect size of 1.0 means that those in the intervention group score, on average, one standard deviation unit higher than those in the control/comparison group. On a standardized IQ test, for example, the intervention group would score 15 points higher than the control/comparison group. An effect size of 0.2 tells us that 58 per cent of those in the intervention groups score above the mean for the control/comparison groups; an effect size of 0.5 tells that 69 per cent of those in the intervention group score above the mean for the control/comparison groups; and an effect size of 0.8 tells us that 79 per cent of those in the intervention groups score above the mean for the control/comparison groups (see Lipsey and Wilson 2001, p.153, Table 8.1). Effect sizes of 0.2 are considered to be small; 0.5 are considered to be medium; and 0.8 are considered to be large (Lipsey and Wilson 2001).

2   Total effect sizes for each domain for each design were obtained by summing the effect sizes across measures.

Chapter 13

Shared Family Care
Child Protection and Family Preservation in Action

Richard Barth and Amy Price

This chapter describes an innovative approach to helping families, in which parents and children are placed in the homes of community members who act as their mentors and work with professionals to help them achieve permanency for their children and move towards self sufficiency. Findings from a trial show that Shared Family Care is not appropriate for all families, but is most effective with participants who are homeless or marginally housed, who are motivated to change, mentally stable, and actively engaged in treatment or recovery programs for substance abuse. Parents who successfully completed the program showed improvements in family stability, income, employment, and housing circumstances; their children were less likely to return to care. Preliminary findings also suggest that where more than one child is involved the program is less costly than treatment foster care, and that there are additional public savings to be gained from the reduction in parental unemployment and homelessness.

Introduction
Shared Family Care (SFC) is an innovative approach to helping families achieve permanency for their children and move toward self sufficiency. Unlike traditional child welfare services, SFC involves the placement of whole families in the homes of community members who act as mentors and work with a team of professionals to help the families achieve these goals. By simultaneously protecting children and preserving families, Shared Family Care fills a critical service gap between traditional family preservation and out-of-home care.

Although this approach builds on a variety of program models in the US and overseas – including adult foster care, residential care for children and families in Sweden, and mother and child houses in Germany (see Price and Barth 1997; Barth and Price 1999), this chapter focuses on implementation and evaluation of the approach in the US. Over the last eight years, the research team had the opportunity to work with colleagues to help develop and evaluate six SFC demonstration programs in California and Colorado. This chapter describes the positive outcomes of the approach and the problems encountered in disseminating the findings to additional US sites. It explores themes that other innovative programs will need to address in response to the widespread premium placed on implementing evidence-based interventions.

Underlying assumptions of shared family care

Shared Family Care (SFC), like all child and family service programs, has a variety of assumptions that deserve appraisal as implementation develops. Although this chapter does not explicitly test each of these 'theories' it does provide some reflection about how they operate in the implementation of SFC. The following five key theories underpin the program:

1. Families are more likely to become stable and self sufficient if their basic needs (e.g. housing) are met and a mentor helps them establish a positive network of community resources and supports.

2. Mentors to families receiving child welfare services, who receive adequate training, support and supervision, and who are carefully matched with participants, play a critical and unique role in helping them meet their goals.

3. Most individuals care for their children the way they were cared for, and many parents in the child welfare system did not receive appropriate or adequate parenting themselves. By nurturing and re-parenting these adults, and modeling and teaching them appropriate parenting and home management skills, SFC helps parents better protect and care for their children and helps families interact in a healthier manner.

4. By keeping families together, SFC minimizes the adverse impact on children and parents caused by separation. At the same time, by providing a secure home and helping families meet their basic needs,

SFC improves the physical and mental well-being of children and their parents.

5. Finally, if after six- to nine-month placements, SFC is successful at keeping families together and preventing subsequent out-of-home care, the long-term cost of the program will be significantly less than traditional foster care options.

The dawning of a new millennium brings renewed hope for breakthroughs in services and science. Much of the discussion among human service researchers focuses on generating new evidence-based methods to assist children and families. Such approaches (e.g. Burns and Hoagwood 2002) should rely on an ordered transition through the following:

1. theory

2. controlled clinical (efficacy) trials

3. single case interventions under real world settings

4. initial effectiveness tests (using randomized clinical trials) under modestly challenging circumstances

5. full scale clinical (effectiveness) trials

6. effectiveness of treatment variations

7. determining the fit with a broad array of service organizations

8. dissemination and development of sustaining supports and policies.

Yet, this is not the typical order of child and family service innovations which tend to jump from Step 1 (theory) to Step 3 (single case interventions under real world conditions) to Step 7 (determining the fit with a broad array of service organizations) which determines whether or not the intervention can be sustained. Although there have been several trials prior to the involvement of UC Berkeley and several small or short efforts to implement SFC in the Bay Area and Colorado, the closest that we have to an in depth single case trial, albeit a non-experimental one, is in Contra Costa County California, as discussed below.

Overall descriptive findings

Between the spring of 1997 and May 2002, a total of 289 families were referred to the Shared Family Care programs in California and Colorado. Of this group,

87 families (with 129 children) were placed in mentor homes.[1] Most families that were never placed chose not to participate or were determined inappropriate for the program for a variety of reasons (e.g. active drug use, demonstrated unwillingness to work on goals or comply with program rules, too many children).

Families are considered successful if they complete (or make substantial progress toward) their placement goals or voluntarily relinquish their parental rights, demonstrating their agreement with child welfare services that they are not sufficiently interested or capable of parenting a child, at this time. We refer to these families as 'graduates.' Families that are asked or choose to leave the program before completing their goals are referred to as 'terminated.'

As of May 2002, 6 families were in placement, 50 successfully graduated from the program, and 31 were terminated early.

Applicant and participant families from all of the SFC programs typically have been single women with two children who have an average age of around four years. Since March 1997, six pregnant women have participated. Although, to date, no couples have been together in placement, eight participants have been married or with a significant other. Additionally, five single men have participated with their children; two graduated from the program and three were terminated early (two for non-compliance and one for parental relinquishment). The mean age for all of the applicants was 28 years. Nearly 12 per cent were 18 years or younger; however, approximately one third of all applicants, and nearly 40 per cent of placed families, were, or had become, parents at 18 years of age or younger. Moreover, parents who terminated were, on average, slightly younger than other applicants and more likely to be teenage parents.

Approximately one third (38%) of all applicants reported a criminal history, and 63 per cent had a history of substance abuse. Most applicants with a history of substance abuse had spent some time in recovery, but few had spent more than one year. Levels of educational achievement were notably low among all applicants, with almost half reporting less than a high school diploma or high school general education equivalence degree (GED) at intake.

The majority of families placed over the past five years had monthly incomes notably below the poverty rate, and only one quarter entered the program with a job. A majority of families were receiving some form of public assistance both at intake and graduation. A greater percentage of graduated families (33%) than terminated families (21%) had employment upon placement in SFC, whereas a greater number of terminated families (69% versus 60%) were receiving some form of public financial or food support (e.g. Temporary Assistance for Needy Families (TANF), Social Security Insurance (SSI), Women's Infants' and

Children's (WIC) Nutrition Program, Food Stamps) upon placement. Only four participants (two graduated and two terminated) reported receiving some financial support from friends or family. This suggests that, although some participants reported living with friends or family, the majority were isolated from their families and community.

The median length of stay for all participants in all programs from 1997 to June 2002 was five and a quarter months. On average, among all SFC programs, graduates stayed in placement three times longer than terminated families (a median of six months and two months, respectively). Terminated family placements ranged from one week to nine and a half months, and graduated family placements ranged from two weeks to fourteen months.

Data are available on 30 of the 31 participants who terminated from all programs during the study period. Of these, non-compliance with the program or house rules was the most frequent reason for termination cited by program staff (18). Other reasons included: the mentee chose to leave the program (6); the child was removed from custody (3); the mentee relapsed (although this was only cited as the primary reason for termination in one case, four mentees had a reported relapse while in placement); a participant was terminated after one week due to never obtaining custody; and one mentor had to leave the program and a replacement was not available.

Like the participants, the majority of the mentors are women and about half are married. Several mentors of fathers are single men. The average age of the mentors is 46 years. Most have some parenting experience, and almost half currently have their own children or grandchildren living with them. About 75 per cent of the mentors have at least some education beyond high school, and most either work full time (69%) or are retired (20%). Whereas 27 per cent of the mentors had previous foster care experience, the most frequently stated reason for becoming a mentor is to strengthen or improve their community. Thus, neighborhood organizations, faith-based organizations, and word of mouth are the most effective resources for mentor recruitment. However, as with foster carers, only about 3.5 per cent of those recruited actually apply, complete the training and become active mentors. About one third of mentors accept subsequent placements after their first family graduates or terminates. The retention rate is even higher in Contra Costa County where, due to extensive ongoing training and support, it has not been necessary to actively recruit new mentors for almost two years.

Progress in meeting anticipated outcomes of Contra Costa County SFC project

Both research findings and anecdotal information suggest that Shared Family Care should be available to families involved, or at risk of involvement, in the child welfare system. Although it is clear that this model does not work for all families, it appears to fill a service gap for those who are ready to make a change and capable of caring for themselves and their children with some guidance, support, and structure. So far, demographic data and the feedback of program staff demonstrate that the clients for whom SFC has been most effective are motivated and open to feedback and mentoring; mentally stable, clean, and sober, and actively participating in a treatment program or recovery support; and homeless or marginally housed.

Child welfare workers overwhelmingly support SFC and appreciate having it as a resource for their clients, but it can only become a standard child welfare service if there is public funding available and public agencies make the commitment to allocate the resources necessary to develop and implement it effectively. This may require policy changes as well as paradigmatic and ideological shifts. It will also require multi-disciplinary public and community-based organizations to collaborate with each other to develop common goals, address turf battles and philosophical differences, define roles and responsibilities, and determine procedures for referring and working with families to ensure continuity and consistency of services. Finally, although SFC clearly is the best service option for some families involved or at risk of involvement in the child welfare system, public agencies must have realistic expectations about the number of families that such a program can effectively serve.

Training of service providers is critical to any innovation, and SFC shares this trait. Prospective mentors in the Contra Costa program must participate in 16 hours of foster parent training that has been tailored to meet their specific needs, as well as eight hours of initial mentor training. They also must attend ongoing monthly trainings/support groups. Since 1997, a total of 28 mentors have had at least one family placed with them in Contra Costa County. An overwhelming majority of them felt that they received enough training, supervision, and support to be a mentor.

Because the relationship between a mentee and mentor appears to be critical to the success of a placement, great effort should be taken to place mentees with the most suitable mentors. To this end, several introductory meetings occur and, in some cases, a trial overnight visit is arranged prior to making a placement. If the match does not seem suitable, placement is delayed until a more suitable match is found. Likewise, if the situation is not working out during placement, every effort is made to relocate the mentee to another home. To date, out of Contra Costa's 39 mentees, there have been only four such transfers, and only one that resulted from mentor/mentee conflict. This may be a reflection of an effective matching process, as well as responsive case managers who were readily available to assist with conflicts or difficulties experienced in the mentor/mentee relationship.

Since 1998, both mentors and mentees reported having generally positive relationships with one another. Nonetheless, more than half of the respondents reported that conflicts in the relationship occurred during their stay. Over time, one third of the mentors reported a decreased ability of the mentee to follow house rules or openly communicate, and almost half reported a decrease in the mentee's ability to receive feedback from the mentor. These decreasing rates were more frequent in the graduated than the terminated group. They may reflect the fact that graduates, who generally are in placement significantly longer than families that do not complete the placement, may become increasingly independent. This also may be indicative of a natural readiness for the relationship to end over time.

The fact that the majority of families stayed with their mentor throughout placement suggests that both parties were able to work through and/or put aside conflicts. Possibly related to the mentors' willingness to continue to work with some mentees despite conflicts, were mentors' excellent relations with the mentees' children. In fact, several mentors report a strong desire to maintain their bond with participant children as the main reason for continued contact with the families. Indeed, a majority of program graduates (70%) have remained in contact with their mentor family after placement, and many talk weekly or daily.

Since 1998, mentors in Contra Costa spent most of their time with mentees on the following activities:

- providing transportation
- talking about program goals and house rules
- spending recreational time (including social and spiritual)
- providing respite and child care
- assisting with parenting and child safety
- teaching life skills.

Only two services decreased notably after the first three months: transportation by mentors reduced from 82 per cent to 68 per cent and involvement in recreational activities from 21 per cent to 5 per cent. The percentage of mentors assisting mentees with job training and employment, on the other hand, increased from 4 per cent in the first three months to 100 per cent in the last four to six months. This is not surprising as the focus at the beginning of placement is on establishing relationships and connections with community resources, while in the latter months, mentees are moving towards independence and financial self sufficiency.

Most child welfare workers commented on the usefulness of the services and the support provided through the Shared Family Care agencies and mentors – particularly the continuity of care, weekly meetings, housing assistance, access to resources (including paid job training), intense supervision, and the role modeling provided by the mentors. These services appeared to help families reach their goals. The most common goals identified by mentees were employment, education, parenting skills, housing, life skills, reunification, and recovery. Graduates attained most or all of their goals, while very few of the terminated mentees did. Most of those who terminated attained one of their goals; four did not attain any.

On average throughout placement, the majority of Contra Costa mentees (over 80%) felt they had as much social and community support as they needed. The vast majority of families reported good access to these services when they entered the program, leaving little room for improvement. It is difficult to know whether this is a function of self reporting, confusion about the questions, or the fact that almost all of the mentees were already involved with child welfare services and/or drug treatment or other community services when they entered SFC.

Many mentees continued to receive services after they completed their placement. Along with sustained post-reunification case management and home-based support, other services most utilized by mentees upon graduation were: employment services, housing, child care, substance abuse recovery services, financial assistance, and transportation. Secondary services accessed after placement completion included infant services, mental health services, food, and clothing.

To date, the research team has remained in contact with 23 of 25 (92%) graduates from the Contra Costa program for up to one year post-placement. Limited efforts to locate the terminated families have been unsuccessful, so there is no post-program information on them. The majority of SFC graduates felt that the SFC program was either 'somewhat helpful' or 'very helpful.' When asked if they would recommend SFC to others in similar life circumstances, all of the graduates replied in the affirmative. Many graduates noted that the program was 'very good' at locating housing and assisting them with making the transition to independent living situations. They also noted that the program helped them to budget and save money, become more stable and independent, get their children back, find employment, become better parents, maintain their recovery, get back on their feet, and start a new life.

Of the 23 graduated families for whom income data were available at intake, the median monthly income was $520. Of the 19 for whom data were available after program participation, the median monthly income had risen to $1100. While this is still at or below the poverty level, the increase in graduates' income is quite substantial and probably reflects an increase in employment. Whereas only nine graduates (36%) were employed at intake, 19 of the 25 families (76%) who have graduated from the Contra Costa program since 1997 were employed at graduation.

Since 1997, 16 of the 25 Contra Costa graduates have made the transition into independent, permanent living situations upon graduation from the mentor home. The remaining families went into transitional housing (3) or lived with friends or family (6). In comparison, at intake, only two families reported living independently. The remaining families were homeless (7), in residential treatment or sober housing (5), living with friends or family (6), or in transitional housing (2). Three families were unaccounted for. Thus, SFC clearly has had success in moving families from homelessness or unstable housing situations to independent living in either permanent or transitional housing, the latter being often necessary for families who are not yet ready to live on their own.

Both mentors and mentees were asked to rate mentees' parenting skills each month in the following areas: talking with their children; setting time aside for their children; using consistent and appropriate discipline techniques; encouraging their children; displaying affection toward their children; and showing approval when their children behaved well. Reports of these parenting skills were quite high throughout placement, and thus there was little room for improvement. This might suggest that mentees' needs and focus were more on becoming stable and self sufficient in order to provide adequately for their children, rather than on improving their parenting skills. On the other hand, it may reflect the nature of mentees' self reporting combined with mentors' desire to protect them by commending their parenting skills.

Perhaps more telling is the extent to which children in families who successfully complete Shared Family Care stay out of the child welfare system. As of December 2002, three children (8% of the total) from one graduated family (4%

of the total) re-entered foster care within one year of completing the program. In comparison, six children (25%) from three terminated families (21%) returned to foster care either during the SFC placement or within one year after participating. Further, an estimated 20 per cent of children in California who go home from foster care are readmitted within three years (Berrick *et al.* 1998). Thus, although the numbers are small, they suggest that SFC may be more effective than regular foster care options at stabilizing families and keeping children out of care.

Although SFC requires a considerable amount of resources, data suggest that it may be as cost-effective as traditional out-of-home placement, and may, in fact, result in cost savings in the long run. Yet this comparison is not an easy one to make, given that SFC provides intensive services and housing to parents and children, whereas foster care provides services primarily for the child.

Costs of SFC

To assess the overall cost of Shared Family Care, the research team quantified the amount being spent on services for the family. To do so, they looked at the number of hours Contra Costa SFC staff reported spending on the following five aspects of the program from June 2001 to May 2002: mentor recruitment and training; pre-placement (team meetings, participant screening, facilitating matching); placement (home and office visits, meetings, and phone calls with mentor and/or family, referral services); aftercare (case management, locating housing and other services); and administrative and miscellaneous costs. The reported number of hours was then multiplied by each individual's hourly salary.

The team calculated that the direct placement services (as defined above) alone cost an average of approximately $533 per family per month, or $3198 per family for the placement duration. When added to the direct payment to the mentor, the average total placement cost is $1733 per family per month, or $10,398 per family for the placement duration. When compared with other out-of-home care options, on a monthly basis, SFC costs just slightly more than treatment foster care ($1589) and considerably more than basic foster care ($425) for one child. Given that, on average, two children are placed in each SFC home, the team also looked at the comparative cost for a family of three (one parent and two children). Because the cost of SFC remains the same, the difference between the monthly cost of basic foster care and SFC decreases when two children are placed ($1733: $887),[2] while treatment foster care for two children is considerably more than the placement cost of SFC ($3237:[3] $1733).

When considering total cost for placement duration, SFC is even more economical. In Contra Costa County, the average length of stay is 10 months for basic foster care, 19 months for treatment foster care, and 6 months for SFC (Needell *et al.* 1996). Based on these average placement durations, the total cost of a SFC placement for a family with two children is comparable to basic foster care for two children and a fraction of the cost of treatment foster care.[4]

Other administrative costs of SFC (e.g. mentor recruitment and training, pre-placement costs, aftercare, and miscellaneous administrative expenses) raise the total cost for a six-month stay for one family to approximately $18,000. We were not able to obtain comparable information for the cost of conventional foster parent recruitment, training, licensing and retention, or aftercare. However, even when factoring in the total available administrative costs of SFC, it costs almost four times more to place two children in treatment foster care than a family of three in SFC.

This still does not tell the complete story. Because, upon entering the program, the majority of families who participate in SFC are either homeless or on the verge of homelessness, we also considered the comparable cost of sheltering a parent. In Contra Costa, the cost to occupy one bed in a homeless shelter is $25 a night. If a parent spends one month there, the cost to the county will be approximately $750. When this is added to the monthly costs for children being placed out-of-home, SFC becomes much more cost-effective in comparison. For example, the placement cost of two children in basic foster care *and* one parent in a homeless shelter is $1600 per month – just slightly less than a SFC placement.

Thus, while SFC is not an inexpensive program to develop or operate, a true cost–benefit analysis is necessary in order to understand its comparative cost-effectiveness. Further, the savings resulting from preventing homelessness and increasing employment earnings must be quantified and incorporated into any comprehensive analysis. The US system for paying for child welfare services is highly categorical in structure and involves different funds for in-home, out-of-home, housing, and health services; overall savings between programs with different budgets (such as housing) are not considered policy-relevant, a situation that is also common in the UK. In settings in which financing is population based, these savings could be significant.

Shared Family Care appears to be a cost-effective and sensible way to help families move toward self sufficiency and achieve permanency for children in a more timely manner. It is not, however, appropriate for all families. It also is a program that takes a considerable amount of time, commitment, and persever-ance to develop.

Nevertheless, over the past five years, Contra Costa County in California has demonstrated that, with strong leadership, commitment, interagency collaboration, sufficient resources, and patience, Shared Family Care can be implemented effectively. Not only can it help promote safety and stability for children, it also helps to stabilize families and, in many cases, creates extended family for those who have none or are estranged from their own. As a result, data suggest that, after participating in SFC, children are less likely to re-enter foster care, their parents are more likely to be employed and to have increased their income, and the family is more likely to move together into stable independent living situations.

SFC gives even those who do not successfully complete the program a chance to try to live together as a family and the opportunity to determine (from the perspective of the family and the child welfare system) whether they are ready and willing to do so on their own. Some families who do not successfully graduate from SFC have their children removed while in placement. However, our limited data suggest that, of those families that leave the program before completing it, the majority of their children do not re-enter care within the first couple of years after their involvement with SFC. Further research would be helpful to determine if this is because they were not really in need of the program to begin with (for instance because they were adequately caring for their children) or because, even though their involvement was relatively brief, the program had some impact on their parenting abilities. This information may have implications for client screening criteria as well as for determining the most effective length of stay.

After five years of demonstrating SFC in various localities, experience strongly suggests that this model should be available to families involved (or at risk of involvement) with the child welfare system. SFC fills an important middle ground for families that need an extensive amount of assistance in resuming the care of their children. This is help that they would not get with brief family preservation services or with weak doses of parent training programs. These families are, after all, those with which the child welfare system has had the least success.

Conclusions

Without a portfolio of rigorous evaluation results to display, selling new program models is increasingly difficult. Decision makers all across the globe are looking for evidence-based interventions (Willinsky 2003), preferably those with tight eligibility criteria and consistent manualized intervention models (Chambless and Ollendick 2001). Such carefully scripted approaches allow for 'training to the book' and replication studies that have high levels of fidelity to the original. Whereas such experimental research is highly desirable, it is very difficult to conduct with a small-scale and innovative program that accepts a diverse clientele endeavoring to meet a variety of needs. The most compelling of these studies are manualized, with detailed instructions about how each treatment session should be delivered, and have narrowly defined populations of concern upon which specific techniques are shown to be effective. Yet, there may be an inverse relationship between the exclusivity with which a treatment focuses on immediate symptom resolution and the stability and breadth of the changes obtained (Chambless and Hollon 1998, p.16).

There may also be an inverse relationship between the acceptability of interventions and the narrowness of their focus and guidelines. Bardach (2000) contends that 'smart practices' (like Shared Family Care) have a greater likelihood of adoption if the interventions are 'not prescriptive and overly precise' (p.79). This is the approach taken in the Shared Family Care manual (Abandoned Infants Assistance 1996). It provides broad consideration of a theoretical and practice framework and identifies details that each implementing agency will have to address. Yet, the flexibility of Shared Family Care to serve families that have not had prior child welfare involvement, as well as families with children placed into foster care and subsequently engaged in reunification, means that agencies must be flexible in the delivery of the service, setting of goals, and assessment of achievement.

More rigorous evaluations involving random assignment are certainly needed, but the strength of the underpinning theory, and the limitations of other available approaches which do not form an adequate continuum of care suggest that there is sufficient evidence now in place to warrant replication of the program. The role of theory is critical to this discussion because the evidence suggests that the intervention can address key risk and protective factors, help to change the mechanisms that underpin them, and includes engagement strategies that enhance change by addressing clients' preferences and providing opportunities for learning and practice. Unfortunately, the lack of rigorous scientific evidence showing that these risk and protective factors change in the desired direction and remain changed leaves the many groups interested in SFC at a stalemate.

The extraordinary congruence between SFC and family and children's services values should be the hammer that breaks the logjam. SFC provides protection and permanency in a family context. It offers families a reasonable opportunity to show that they are motivated to achieve permanency and to learn the necessary skills. Unlike most parent training programs that are classroom bound, didactic, diluted, and childless (Barth *et al.* in press), SFC is dynamic, intensive, involves children, and operates under realistic circumstances. SFC provides an alternative to the conventional services that often lack the fairness and efficacy that child welfare workers, judges, and families desperately want. The least we can do is figure out how to finance SFC, to build on the available training materials, and to begin new trials implementing this very possible, deliciously sensible and cost-reasonable approach. In our demanding work, value-based approaches which can, demonstrably, be implemented deserve a long and careful look.

Acknowledgements

The authors gratefully acknowledge the efforts of Christie Clovis and Lauren Wichterman in the conduct of research in Contra Costa County. We also thank Ellen Walker and the Zellerbach Family Foundation for their commitment to Shared Family Care, for recognizing the importance of innovation and evaluation, and for their support of the SFC evaluation project – without which this chapter would not exist. We also thank the National Abandoned Infants Assistance Resource Center, of the School of Social Welfare, at University of California at Berkeley.

Notes

1   The referral process involves two steps. Families are first referred by county child welfare workers to the Shared Family Care program. Then the program further evaluates appropriateness through its own intake process, which involves completing an intake application form on the family being referred. Not all families initially referred by child welfare workers make it to this point in the process. The data in this report is only collected on those families who completed an intake application form.

2   The figure for two children in basic foster care, $887, reflects the cost for one child aged 0–4 ($425), and one child aged 5–8 ($462).

3   Likewise, the figure for treatment foster care, $3237, reflects the cost for one child aged 0–4 ($1589), and one child aged 5–8 ($1648).

4   These figures are for children under the age of five.

Part IV

Promoting the Well-being of Vulnerable Communities

Chapter 14

Housing Issues in Child Welfare

A Practice Response with Service and Policy Implications

Bruce Leslie

Child welfare services in Western societies are united through their concerns for the protection, safety, well-being and family relations of children. These services are socially defined and locally refined, supporting community standards for protecting children from maltreatment and the risk of maltreatment. Although it is widely accepted that diverse layers and aspects of society influence the definition of child welfare problems, there is less consensus about their contribution to the actual occurrence of child maltreatment and their potential for reducing its incidence.

Introduction

Systemic, ecological models for understanding the context and development of child welfare problems identify numerous factors emanating from diverse layers of society operative in the incidence of child maltreatment (Zuravin 1989). These ecological models highlight a broad basis for creating effective interventions aimed at a variety of outcomes, both short and long term, and impacting on more than just an individual child or family. In contrast, the vast majority of child welfare services direct their change efforts at the child/parental/familial levels of influence, with solutions being driven by immediate safety needs of children and the resolution of parenting issues (Pelton 1992).

Factors in the wider family and environment – the third side of the Assessment Triangle – are often ignored. Their influence is explored in the chapters in this part of the book.

Even though there has been an expansion in the scope of explanatory models, first from connecting abuse with a parent to including family relationships, and then extending to the identification of relationship and interactive effects for system factors (Wolfe 1987), frontline workers (and service planners) often appear to have an ambivalent/conflicted relationship with these models in a practice environment. Ecological models appear to be accepted in principle, but their implementation in direct service agencies is tenuous, due to their limited utility when it comes to affecting the urgent safety issues of a child or trying to optimize his or her well-being in the short term. Lack of focus in these agencies on the broader ecological issues that affect their clients, which have been found associated with child maltreatment by many researchers (e.g. Trocmé *et al.* 2001), is further complicated because the means to their effective solutions are not clear and the likelihood of success with regard to community and political change too far removed and uncertain. There is evidence from both sides of the Atlantic that environmental issues, which form the third of three interlocking domains that provide the Framework for the Assessment of Children in Need and their Families (Department of Health, Department for Education and Skills and Home Office 2000), are the most frequently overlooked in social care assessments.

A narrow short-term perspective on resolving child welfare problems has been criticized for being overly restrictive (e.g. Pelton 1992). The effective promotion and maintenance of the welfare and well-being of children is seen by many to require the development and support of a continuum of linked options from prevention to investigation and assessment to protection, incorporating levels of intervention from an individual child, to family, to community, and to the political arena (Wolfe 1987). Such a continuum would have local variations in the specific definitions of 'adequate housing' but would share common ground in a concern for housing as an environmental risk.

Feedback loops are an important part of the effective development of this continuum. Child welfare services are in a unique position to identify areas of exclusion and to access problems and successes associated with social programs designed to assist needy, vulnerable and disadvantaged families. Problems and issues identified at the front line of services do have immediate solutions but they are of limited scope with regard to predisposing or precipitating factors involved in child maltreatment. A constricted focus on children and families is also problematic because it can reinforce the marginalization of already disadvantaged families and does not facilitate inclusive societal solutions. Some of the problems identified in connection with a family or parent's actions are more correctly attributed to developments in the environment and social systems around them (Terling-Watt 2000).

In addition to the issues identified above, two key frames of reference were used in the development of the present study and the analysis of the results. The first focuses on the significant influence the parameters of a definition have in directing the creation of solutions and the importance of including ecological/ systemic models in assessing and advancing alternative solutions to child maltreatment. The second highlights the inter-relationships between individual needs, parenting capacity influences and social program priorities.

A multi-layered, interactive definition of child welfare issues

When specific causes are not known, the identification of problem determinants and their relationship to the composition of solutions has many influences. It would often seem that if something has not been identified as part of a problem it would not be considered part of the solution. If the exact amount and direction of the influence social housing policies have on incidents of child maltreatment remains unknown, there is less reason for those policies to change.

The definitional characteristics and parameters of human problems and their solutions are also influenced by such factors as ascribed role, controllability, stage of development and age of those affected. The formulations created in response to the question, 'Who is responsible for a family's housing?' are many and vary along a continuum influenced by such factors as perceived influence, control and ability: for example, some attach blame to parents and others identify more socio-political solutions.

Problem solutions can also be influenced by the simplicity or complexity of their underlying definitions. In Ontario, child welfare services are emerging from an intensive period of public scrutiny following several inquest reviews in which there has been an intensified focus on the workload and casework practices of frontline workers. These reviews have studied situations in which there has been a death of a child and at least some involvement of child welfare services. Researchers have found that this type of inquiry has often resulted in efforts to resolve child welfare problems through reducing caseloads, increasing staffing and the provision of better training (Gelles 1996; Regehr *et al.* 2000). Other more conservatively oriented critics have seen a need for more prosecution of parents and easier termination of parental rights (Gelles 1996). This focus on individual workers and parents has been criticized for being overly narrow and ignoring the role of broader influences contributing to the problems and consequently omitted in their solutions (Etzioni 1994; Terling-Watt 2000). The pressure to maintain such a narrow focus has been supported by notions of expediency; it is often considered easier and less expensive to change individuals than systems. As many have noted, child welfare services are most often aimed at changing people rather than changing the environment (e.g. Pelton 1992; Wakefield 1996).

Families are surrounded by neighbours, communities, municipalities and townships, each layer adding complexity that can lead to a range of directions, from encouraging growth and providing pathways to higher achievements, to stifling growth through limits and restrictions, leading to dead ends. If one accepts a multi-layered and textured model of child welfare problems that involves diverse sectors and elements of society, the question emerges, 'Why do our attempts to assist children and families negatively impacted by social problems focus so much on individual children, parents and frontline workers?'

Recently in Ontario, frontline staff have struggled with a shrinking core of service activities, affected by growing concerns about risks to children and increased competing work demands. The functional operating space for workers is being effectively reduced (Hetherington *et al.* 1997). Their time and strategies to maneuver with families are being restricted by other priorities and intervention standards and, consequently, they quickly move from assessment to statutory interventions aimed at reducing imminent risks to the children. Child welfare agencies appear to be more frequently using a reactive pattern of intervention that is guided by elements of the presenting situation with the complexity of associated factors somehow becoming a background blur.

Such an approach to the work tends to ignore the effects of a plethora of social issues that have been identified as associated with child maltreatment – poverty, income equity, education, employment and working conditions, and housing (Garbarino and Kostelny 1992; Trocmé *et al.* 2001).

Community policies that negatively affect child welfare clients can leave staff delivering frontline services in child welfare agencies feeling helpless and stressed (Regehr *et al.* 2000). The weight of the unaddressed, broader social issues can be another factor driving these workers from the field. Micro-managing of macro-level problems is ineffective and disheartening. In these days of recruitment and retention problems, every advantage needs to be pursued.

In contrast to the UK, where prevention is a fundamental element in the policy agenda (see Chapter 3), child welfare services in Ontario and elsewhere in Canada have become more protection-focused with less, or no, financial support for prevention services. This might prove to be a shortsighted attempt at saving costs or be representative of less egalitarian legislation and policies.

The Children's Aid Society of Toronto (CAST), where the present study was conducted, is one of the few child welfare organizations in Ontario that has developed and maintained community work and advocacy roles as vital aspects of its services. The inclusion of these supportive activities is well received by staff and contributes significantly to the available options for addressing family difficulties. The organizational vision includes a continuum of child welfare services that helps provide a more balanced perspective in service planning.

Maslow's hierarchy

The second major frame of reference that was influential in shaping the present study was Maslow's hierarchy of needs. His theory organized basic needs in a hierarchy of 'prepotency', according to their priority of gratification (Maslow 1970). The five ranked categories of need – Physiological, Safety, Belongingness and Love, Self-esteem, and Self-actualization – are often presented visually with the broad, solid base of a pyramid at the bottom of the hierarchy, reflecting a secure basis for growth emanating from the more basic biological needs. But for many children and families seen in child welfare services, achievement of even the most basic needs is not assured and the pyramid turned upside down, balancing on the tip, more accurately represents their precarious state (see Figure 14.1).

The hierarchy elegantly depicts struggles that are seen in child welfare situations. Needs like housing, food and shelter are of greater priority than the higher order needs such as self-actualization. When lower order needs are not gratified they become the operative force motivating action (Maslow 1970). Competition, divisiveness and the likelihood of child maltreatment within a family are greater when resources to satisfy the physiological needs are scarce. The ability of a parent to achieve such higher order needs as a 'caring family', as part of the need for belongingness, is seen to be based in part on the achievement of the lower order needs. Parents who are struggling with basic physiological needs are, within this model, seen to be limited in their ability to achieve more altruistic and empathic ways of relating to family members.

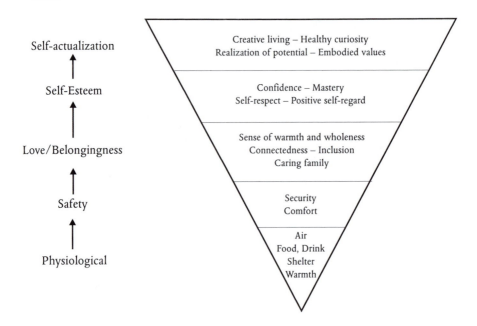

Self-actualization ↑

Self-Esteem ↑

Love/Belongingness ↑

Safety ↑

Physiological

Creative living – Healthy curiosity
Realization of potential – Embodied values

Confidence – Mastery
Self-respect – Positive self-regard

Sense of warmth and wholeness
Connectedness – Inclusion
Caring family

Security
Comfort

Air
Food, Drink
Shelter
Warmth

Figure 14.1: Inverted pyramid model based on Maslow's hierarchy of needs

Housing study development from 1992 to 2000

In the context of the considerations referenced above, a housing study was first conducted at the Children's Aid Society of Toronto (CAST) in 1992. A group of staff at CAST and researchers at the University of Toronto were concerned about the impact that housing conditions were having on the children and families seen by social workers. A review of the existing research at that time showed it was very limited (Cohen-Schlanger *et al.* 1995) and there was a desire to examine more thoroughly the breadth of influence across family service cases and types of housing problems.

This was practice-based research with policy intentions. Identifying the degree of influence that housing-related issues had in all the many types of family service cases was not seen to be as convincing to funders as exploring how far they affected the decisions to admit or discharge a child from care. The emotional, developmental and familial concerns for children are greater in these latter situations and the financial costs of services considerably higher. In 1992, the cost of working with a child living with his or her family in the community was estimated to be $94 a month, whereas the average cost of maintaining a child in care for a month was estimated to be $1528.

Eight years later, in 2000, there were concerns that the housing conditions in Toronto had deteriorated and child welfare reform in Ontario – by more clearly identifying child protection concerns related to neglect and emotional harm – had made housing an even more important consideration for the protection of children. In Toronto, rents had been rising faster than incomes and more families were being evicted because of arrears. An increasing number of families were unable to find stable affordable housing and drifted between shelters, relatives and other shared accommodations (City of Toronto 2000).

The present study was conducted in 2000 to re-examine the links between inadequate housing supports for families with limited financial means and the placement of children in care. The present study replicated the 1992 study, facilitating comparisons between the two.

Method

The study was conducted at the Children's Aid Society of Toronto (CAST), one of the largest board operated, government funded child welfare agencies in North America. There are approximately 735 staff with a budget of about $120 million. The agency serves the non-Catholic, non-Jewish population of the city of Toronto and this target population constitutes about 60 per cent of the 2.5 million residents. CAST served 24,512 children and 10,838 families in the community during 2001. Additionally, the agency admitted or re-admitted 1289 children to care during the year. In total, it provided services to 3481 children in care through the year. Approximately 57 per cent of the families served by the agency received some form of government financial assistance and 53 per cent were single parent households.

The aims of the study were to identify whether or not housing difficulties were a factor prevalent during admissions and discharges of children from care, to estimate their incidence in the agency's in-care population and to highlight the common types of housing difficulties faced by families involved with child welfare. The study design essentially replicated the methodology from the 1992 study and the present research team included two of the original members.

Family Service Workers at the agency were selected as the key informants because of their unique role and skills. They are central figures in a team setting that make assessments and recommendations on a daily basis regarding the welfare of children, admitting children into care and returning them home. They visit families in their homes as a routine practice, and have first hand information to assess family living conditions and circumstances. Of the 13 major areas covered in the survey, two key questions were:

- 'In your opinion, was the family's housing situation one of the factors that resulted in temporary placement of a child/children into care?'

- 'In your opinion, was there any delay of the return home of the child from care due to any housing related problem?'

All open family service cases with children in temporary care during the months of September to December 2000 (a few months prior to questionnaire distribution) were initially identified as part of the study sample. Some of these children had been in care for a few weeks and some for many months.

About 950 children were identified in each of these four months, and excluding repeating cases, a total sample of 1331 was produced. A randomized selection from this sample led to 323 cases being identified. Fifty-two cases proved ineligible and the final sample totalled 271 cases. This process of selection was designed to maximize the potential number of workers involved in completing the questionnaire and produced a 32 per cent increase in sample size from the earlier study. To limit workload implications, the respondents were asked to complete questionnaires on only two or three children's files, randomly selected from their caseload.

Results

Participation and response rates

At the time of the 2000 study there were 128 Family Service Workers at CAST and a good staff participation rate of 83 per cent was achieved, with 106 returning questionnaires. The total number of questionnaires distributed was 271 and 191 were returned (a 70% return rate). This is an increase on the 1992 study where 108 Family Service Workers were surveyed, and 69 returned their completed questionnaires (a 64% return rate).

The sample

Table 14.1 shows how the characteristics of the children's families differed between the two studies.

Table 14.1: Comparison of 1992 and 2000 sample characteristics

	1992	2000
Children from single parent households	68	74
Estimated monthly family income (median) ($)	1225	1500
Families receiving government financial support (%)	70	56
Families receiving unemployment insurance (%)	5	1.6
Families living in government supported housing (%)	23	30
Median age of the child placed into care	6.5	11
The child's gender: Male (%)	53	48
Female (%)	47	52

Overall, the two samples appear fairly similar. However, the increased numbers of families residing in public housing in the 2000 sample is noteworthy, given the declining availability of this type of government-supported housing from 1992. The lower number of families receiving some form of government financial assistance reflects the provincial pattern following a 21.6 per cent decrease in the amount of money provided by the government and other changes to the program eligibility criteria implemented in 1995. It is also noteworthy that, although more families have 'earned income' in 2000, the estimated monthly average does not reflect a large increase, especially when cost of living changes are factored in. These family characteristics are also similar to the profile of total cases receiving family services from the agency, except that the study sample had a slightly higher percentage of single parent households and those living in public housing.

Table 14.2 compares the study sample with findings of the Canadian Incidence Study of Child Maltreatment (CIS) (Trocmé *et al.* 2001) and the Ontario Incidence Study of Child Maltreatment (OIS) (Trocmé *et al.* 2002). The present study sample is characterized by greater use of rental and public housing and more transient forms of living arrangements than the larger national and provincial studies.

Table 14.2: Comparison of the housing situations of samples from the Canadian Incidence Study (CIS), Ontario Incidence Study (OIS) and CAST 2000 Study

	CIS	OIS	CAST
Private rental (%)	47	50	61.7
Government-supported housing (%)	10	8	23.9
Purchased home (%)	26	29	10.2
Hotel/Shelter/Homeless (%)	1	2	3.7
Other (%)	6	3	1.5

The CAST study sample was also found to be living in higher risk living situations overall than the samples from the CIS and the OIS, as shown in Table 14.3. However, the present study sample of cases, based on children in care, would be a sub-sample in the larger studies that included a representative sample of all forms of investigated child maltreatment, not just those where children were placed away from home. Moreover, the CAST study sample ratings were based on the workers' assessments of the family living conditions, as documented using the provincial Risk Assessment Tool. The CIS and OIS studies used staff ratings based on file reviews and had to rely on the documented descriptions of living conditions that might not have conveyed the same level of risk and hazard, without first hand observation.

Table 14.3: Comparison of the CIS, OIS and CAST 2000 samples with regard to safe/unsafe home conditions

	CIS	OIS	CAST
Safe conditions (%)	64	78	32
Unsafe conditions (%)	18	9	68

Care admissions and discharges

In the present study, housing situations influenced the decision to have a child admitted to care in 39 families (20.7% in 2000; 18.6% in 1992). For these cases, the respondent was asked in a subsequent question to identify what type of housing problem or problems were involved. The most common housing problems for these families were eviction, difficulty in paying the rent, and no permanent family home (e.g. transient, or living in a shelter).

At the time of the study there were 134 cases in which the child had not been returned to the family since initial placement. For these cases, the respondent was asked to identify whether housing was a factor delaying the return. Returning children home was found to be delayed due to housing-related problems in 11.5 per cent of cases (8.6% in 1992). The major problems creating delays included inadequate income, inadequate amount of living space, inadequate health standards, no affordable home for the family, and no permanent home for the family.

In total, 44 families had their lives disrupted and their children's stay in care influenced by their living situations; 39 families on admission and an additional five on return of their child. Ten families had both the admission and discharge of their children from care influenced by their housing situation. The 44 families represent 23 per cent of the study sample.

Although the percentage increase of delayed returns due to housing-related problems between 1992 and 2000 does not appear large, when the dramatic increase in the overall agency children in care population is factored in, the significance is more apparent. At the end of 1992, there were 1568 children in care of the agency, 2250 at the end of the year 2000. The increase from 8.6 per cent to 11.5 per cent of children estimated to have their return home delayed as a result of housing problems suggests that the figure rose from 135 in 1992 to 258 in 2000, a 91 per cent increase overall.

A comparison of the 1992 and 2000 agency population data with regard to the responses to the survey question on admissions similarly amplifies the impact of the present findings. In 1992, the percentage of families identified from the survey with housing problems influencing the workers' decision to admit a child was 18.6 per cent, increasing to 20.7 per cent in the year 2000. When these percentages are applied to the full agency population, this change produces an estimate 61 per cent higher for the number of children in care in the year 2000 – from 289 in 1992 to 466 in 2000.

Another major change that significantly increases the importance of the findings is in relation to the financial costs of a child in care. In 1992, the average costs for a child in care were estimated to be $1528 per month but by 2000 these had increased to $1941. Applying these costs to the estimated 466 children with their admissions to care influenced by their family living situation, a maximum monthly expense estimate of $904,506 is produced. With the addition of the costs attributable to delays in exiting care, housing problems contribute up to about a $1,000,000 monthly expense for CAST.

Implications of findings

Evaluations of costs and benefits of social programs are frequently identified as problematic because of the complexity of influences operating on the outcome of interest. The present study has produced findings that reflect the impact of social housing policies on the welfare of children and child welfare services. Housing problems for this group of children and families were most commonly identified in relation to the lack of affordability and availability. The methodology has strengthened the rigour of relevant information supporting the perception of many frontline staff and managers that, in Toronto, government housing policies are increasing instability for already disadvantaged families, disrupting family connections and contributing added risks to children.

The study aimed to estimate the incidence of housing problems in the decisions of child protection workers to admit children to care and plan for their discharge. It is recognized that these decisions are multi-dimensional and multi-factored and this study cannot state that housing-related factors directly caused the admissions of children to care. The workers surveyed identified housing as a factor in about one in five cases in which a child was admitted. The casework decision to remove a child from home is one of the more serious ones affecting children and parents and reflects a high level of child protection concern resulting from an assessment of the family housing conditions in conjunction with other factors. This casework decision reflects more than a worker's concern about health hazards, or parents' stress as a result of using more than 60 per cent of their income on housing costs. This decision to admit children is seen to be significant from the perspectives of the children, the families, the service and social policy.

Housing is intimately connected to children's sense of permanence and well-being. Children are being removed from their families to ensure their protection, a decision at least partly attributed to their family living situations. This study suggests that access to safe and affordable housing may reduce both the number of children brought into care and also housing-related delays in the return of children home, thereby stabilizing the family's living situation in ways that promote children's well-being. Unfortunately, this study reveals that progress on related social policies was not made in the eight years following the 1992 study.

The survey findings indicate that Toronto's housing situation continues to have a detrimental impact on the safety, stability and well-being of many families with children who are clients of CAST. Comparisons with the broader geographically based findings of the Canadian and Ontario Incidence studies show higher levels of risk related to unsafe housing in Toronto. These families face substantial barriers in securing adequate and appropriate housing to meet their needs and this may have an impact on parents' abilities to care adequately for their children. Not having permanent affordable housing can lead parents to feel insecure, anxious, stressed and possibly depressed and this contributes to the neglect of their children (Zuravin and Taylor 1987). This stress can then be passed on to children who may become depressed, aggressive and difficult for parents to manage, creating a cycle of stressors. This unfolding situation may be further compounded if parents become overwhelmed and unable to focus on working with child welfare staff in gaining the skills needed to safeguard their children. If parents are focused on basic needs for shelter and food, they have less energy to support a caring family environment (Maslow 1970).

These ripple effects are expanded on in the theory of motivation that is behind Maslow's hierarchy. It explores the inter-relationship between needs and makes connections between choices, priorities and values, whether on a day-to-day personal basis or in policy decisions (Maslow 1970). Policies are seen to be the means by which societies implement these needful considerations and reflect social priorities. Since 1992 the numbers of children in care and families served by child welfare agencies across Ontario have increased substantially. If the admission of children to care is seen to reflect the breakdown of other community and familial attempts to protect children, one factor appears to be a decline from 1992 to 2000 in social supports related to family housing. More specifically, if the number of children whose admission to care is influenced by their family's housing situation is accepted as an indicator of the effectiveness of social housing polices, children appear to be becoming a lower priority and family stability less of a concern for government policy makers.

In Ontario, there has been no new social housing created in the last few years, producing extensive waiting lists, with some estimates of ten years' delay (City of Toronto 2000). Rent controls have been lifted leading to higher rents. A slowing rate of construction and a growing population has led to lower vacancy rates. The reduction in government-supported financial assistance by 21.6 per cent in the mid 1990s continues to add stress to disadvantaged families. The combination of these factors has led to evictions increasing, and deteriorating housing and neighbourhood conditions; children and families are the fastest growing group of shelter users (City of Toronto 2000).

Ontario's housing policies might have saved money for their own government ministry but this study suggests that they have contributed to increased costs for others. This study also suggests that the incidence of child abuse and neglect could be reduced if more families had access to affordable and adequate housing; that government investments in housing supports for economically insecure families could reduce the incidence of admission to care where housing is a factor; and that these investments could also reduce the delays in returning children home.

Child welfare services can be actively involved in promoting the best interests of the children and young people and the families they serve through participation in studies examining such influences. At times, they need to look past the pressing, short-term frontline issues to more long-term, preventative strategies. Child welfare services need to uphold primary prevention actions, at least through the contribution of relevant information about factors affecting major case decisions. This study has provided more evidence for the inclusion of family housing issues as a contributing influence in child maltreatment definitions, especially with regard to the admission of children to care. The challenge for child welfare services is to create a plan that will adequately address the impact of factors that appear to be at least in part attributable to government policies developed in other ministries.

The importance of addressing housing on child welfare services is growing as they are now more strongly mandated to protect children from forms of maltreatment related to neglect, in addition to abuse. These services need to improve their ability to differentiate the sources of this neglect. Children's Aid Societies are mandated to protect children and appear to be providing 'catch-all services', preventing them from falling further as a result of gaps present in other social programs. This use of child welfare services might have some short-term gains in terms of the protection of children but there are also long-term, negative consequences for many children and families in terms of outcomes such as permanency and well-being.

We need to look at capacity building within the child welfare field to improve our ability to challenge social factors negatively impacting children and families. This does not mean skill building for workers but more effective inter-governmental and policy collaborations. We need macro-level solutions for macro-level problems. Child welfare services need to participate actively in health promotion to support, enhance and sustain appropriate changes to achieve better outcomes for children. Promoting improved housing policies for children and families with limited financial means will promote child, family and community well-being.

Children's Aid Societies must address precipitating and predisposing factors to provide a comprehensive protection plan for children. Without such a plan, child welfare services will continue to protect children who have *been* harmed, rather than safeguarding children *from* harm. If neglect is to be accepted as a recognized form of child maltreatment, we need to be clear in formulating solutions that address where the neglect begins, not just where it ends.

Acknowledgements

This study was conducted at the Children's Aid Society of Toronto: we thank the family services workers who completed the survey and the organizational support that made the study possible.

The study team included Dr J.D. Hulchanski, Chair in Housing, Faculty of Social Work, Director for Urban and Community Studies at the University of Toronto; Ann Fitzpatrick, Community Worker at the Children's Aid Society of Toronto; Shirley Chau, Research Associate and doctoral candidate, Centre for Applied Social Research, Faculty of Social Work, University of Toronto; Debbie Schatia, Family Services Supervisor, Children's Aid Society of Toronto; and Bruce Leslie, Research and Quality Improvement Analyst at the Children's Aid Society of Toronto.

Shirley Chau was the recipient of a Royal Bank Doctoral Student Research Internship that supported her involvement in the study. We thank Dr Chow Yei Ching who endowed a Chair in Housing which has enabled the Faculty of Social Work, University of Toronto, to focus on housing research, and Joanne Daciuk at the Centre for Applied Social Research at the University of Toronto who assisted with sampling considerations.

Chapter 15

Searching for Impacts of a Community-based Initiative
The Evaluation of '1,2,3 GO!'

Camil Bouchard

This chapter introduces a multi-sectoral demonstration initiative, implemented in 1995 in the Montreal region of Canada in six vulnerable areas with the aim of building stronger, more cohesive communities oriented towards promoting children's well-being and development. The chapter covers the theoretical model and the evaluation design as well as exploring the findings. Data, collected at two-year intervals, reflect the level and the nature of collaboration between child and family services as well as the parents' perception of their neighbourhood and their utilization of local resources. They also portray parents' levels of stress and disciplinary behaviours, social support systems and the cognitive development of their children. Except for some of the collaboration measures, pre–post and comparison scores with matched communities show no significant improvement on almost all indicators and the chapter explores the reasons for these findings.

Introduction

The importance of neighbourhoods in supporting parenting and promoting or inhibiting children's development has gained considerable scientific recognition over the last 15 years (Brooks-Gunn, Duncan and Aber 1997). The depletion of neighbourhoods, linked with concentrations of poor families in the same living areas, has been associated with elevated rates of low birthweight, infant mortality, teenage childbearing, dropping out of school, child maltreatment and adolescent delinquency (Garbarino and Kostelny 1992). The absence of affluent neighbours has more recently been related to problems in cognitive competence for pre-school as well as school-age children (Brooks-Gunn, Duncan and Aber 1997). A recent Canadian study, completed on a very large representative sample of four- and five-year-olds, has confirmed a modest but significant correlation between indicators of neighbourhood affluence and levels of social cohesion and children's behaviour problem scores after controlling for families' and mothers' characteristics (Kohen *et al.* 2002).

Mechanisms that would account for the impact of the neighbourhood on children's development and well-being over and above the direct influence of parents are still not well known. Sociologists have proposed different theoretical explanations, in which available role models, processes of collective socialization, the availability of institutional resources and competition for them would play complementary or contradictory roles (Furstenberg and Hugues 1997). Recent theoretical efforts have tried to integrate these fragmentary models in the context of a very large study of Chicago neighbourhoods (Sampson, Raudenbush and Earls 1997). Sampson (2001) advances the integrative concept of *community organization* which refers to 'the ability of a community structure to realize common values of its residents and maintain effective social controls' (p.8). One important component of social organization, 'collective efficacy' or the capacity of a community to enforce common norms and values (e.g. protect and monitor its children), would rest on the presence of a strong social capital, dense interconnected networks, trust among residents, social cohesion and shared willingness to intervene for the common good. Chicago researchers have demonstrated that weak collective efficacy has a very strong relationship with violence and also with low birthweight rates after controlling for concentrated disadvantage and other neighbourhood structural characteristics (Sampson 2001).

Such conceptual and empirical studies, coupled with observations on the inefficacy of traditional service approaches (see Schoor 1997), have fuelled the impetus for alternative models of intervention in the lives of children and their families. Inspired by Bronfenbrenner's ecological approach (1979), new community-based initiatives have been piloted in the US, Canada and the UK. These initiatives take different shapes (Leventhal, Brooks-Gunn and Kamerman 1997). In Model One, initiatives rely on categorical programs but add to them a community component to facilitate access to families in need and their children, to build trust with them and to provide relevant, more flexible interventions. Reforming services is the main issue. In Model Two, the emphasis is put on service integration: energy is dedicated to building stronger and denser links between service providers, between families and services and within the community at large. The main underlying concept of this model is the consolidation of relationships and networks. In Model Three, communities prefer to invest in housing and in the strenghtening of the local economy (Community Development Corporations); the emphasis is on social habitability and life spaces. Model Four is the Comprehensive Community Initiatives model, in which promoters try to integrate the first three models so as to tackle several layers of the ecological system simultaneously. This chapter explores one of these community-based initiatives currently being piloted in Montreal: *1,2,3 GO!*

The '1,2,3 GO!' initiative

'1,2,3 GO!' is a community-based demonstration project initiated and supported by a large philanthropic organization (see Bouchard 1999 for a detailed description). The initiative was implemented in 1995 in the large Montreal regional area of Canada. It involves six communities. Three of these are small neighbourhoods located in dense urban environments, two others are located in the suburbs and one is a rural municipality. In each of those communities there are between 600 and 800 children aged nought to three. The urban and suburban neighbourhoods were selected because they presented high levels of impoverishment and social risks. The rural community, although the poorest in its area, is not as impoverished. Its presence in the initiative was mainly to test the viability of this type of intervention in a rural surrounding.

The theoretical model

At the core of the initiative is the commitment to build stronger, more cohesive local communities oriented towards promoting children's well-being and development.

The conceptual model proposes that, under the leadership of a local consortium of partners, communities will succeed in improving children's development and well-being. First, fostering collaboration between community resources and services will lead to more relevant and better quality activities for children and parents. Greater participation of parents in community life will also be expected and this in turn will strengthen their sense of community. Parents' positive perceptions of community cohesion, of collective efficacy and of community services will follow from greater participation and denser social networks. It is worth noting that the main direct effects on child development (See Generated activities in Figure 15.1) are associated with the creation of high

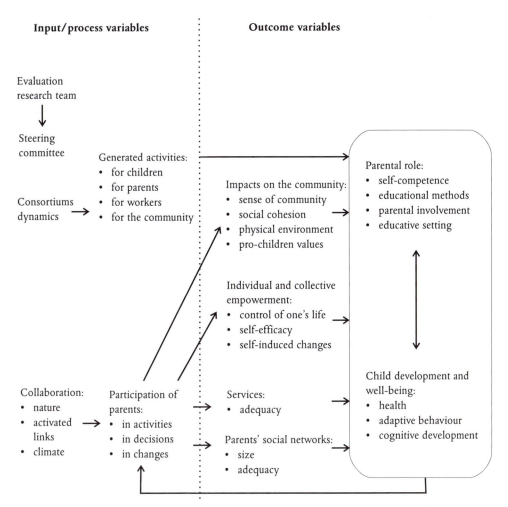

Figure 15.1: Models of predicted impacts and of relations among variables

quality activities and environments for children, families and professionals. This is in accordance with recent analyses that propose that the outcomes for children at risk improve when services are intense, continuous and of high quality, and when they involve children directly (St Pierre and Layser 1998).

The way it works

In 1,2,3 GO! communities identify their own priorities. Local consortia design and implement annual action plans specific to their neighbourhoods. For example, in one of the urban neighbourhoods, the local consortium has chosen to ensure food security for babies and their parents and to facilitate access to various services in locating several child and family resources in the same physical space. One of the suburban communities has opted to tackle the problem of the lack of stimulation for their nought- to three-year-old children, to facilitate training and back-to-work efforts for very young mothers and to improve access to family services for parents. In the rural municipality, priority was given to language acquisition, and a formal community-wide program in infant/child interactive reading was developed and offered to both parents and child care workers.

Although each local consortium is allowed to develop and implement its own action plan, it nevertheless has to comply with general guidelines such as the mobilization of large coalitions of citizens, collaboration between local institutions, services, and citizens, reaching out to vulnerable families, the direct involvement of children in enriched environments, the participation of parents in the design, management and execution of the projects, and the provision of adequate support to community workers. The underlying model for this community initiative most closely corresponds to Leventhal and colleagues' (1997) Model Two: the consolidation of relationships between providers, families and services and within the entire community is in the forefront of the project.

Evaluating 1,2,3 GO!

The design

As is evident from the above, 1,2,3 GO! is a theory-driven project; evaluating it is thus a matter of asking two types of question: (1) Is the theory well founded? and (2) Does it deliver the expected outcomes? The discussion in this chapter addresses this last question only. In order to answer it a quasi-experimental design using non-intervention communities as comparisons was adopted. A series of four biennial data collections was undertaken. During each collection wave, the researchers surveyed parents and frontline workers in intervention and comparison communities, and local consortium members in the 1,2,3 GO! communities only. We report here on two full cycles of data collection, both completed before November 2001.

The parents' survey

Every two years, a new cohort of parents of 20- to 40-month-old children is recruited through personal letters and telephone calls. There are 535 in each wave, with participation rates varying from 42 to 45 per cent. The research team elected to test the various impacts of the initiative by recruiting samples of families from a population list (Universal Family Allowances List) and *not* from a pool of families who would have attended 1,2,3 GO! Indeed, 1,2,3 GO! is not a specific program or service accessed by families. It is rather a collective collaborative initiative, aimed at improving various dimensions of the communities including, but not exclusive to, family and children's services and institutions. The researchers were also sensitive to the assumption that the initiative should impact on children of subsequent cohorts. For this reason a new cohort of families with children aged 20 to 40 months is recruited at each of the four biennial surveys.

In order to monitor impacts on the various parts of the model, the parents' survey covers a vast array of domains: the degree of their participation in community life, their perception of the community as a place to raise children, their perception of its cohesion and capacity for collective action (Sampson *et al.* 1997), their evaluation of the quality of services offered, as well as their own sense of community. The team also investigates the utilization of community resources by parents and the size and nature of their social support networks (Barrera 1980). Parental stress (Abidin 1995) and parental disciplinary strategies (Tessier, Pilon and Fecteau 1985) are also examined. Parents also answer questions on their child's health and behavioural adaptation (Behavior Problem Index: Achenbach, Edelbrock and Howell 1987). During the same home session, which lasts about three and a half hours, a trained research assistant evaluates the child, using the Bayley Scales of Infant Development (Bayley 1993). Finally, parents answer questions pertaining to their socio-economic circumstances that seek to identify three major risk factors: financial insecurity, single parenting, and low levels of parental education. These three variables constitute an important anchor in our statistical analyses.

The frontline workers and services providers survey

The second survey is completed with frontline workers and service providers, recruited from an inventory of all local community resources for children in both 1,2,3 GO! and comparison communities. The size of the two survey groups are 163 and 167 respectively, with participation rates varying from 73 to 76 per cent. In addition to several other dimensions that are not reported here, this face-to-face survey mainly addresses the question of how far the initiative impacts on the nature and intensity of collaboration between local agencies. The focus is on the participants' perceptions of the nature and climate of collaboration

234 / Safeguarding and Promoting the Well-being of Children, Families and Communities

between the various community resources for pre-school children. This is measured using the Montreal Collaboration Scale, developed from work by Himmelman (1992). The researchers also identify participants' access to any other local children's services during the year preceding the survey, and their reasons for doing so.

The local consortium survey

The researchers also monitor the evolution of local 1,2,3 GO! consortia. A mailed questionnaire is sent to all consortium members; 88 (72%) have responded. This addresses seven dimensions of the functioning of local consortia (organization, cohesion, role clarity, diversity of membership, perceived impacts, networking, planning) as well as the nature and the quality of the leadership. Members also indicate which of the following stages their consortium has reached by the time of the survey: planning, implementation of the plan, evaluation or reorientation. These evolutionary stages are discussed later in this chapter.

Findings

Collaboration data

Visual inspection of the data shows that the presence of 1,2,3 GO! may have accelerated the formalization of collaborative structures between the community resources.

Inventories of official consortiums, coalitions or concentration tables aiming to safeguard and promote the well-being of young children depict more extensive formal collaborative arrangements between child and family resources in the 1,2,3 GO! communities than in the comparison communities. This is true for almost all of the 1,2,3 GO! areas. We cannot of course completely discard the possibility that this could be due to the presence of higher needs in the 1,2,3 GO! communities resulting in earlier or simultaneous efforts initiated by other actors in these neighbourhoods.

The story is somewhat different when we look at the perception of the climate of collaboration (see Figure 15.2). Frontline workers and service providers perceive a better climate among all of the communities at Time 2 as compared with Time 1 (F=7.87; p<0.01). Perceived efforts at coordinating services do not change over time and remain similar between 1,2,3 GO! and comparison communities. However, the development of a shared vision is amplified in comparison communities, though not in 1,2,3 GO! communities at Time 2 (χ^2=6.6; p<0.01). Collaborating in a new accountable decision-making

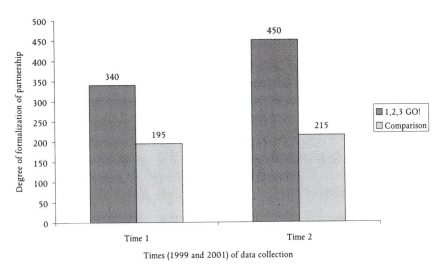

Figure 15.2: Level of formalization of partnerships among the resources of the community

environment can be seen as a long struggle to resolve divergences among organizations, at least for a transition period, and these results may, of course, reflect an increase in conflicts or misunderstandings in the 1,2,3 GO! communities as agencies plunge heavily into collaborating.

Data from parents

PARENTS' PERCEPTIONS OF THEIR COMMUNITY

Despite vigorous efforts at matching, the respective samples of families in the comparison and 1,2,3 GO! communities are not as similar as we had wished.

As Figure 15.3 shows, the proportion of families coping with two or more risk conditions is higher in the samples from the 1,2,3 GO! communities than in the comparison groups ($\chi^2 = 35.87$; p=0.000). Scores on most variables correlate with the presence of these risk factors in the lives of families, so this could constitute a bias in favour of the comparison communities when the impacts of the initiative are measured. Such a bias could make it very difficult to identify the presence of specific impacts, and we have therefore opted to use Ancovas or partial correlations in order to control at least partially for this.

Globally, parents who experience more risk factors tend to express a more negative view of their community. For example, parents coping with multiple risk conditions are less appreciative of their community as an environment in which to raise their children (F=12.56; p=0.00). On this specific measure, negative

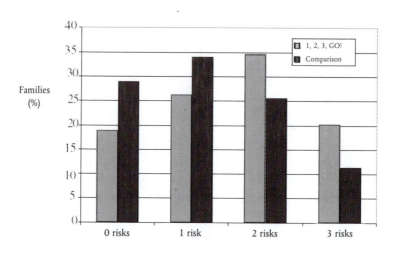

Figure 15.3: Number of risk factors present in families

perceptions are particularly evident in 1,2,3 GO! communities, even after controlling for the presence of risk factors (F=25.23; p=0.00).

Moreover this does not change with time. Parents in 1,2,3 GO! communities also show less attachment to their community at both time points (Covariance analysis: F=8.36; p<0.004). The findings also show that the more risks parents face, the less they believe that their community is cohesive and articulate enough to intervene to protect their children (collective efficacy) (F=6.66; p<0.01). There is no difference between 1,2,3 GO! and comparison communities on this issue.

As expected, parents who experience one or no risk conditions are more likely (84%) to use child care services or other community children's resources than those who are coping with three (47%) (F=58.01; p=0.00). Here again 1,2,3 GO! does not seem to make a difference over time or in comparison with matched communities.

PARENTAL ROLES AND BEHAVIOURS

Parental stress is closely related to the presence of risk factors (F=64.63; p=0.000). Parents experiencing two or three such areas of vulnerability evaluate their children as more difficult and express more doubts about their own competence. Their social networks are smaller (6.2 persons) than those of parents with only one or no risk conditions (10.4 persons) in their lives ($F=119.68$; $p=0.000$). Their networks are also more conflictual, a finding which brings us back to the notion of maternal insularity (Whaler and Dumas 1989). There is no difference between parents from 1,2,3 GO! communities and those from the comparison areas on these stress and social network variables; nor is there any evidence of change between the two time points.

The presence of multiple risk factors is also associated with the use of coercive disciplinary behaviours by parents ($F=35.09$; $p=0.000$). This is true for parents from both types of communities and at both time points.

CHILD DEVELOPMENT AND WELL-BEING

Parents who experience greater numbers of risk factors tend to report more adaptation problems with their children ($F=34.10$; $p<0.01$). There is, however, no difference between children in 1,2,3 GO! communities and those in the comparison groups. This is also true for children's scores on measures of cognitive development.

Even very young children showed highly significant differences on Bayley cognitive scores between those whose families were economically and socially secure (98) and those whose families were coping with several risk factors (85) ($F=161.79$; $p=0.000$). The data also show that the home environment of children living in multiple risk families is impoverished by a paucity of books, puzzles, toys and reading interactions with their parents (Bastien *et al.* 2002). 1,2 3 GO! does not seem to have made a difference to this situation at this point in time; 1,2,3 GO! areas show no indicators of improved stimulus in the home environment in comparison with their matched communities.

Implications of the findings

According to the 1,2,3 GO! model, and to numerous hypotheses developed in the contemporary literature (for instance, Foster-Fishman *et al.* 2001), improvements in the level and formalization of collaboration between service providers should be associated with improvements in services and ultimately with an amelioration of family well-being. However, indicators that reflect the way parents regard and relate to their community and services, the way they view themselves and their children, and scores of child well-being and cognitive development all tell a different story.

Accumulation of risk factors remains a very robust predictor of parental functioning both in regard to their community and their children. Risk factors are also heavily associated with slower cognitive development in the sample of very young children. These last results are in line with the numerous aetiological findings which show that economic pressures and the absence of cognitively stimulating material or child-centred activities in the home directly or indirectly increase the probability of slower cognitive development and the presence of adaptation problems in children (Huston, McCloyd and Garcia Coll 1994; Jean Yeung, Linver and Brooks-Gunn 2002). According to the same studies, economic pressures trigger parental depressive moods, leading to the utilization of more coercive disciplinary behaviours and the absence of stimulating activities with the child. Our data fit well with this perspective. But they also raise doubts about the capacity of an approach such as 1,2,3 GO! to trigger any significant changes in the lives of children and families exposed to such circumstances. Pre–post measures do not show any improvement and there are no noticeable differences between 1,2,3 GO! communities and their matched comparisons. All in all, the message is that 1,2,3 GO! does not make a difference, at least at this point in time.

In view of the rather disappointing findings from this study, one could be tempted to conclude that community-based initiatives should be written off as strategies to change the fate of children and families experiencing multiple conditions of risk. After all, this is yet another evaluation of such initiatives that fails to record a significant impact on the health or well-being of the target population (Kreuter, Lezin and Young 2000). However, others have reported significant improvements both at the child and family levels following the same approach. Chapter 12 discusses the introduction of one such successful initiative in Ontario. Two questions emerge in confronting the absence of significant effects in the case of 1,2,3 GO!:

1.   Do community consortia have access to the best available knowledge and do they use it in their action plan?

2.   Are we using the most appropriate research approach in evaluating such initiatives?

Do community consortia have access to the best available knowledge and do they use it?

The overall message delivered by contemporary research is quite clear: to make a significant impact on the development of vulnerable children, we need to invest in programs which offer intensive, early intervention services that offer continuity, and that are tailored to children's developmental needs and their parents' culture (Ramey and Landesman Ramey 1998; St Pierre and Layser

1998). Many programs have been designed, tested and are available for dissemination (see for instance those described in Chapters 7 and 11). At the same time, the literature identifies clear limits to the traditional institutional model of dissemination (Schoor 1997). One major problem, among several, is the difficulty in delivering these programs to those children and parents who are experiencing high or multiple risk conditions (Leventhal *et al.* 1997).

Community-based local consortia are looked at as an alternative means of reaching out to these families and solving problems related to mismanagement of local resources (Schoor 1997). In the case of 1,2,3 GO!, as in many such initiatives, grass-roots organizations and parents participate the most in local consortia. These groups are regarded as very efficient in their capacity for reaching vulnerable families. They hold values such has citizen empowerment and participation, community ownership and cultural diversity that make them very receptive to local knowledge and sensitive to cultural differences. Researchers and administrators of statutory services, without necessarily dismissing these values and assets, are more likely to favour clear lines of power and communication and evidence-based knowledge. Discussions and trade-offs then arise between administrators of statutory services, researchers and grass-roots organizations about what type of expertise might be considered most valuable. Compromises have to be reached concerning the objectives and strategies to be adopted. These compromises can, as we have been able to observe in the annual plans of local consortia, generate a multiplicity of objectives and strategies that can dilute the intensity of the intervention. Sustaining consortium members in their capacity to act effectively, to focus on the main targets, and to invest in tested approaches thus becomes a high priority. New models of intervention, such as Communities that Care, which base community decision-making processes on data about local risk and protective factors and propose a menu of best practices to local consortia may well improve community capacities in this area (Greenberg 2001; Hawkins, Catalano and Associates 1992).

Are we using the most appropriate research methods?

There are also several important issues to be discussed concerning the choice of a quasi-experimental methodology to evaluate initiatives such as these (see Berkowitz 2001 for a review). As has been evident throughout the implementation process of 1,2,3 GO!, communities do not stand still. They change along the way. The comparison communities, which had been chosen from census data as being equivalent to those implementing 1,2,3 GO!, showed important differences in the profiles of supposedly matched samples at both data collection points. This is an issue that is by no means unique to this study (see Ward *et al.* 2004), but it considerably limits the conclusions that can be drawn from the findings.

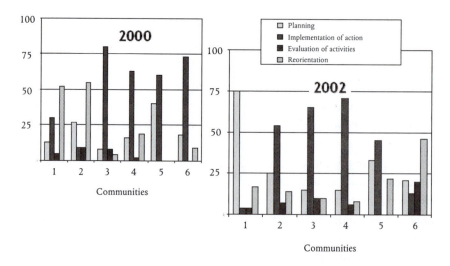

Figure 15.4: Stage of the initiative in January 2000 and 2002 according to consortium members

Initiatives can change as well as neighbourhoods (Foster-Fishman *et al.* 2001). Members of the local consortia of 1,2,3 GO! were asked to identify which of the four stages (planning, implementation, evaluation and reorientation) their initiative had reached at the time of each survey. As can be seen in Figure 15.4, things do not stand still, nor do they follow a linear path. For example, in 2000, the initiative in Community 1 was mostly perceived by its members as being in a reorientation mode. Two years later, after a period of intense reflection and struggle with unexpected challenges, the community wrote up a new plan of action. Proceeding with concrete, tangible projects had to be put on hold for a lengthy period. On the other hand, Community 2 had quite clearly begun to question its future direction by 2000 (reorientation phase). In 2002, it had returned to an active mode, though there was still some planning to complete. Community 6 passed from an implementation mode in 2000 to a reorientation phase in 2002. Only Communities 3, 4 and 5 presented a stable pattern throughout the study period. These data point to two important phenomena. First, the dynamics of communities are complex and may unfold in an apparently chaotic way; traditional methodologies for evaluation may not be suited to grasping this type of complexity. Second, in this context, changes and impacts may be slow to manifest themselves in a model of service integration such as 1,2,3, GO! (Casey Foundation 1995). If we consider that 1,2,3 GO! was first introduced in 1995, that the first stage of setting up the consortium, assessing needs, planning and writing the action agenda takes from one and a half to two years, it could be that significant changes in families and children will be detectable only at a later time point.

Figure 15.4 also reveals a very important but easily forgotten characteristic of community-based projects: their uniqueness. Considering them as a group, as we have chosen to do for this round of analysis, ignores their local evolution and may mean that subtle outcomes occurring in one or two communities pass unnoticed. However reverting to the analysis of individual case studies does not really allow us to test apparent contradictions or to answer the question: 'But what if the intervention had not been there?' The number of participants varies between 43 and 55 in each community; such small numbers would present a threat to internal validity if each community were to be evaluated separately. Moreover, qualitative appraisal of changes through key informants or focus groups suffers from the reputed bias of perceptions that have to be counterbalanced or triangulated with other methods. Finding the right methodological balance to evaluate such community-based outcomes has now become a challenge for the entire scientific community (Berkowitz 2001).

Acknowledgements

This study was supported by generous grants offered by the Fonds québécois de recherche sur la société et la culture, the Canadian Institutes for Health Research, and the Québec Ministry of Health and Social Services. The McConell Family Foundation also contributed very generously in supporting the first phases of the study.

The author wishes to thank the following colleagues and students who contributed comments and suggestions: Marie-France Bastien, Nathalie Bastien, Natalie Cormier, Eliza Denis, Mireille Desrochers, Julie Goulet, Geneviève Gratton, Gérard Malcuit, Jacques Moreau, Andrée Pomerleau and Julie-Anne Risler. Special thanks to Danielle Blanchard who planned and completed the statistical analyses.

Part V

Conclusion

Chapter 16

Dude, Where's My Outcomes?

Partnership Working and Outcome-based Accountability in the UK

Mark Friedman, Louise Garnett and Mike Pinnock

This chapter describes the experience of applying the ideas of outcome-based accountability to partnership working in an English setting. It describes the characteristics of this approach, explores how it has been used within a local strategic partnership (LSP) in the UK and outlines some of the lessons that might be drawn from the experience. Finally, the chapter explores how these ideas have influenced the way in which one partner agency within the LSP has designed its approach to performance review and service development.

Introduction

Earlier chapters in this book have explored the prevalence of need and its consequences, and the effectiveness of specific policies and programmes designed to promote the well-being of children, families and communities. The two concluding chapters consider how outcomes can be routinely monitored.

The idea of outcome-based accountability introduces a more disciplined way of thinking about how partnerships can move from talk to action in delivering better outcomes for children and families. It presents a way of organizing the process of policy decision-making around a clear set of desired outcomes. The approach described in this chapter has now been used, in whole or in part, in over 40 states in the US and in a number of states and municipalities in countries such as Australia, Holland, Ireland, Norway and Chile.

The approach has a number of distinctive features. First, it recognizes that, to be effective, partnerships must share a common language to which people ascribe common meaning. Second, it stresses the importance of making a clear distinction between measuring outcomes at population level and measuring performance at an agency level. Third, it insists that accountability processes should involve a minimum of bureaucracy. Finally, the approach assumes the involvement of stakeholders and communities at each stage of the process and at all levels of decision making. Hence, the term partnership used in this context describes any collaboration of local agencies and local people that might play a part in bringing about better outcomes for local children and young people. Although this chapter focuses on the well-being of children, the framework described here can be applied to any sub-population (for example, older people, people with learning disabilities) and to the well-being of the whole population of a town, city, county or country.

Background

This chapter explores the experiences of working with the ideas of outcome-based accountability[1] in North Lincolnshire Social Services, a department of an English unitary authority providing adult and children's social services to a population of about 152,000. Interest within the authority focused on developing an approach to performance review and service improvement that moved from the traditional concerns of economy and efficiency towards effectiveness. The work began in 1998 and initially focused primarily on children in care, children on the child protection register and other children in need (including children with disabilities).

There were three main influences on the design of the approach: first, the authority's involvement in a government-funded research project looking at how data about the outcomes of individual children in public care might be collected, aggregated and used to support decision making within agencies (Ward *et al.* 2002); second, work on results and performance-based accountability that was emerging from the US, principally from the Annie E. Casey Foundation, the Finance Project, and the Fiscal Policies Studies Institute;[2] third, the authority was influenced by its own experiences of trying to find ways of engaging operational staff and managers in systematically assessing outcomes for service users. This had led to the development of a process of quarterly performance review that was centred on a clear set of desired outcomes. This approach is now used routinely to review performance across all services areas in the North Lincolnshire Council.

Although the approach to performance review proved to be a successful way of stimulating work to improve outcomes for specific groups of service users, it did not transfer easily to partnership working directed towards bringing better outcomes for children and young people at a population level. In order to do this, more attention was given to the distinction that writers in the US were making between performance- and outcome-based accountability. Such ideas are now being used by a small number of local authorities in the UK as a way of structuring the work of local strategic partnerships. For example, North East Lincolnshire LSP is using this approach to help integrate the desired outcomes and actions of all strategic partnerships operating in their area and to monitor the health, social, economic and environmental well-being of its resident population.

There has also been a movement at a national level towards knowledge-based, outcome-focused policy making and programme design. Initiatives such as Sure Start (HM Treasury 1998) and Quality Protects (Department of Health 1999) are two such examples. Both are based on an explicit body of research knowledge and both have their own arrangements for performance monitoring and evaluation.

Recently, there has also been a move by central government away from simply collecting data about inputs and outputs (and therefore measuring effort) in favour of national returns that attempt to measure the outcomes (and therefore effectiveness) of local services. This is not just about counting different things. As Power (1997) points out, it represents a shift from the logic of audit to the logic of evaluation:

> One logic has developed from a home base in input auditing, focusing on the regularity of transactions, towards the audit of measurable outputs. The other, though not without problems and much less coherent than audit as a practice, is traditionally more sensitive to the complexities of connecting service processes to outcomes. (p.115)

Data from these processes are now being actively used to judge, control and regulate the work of local authorities through the introduction of the national Performance Assessment Frameworks (PAF) (Department of Health 2000a).

National returns include data about progress towards population-level outcomes; the effectiveness of partnership working on issues such as teenage pregnancies, educational attainment and child health; as well as data about the performance of individual agencies. Measures that track the performance of specific services such as child welfare, education and health include performance indicators on compliance, service take up, service volume and process management. Both outcome and performance-based data from local returns are aggregated at a national level in the UK to assess improvements in the overall quality of life for children and families and to provide a national picture of the performance of individual agencies.

Talking the talk – the language of accountability

> The first step to wisdom is getting things by their right name.
>
> *Chinese saying*

Language is often the first barrier faced when we commit ourselves to partnership working. Past reviews and inspections of joint planning have shown how lack of clarity often hinders progress between agencies involved in planning children's services (see Audit Commission 1994; Department of Health 1998a). Typically a children's planning group that is working at a population level brings together people from a wide range of lay and professional backgrounds: social workers, community leaders, nurses, teachers, police officers, accountants and so on. Efforts at partnership working can easily turn into a Tower of Babel. We hear words that are unfamiliar or words that are familiar used in unfamiliar ways. This problem is not just one of jargon and technical language. Often we are simply lazy in our use of language – words lack precision or are applied inconsistently. Imprecise terminology becomes a barrier to partnership working.

However it is possible to help partnerships develop self-discipline in their use of language, for 'words are just labels for ideas. And the same idea can have many different labels' (Friedman 2000). A lack of progress can often reflect a failure to develop an effective means of communicating. If left unattended, this problem will limit the effectiveness of partnership working. Focusing on language allows us to bring to the surface the differences of beliefs, values and aspirations that can prevent the partnership from moving on.

Outcome and performance accountability

The ideas of outcome and performance accountability are based around four key ideas: outcomes; outcome indicators; strategy; and performance indicators.

Outcomes

Outcomes describe conditions of well-being for children and families or for whole communities. For example desired outcomes are that: children are safe;

young people are prepared for adulthood; children live in families. These simple aspirations are the central purposes of public services.

Outcomes can help partnership working in three ways:

- They tell us where we are trying to get to – partnerships can define their purpose around a clear set of 'desired outcomes' that describe aspirations for the future and define what success would look like.

- They help focus collective attention on how we might get there – once we understand our clear set of desired outcomes (the ends), we can focus on the best way of getting there (the means) by identifying 'what works' in bringing about the sorts of outcomes that local people have identified as desirable.

- They help us understand whether we are getting there – partnerships can learn by measuring progress towards the desired outcomes. This process also provides a way of exercising accountability to funders and taxpayers. The feedback can have both an internal purpose (learning) and an external purpose (accountability).

Desired outcomes must be stated in plain language, for example: children are ready to start school; communities feel safe and so on. They describe the things that matter to the well-being of whole populations, irrespective of whether they are directly receiving services.

Outcome indicators

> If you do not know where you are going, any road will take you there.
>
> *Paraphrased from The Cheshire Cat in*
> Alice's Adventures in Wonderland *by Lewis Carroll*

Indicators help us to judge the overall effect of our collective efforts towards achieving a given outcome. Indicators can apply to whole populations or sub-populations that may, for instance, include people who live within a specific ethnic community or locality. In the UK, Sure Start began by focusing resources on young children who lived in particular neighbourhoods. The indicators assess the collective efforts of partnership members in improving their health and readiness for school. In contrast, the Quality Protects initiative focused on improving the effectiveness of partnership working for a sub-group of the local population: vulnerable children and young people who may be in need of family support services.

Strategies

> I am convinced more and more day by day that fine writing
> is, next to fine doing, the top thing in the world.
>
> *John Keats (1795–1821)*

Whilst recognizing the importance of 'fine writing', the ultimate test of a strategy is in 'fine doing'. The commonly held view that planning is something that is separated from doing is neither sustainable nor desirable. There is more value in seeing planning as a form of collective learning. It forms an integral part of strategy which can be defined as the process of collective learning towards actions that stand a *reasoned chance* of bringing about desired outcomes in any given situation. Kubisch and Connell (1998) refer to this reasoning process as 'a theory of change', and emphasize how strategy should be based on a theory of change that is:

- *plausible* – what evidence do we have that the actions will deliver the desired outcomes?

- *do-able* – what collective resources are available to deliver the actions?

- *testable* – how will we know if it is working?

The logic of this approach requires partnerships to consider the evidence base on which their collective actions are predicated. They must also be transparent in demonstrating their selection and use of evidence. This brings a useful discipline to partnership working. It also helps avoid the strategy becoming a disparate collection of 'pet projects'.

Performance indicators

> Weighing the pig won't make it fatter.
>
> *Popular witticism*

Experience of public sector performance management systems in the UK and the US has led to growing cynicism with systems that concentrate on 'weighing the pig'. If the aim is to develop systems that support learning within partner agencies and provide fair and transparent measures of accountability, attention should be directed towards 'nutrition' and 'weight gain'.

Performance indicators are measures of how well public, private and not-for-profit agencies, programmes and service systems are managing the processes that contribute to overall outcomes. They can be divided into three simple categories: 'How much did we do?', 'How well did we do it?' and 'Is anyone better off?' The last category covers customer outcomes for the programme, agency or service system, as distinct from whole-population outcomes that span beyond this group. Service-user outcomes are the key performance measures: they focus on what individual partner agencies or service systems must get right as their contribution toward the achievement of agreed population outcomes. Within performance management systems, service-user outcomes are the ends and service delivery methods are the means.

This local-level approach to performance measurement again emphasizes the interdependence of local agencies in bringing about better outcomes for local children. For example, a partnership might aspire to ensure that children achieve their potential at school. Traditionally in the UK, people would hold the local educational authority (LEA) to account for this outcome. However, success depends on many other critical factors beyond the control and influence of the local education authority, including the child's health status, his or her experience of family life, family income, availability of transport and decent housing. The linkages between these factors are by no means tenuous or contrived. For example, as Chapter 14 has demonstrated, overcrowding, poor structural conditions, poor ventilation, lack of affordable warmth, frequent moves, location and proximity to schools and homelessness all influence the likelihood of a child enjoying and achieving at school.

The next section describes in more detail the experience of the unitary authority in applying these ideas.

Walking the walk: Applying the ideas of outcome-based accountability

A very simple and logical thinking process can help direct the work of a local partnership in developing an inclusive, bottom-up approach to constructing strategies that make a difference. In the following example, outlined schematically in Figure 16.1, the population of interest is infants and pre-school children, but the same thinking process could be applied to many other population groups and inter-agency partnerships (for further details see www.raguide.org).

The process can be summarized as follows:

- What do we want to achieve for infants and pre-school children?
- How would we recognize it in measurable terms?
- What will it take to get us there and who ar the partners that have a role to play?

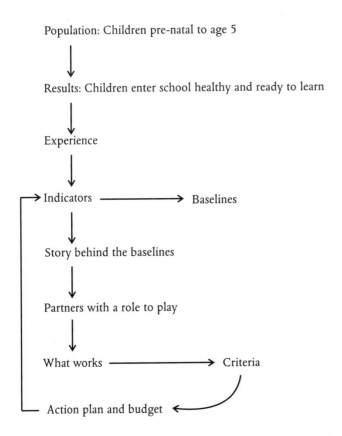

Population: Children pre-natal to age 5

Results: Children enter school healthy and ready to learn

Experience

Indicators ——————————→ Baselines

Story behind the baselines

Partners with a role to play

What works ——————————→ Criteria

Action plan and budget

Figure 16.1: Outcome-based decision making: Getting from talk to action

What do we want to achieve?

Outcome-based accountability starts by identifying a population of interest, for example, all pre-school children. Anchoring strategies in simple statements of desired well-being such as, 'Children are born healthy and flourish, and enter school ready and able to learn', can help communicate the basic purpose of a partnership's actions in ways that the public can understand, and with which all stakeholders would readily agree. Some local policymakers are attracted to using 'off-the-peg' outcome statements on the grounds that they save time and, they believe, carry greater weight. However, drafting and agreeing locally desired outcomes is an important part of the process, not only in terms of securing ownership and commitment, but also in establishing common meaning.

How will we know if we are making a difference?

First, there is what the whole community can experience and observe. For example, we can recognize that children are healthy and flourishing by seeing more young children playing in our parks and playgrounds, fewer living in poor housing conditions, and so on.

As well as generating local ownership of outcome measures, going through this 'how would we know' exercise with parents and other residents may highlight issues of local concern that are not routinely reported. It may also suggest a more diverse group of partners with a critical role to play than might otherwise have been considered.

The next step is to select data that demonstrate, in measurable terms, whether these conditions of well-being exist in the population. The best indicators are those that come closest to measuring the achievement of the desired outcome (proxy power), have resonance with local residents and other stakeholders (communication power) and have a track record of robust, local data behind them (data power). These will typically draw on perceptions and experiences, as well as objective measures. Some data will be available and some will need to be collected. It may be useful to identify which items need to be collected within the main work of the partnership. This maintains a link between the identification of indicators and the overall partnership strategy. It also helps those staff involved in data management to identify their responsibilities.

In the case of pre-school children, most statutory agencies will already collect a range of data that could be used to monitor outcomes at a population level. In the UK the indicators routinely monitored by NHS Primary Care Trusts include: infant deaths per 1000 live births, dental decay in five-year-olds, low weight births, child immunization rates and accidental child deaths (Department of Health 2002a). Housing departments hold data on the number of homeless families in temporary accommodation, whilst national data sets routinely report on the number of young children in low income families at local authority and ward level (National Statistics 2003). Local education authorities also gather information about children's achievements towards early learning goals and will provide indicators of their readiness for school at a local authority level.
The perceptions of parents and other local residents are also important barometers of children's well-being and may already be collected via local surveys.

Establishing a matrix of potential data sources makes it easier to shortlist candidate indicators and highlights priorities for further development. One important factor will be the frequency with which data are reported. Is this often enough to allow partners to monitor progress? Are data sufficient to allow changes to be measured? Other factors include whether indicators have resonance with the local community, and how well they link with the local priorities and Public Service Agreement targets.

The next stage is to present a picture for each indicator of where we have been and where we are headed if we stay on our current course. These baseline pictures allow success to be defined as doing better than previously. They can also stimulate shared learning at a local level and help agencies and the community develop a shared understanding of how each can contribute to better outcomes.

What will it take to get us there?

It is important to explore the stories behind the baseline data. As this work develops there will inevitably be unresolved questions; these may form part of a local information/research agenda.

Questions to explore include: What do we *think* would work? What would it *take* to do better than the observed baselines in *this* area? What has worked in other places? What does research evidence tell us is effective? Just as importantly, what does our own personal experience tell us about what would work here? The answers should draw on the possible contributions of all partners, including public and private agencies, and should include no-cost and low-cost ideas. For example, research evidence from this country and from the US suggests that home visiting can significantly reduce accidental injuries to under-twos in the home, especially those living in areas with high social deprivation (Lucas 2003). Local knowledge about what might work in a specific area might include evidence of what local parents and families say are the barriers to changing safety practices; the type and tenure of housing; and the feasibility of using lay visitors.

The process may result in a long list of things that might work. So what criteria should guide the selection process? These might include *specificity* (is the idea about specific action, not rhetoric?), *leverage* (will it make a large or small difference?), *values* (is it consistent with our personal and community values?), and *reach* (when can this be done?).

A long-term action plan should be developed, specifying what is to be accomplished by when. Responsibilities can then be assigned and work started. Once decisions have been made, performance measures can be used to track progress. One outcome of this process should be the development of a coherent and comprehensive strategy. This process can be repeated at routine intervals, each time refining the strategy and action plan.

Learning points in applying the idea of outcome-based accountability

Building capacity

Whilst the process summarized above may appear simple and straightforward, the resources required to implement it should not be underestimated. Partnerships need to be nurtured and so the process of developing a common language, common outcomes and indicators as well as a common system for sharing ideas and reviewing evidence of effectiveness will inevitably take time. Keeping partners engaged can be difficult when there are so many competing demands on their time.

The key issue is to coordinate, rationalize and monitor the contribution of each partner to children's well-being. This is likely to require a dedicated member of staff. Resources may also be required to develop local databases so outcomes can be monitored over time.

It is important to accept the limitations of our attempts to define the collective experience of peoples' lives in mere numbers. Constructs such as well-being, social inclusion, autonomy and happiness do not lend themselves to the measurement of success in the way that profitability, share value and sales volume do in the business world. Nevertheless, some limitations can be overcome by seeing measures and indicators as a starting place for inquiry and not the end, by working with local residents in the review of partnership performance on outcomes, and by always presenting quantitative data alongside other forms of feedback which allow people to tell the underlying story. Data can be powerful tools for opening up a discussion with local people. To keep this dialogue alive, the experiences and perceptions of the local community should be adequately represented in the ongoing monitoring and presentation of evidence.

Using performance accountability to improve programme performance

Performance accountability focuses on the contribution individual agencies, service systems and programmes make to the realization of desired outcomes. The emphasis is on developing feedback systems that work for the people who actually deliver and manage front-line services (see www.raguide.org for further guidance). Since the late 1980s various models have emerged to encourage managers to see performance as something more than counting inputs and outputs, the most notable of these being Kaplan and Norton's Balanced Scorecard (1992). This proposes a multi-dimensional view of performance, typically based around Customer Results, Internal Processes, Innovation and Learning and Financial, and is being increasingly used in the public sector.

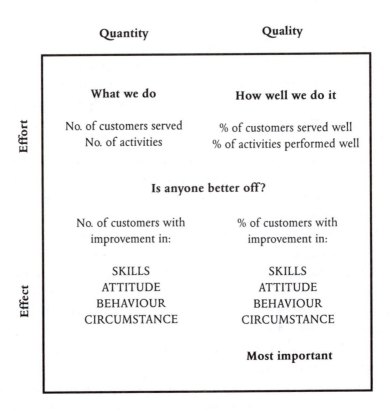

Figure 16.2: Four types of performance measures

Our overall approach can be summarized by Figure 16.2. It suggests that the three key routine questions are:

- How much did we do? For instance how many people used the service over a given period?

- How well did we do it? What did users think about the service? Was it accessible? Did it offer the right sort of help? What do those who did not use the service think? How could it be made more attractive to prospective users?

- Is anyone better off? Has the service addressed a specific problem? Is there any evidence that it has combined with other services (such as education and training, welfare benefits advice, counselling services, leisure and recreational activities) and contributed to better outcomes?

Some local authorities are now routinely using these exact questions to classify performance measures. This simple, comprehensive categorization has allowed them to drop the jargon-laden and overly complex categories. This in turn makes the process of accountability more accessible to the public they are seeking to serve.

The latter two questions are the most important. These help operational managers to steer and judge the performance of the areas for which they are responsible. 'How well did we do it' (upper right quadrant) indicators include:

- Performance indicators to support the good management of the resources that produce the service, i.e. people, budgets, buildings and so on. These could include indicators relating to staff recruitment and retention, the contribution of volunteers, the management of costs, investment in training and learning.

- Performance indicators that support the good management of service quality and processes, i.e. timeliness, accessibility, reliability and cultural competence. These could include indicators of service-user perceptions of agency staff attitudes, response times and any other measurements of the attributes that users have said they value.

The most important (lower quadrants) measures tell us whether users are better off as a consequence of receiving the service. Effectiveness can be measured along four dimensions: Did *skills* improve? Did *attitudes* change for the better? Did *behaviour* change for the better? Are *life circumstances* improved in some demonstrable way? So, for example, a manager overseeing a child care program might want to measure such things as:

- the percentage of children with basic literacy skills (skills)
- the percentage of children with a positive self image (attitude)
- the percentage of children exhibiting disruptive behaviour (behaviour)
- the percentage who go on to succeed in their first years at school (circumstance).

Asking 'What needs to go well?' should prevent us from falling into the trap of defining solutions purely in terms of arrangements that already exist. Questions about performance need to be addressed to both *existing* and *prospective* service users, otherwise there is a danger that we lose sight of the things that are preventing people from accessing services. Potential clients or customers may not use a service for a variety of reasons: it may lack cultural competence, be stigmatizing, be inaccessible – or they may simply be unaware of it. There is a danger that by focusing on service activity, performance measurement systems simply overlook this latent demand.

Learning points from applying the ideas of performance accountability

The ideas of performance accountability bring us on to more familiar ground. New Labour has made extensive use of performance measurement frameworks in the public sector as a means of regulating the implementation of their policies and restoring confidence in public services. Critics argue that far from building trust, these systems might actually have the reverse effect.

> The pursuit of ever more perfect accountability provides citizens and consumers, patients and parents with more information, more comparisons, more complaints systems; but it also builds a culture of suspicion, low morale and may ultimately lead to professional cynicism, and then we would have grounds for public mistrust. (O'Neill 2002)

Harris (2003, p.40) has argued that this 'new accountability' is creating a further erosion of trust and confidence in professional social work, placing additional financial costs on agencies and diverting capacity away from work to actually improve services and develop practice.

It is quite likely that adverse experiences of 'performance management' have already created resistance to the sort of ideas described in this chapter. However experience suggests that, under the right conditions, well-designed performance reports can be effective in supporting organizational learning within child welfare agencies (see Moore, Rapp and Roberts 2000, p.491; Pinnock and Dimmock 2003, p.280). The antecedents for the approach proposed can be traced to the quiet, prescient work of child care researchers such as Packman, Rowe and Parker who, in the 1970s and 80s, anticipated the possibility of child care agencies routinely collecting data in order to evaluate their own practice.

The approach used by the authority has a number of distinctive features:

- Local systems are being designed to help local people judge and understand the effectiveness of local services. This has involved developing and reporting on local indicators which 'fill the gaps' left by national performance frameworks.

- The 'design and build process' has been inclusive. Local service users, their advocates, and front-line staff have been involved in the processes outlined. For example, each of the outcome statements has been the subject of consultation with service users, their carers and advocates.

- Ways of involving service users, their carers and their advocates in the review of feedback information and in decisions about the development of the service are being developed. For example, at service review meetings, young people with a learning disability present their experiences of services alongside the statistical information.

- The information collected is used to help find ways to improve the design of services and develop practice. It is not used to 'name and shame'.

- Individual partners build their ideas of performance around the conditions of well-being that they hope to achieve for service users. When done properly, the outcomes set for services align naturally with the population-level outcomes the local strategic partnership is collectively seeking to achieve at a community level.

A distinction should be made between the internal and external purposes of performance measurement. The internal purpose is served when feedback data are used as a source of learning, the external purpose when data are used to hold agencies to account for their performance. There needs to be a balance between the two. However, little use is currently made of structured feedback within social care agencies and many managers view the production of performance data purely in terms of completing apparently meaningless government returns (Gatehouse, Statham and Ward 2004). Moreover, when individual agencies are held accountable for outcomes that are a collective responsibility, we see evidence of the 'dysfunctional effects' that writers such as Smith (1993) predicted.

By working with the ideas of performance accountability, the unitary authority has tried to develop systems at an agency level that staff actually value and trust. The key learning points were:

- Start with a set of desired outcomes and work forward from there. Often the enthusiasm of front-line staff and managers for the ideas of outcome- and performance-based accountability lies not so much in the fact that they can see where they have been, but that often for the first time they have a clear idea of where they are supposed to be going (see also Casey Family Foundation 1999).

- Staff and service users must be involved at all stages. If staff are encouraged to work with service users to agree outcomes and design their own indicators and measures they will develop a greater sense of ownership and a deeper level of understanding.

- Focus on outcomes for local people, not data for bureaucracy. A recent survey concluded that people come into public service because they want to 'make a difference', specifically with children and people vulnerable to social exclusion. The principal reason for leaving public sector work is excessive bureaucracy and lack of resources (Audit Commission 2002). We must accept that public servants want to make a difference to the quality of people's lives – not to some arbitrary measure of their performance.

- Be alert to the risks and dysfunctional behaviours. As with any performance measurement system, this approach carries its own risks and potential for abuse. If implemented badly it can create the sort of perverse incentives and dysfunctional behaviours that have been seen in other systems (Goddard and Smith 2001). As Schorr (1995, p.6) points out, the important thing is to anticipate and minimize these risks.

- Process makes perfect. It is important to make sure that in our enthusiasm to develop outcome-based measures, we do not overlook the importance of data on inputs (such as human resources and finance) and key processes (such as screening and assessment). Good service-user outcomes are dependent on good inputs. In family support, for instance, these are largely dependent on the quality of the relationship between the agency staff and the service user, rather than on the actual design of the service (Dunst, Trivette and Deal 1994). Unless data about process can be captured, it is not possible to understand whether those things that are expected to contribute to better outcomes are actually happening. Moreover, because of the lag between service actions and service-user outcomes, process data are often all that is available to help us judge whether things are heading in the right direction.

Conclusion

This chapter gives an account of one English local authority's experiences of working with the ideas of outcome- and performance-based accountability. It sets out ideas that can be used to help local partnerships engage with local communities to realize their collective ambitions.

Public sector agencies in the UK have experience of heavily centralized command and control style management that has led to conditions in which it may be difficult to engage interest in these ideas – particularly in areas such as health care, education and, to a lesser extent, social care. For this reason this chapter has emphasized the need to see both outcome-based work at a population level and performance accountability at an agency level as processes that guide and enrich partnership learning.

Notes

1   The term 'result' is often used an alternative to 'outcome'. For the sake of clarity and consistency, we will use the term outcome as this is more familiar to readers outside of the US.

2   See www.aecf.org; www.financeproject.org; www.resultsaccountability.com.

Chapter 17

Evaluating Interventions and Monitoring Outcomes

Jane Scott, Terry Moore and Harriet Ward

This concluding chapter explores a growing trend on both sides of the Atlantic to introduce routine evaluation of services and monitoring of outcomes into child welfare agencies. Practical and technical approaches to the use and analysis of data are discussed, together with the importance of valuing the skills and experience of practitioners and developing an organizational culture that supports learning. The Integrated Children's System, a comprehensive methodology for assessing need, making plans, monitoring interventions and assessing outcomes, is introduced. Systems such as this may help organizations develop a better understanding of need and the effectiveness of interventions designed to safeguard and promote the well-being of children, families and communities.

Introduction

Chapter 1 of this book has demonstrated how, in spite of their affluence, many Western societies still need to take action to meet the United Nations millennium goals for the well-being of children. Subsequent chapters have explored further the evidence of need and its consequences, and considered how effective interventions can contribute to safeguarding and improving the well-being of children, families and communities.

On both sides of the Atlantic there has been a growing consensus among politicians and policymakers that public welfare agencies should routinely evaluate their performance and monitor outcomes for the population they serve. In the US, an important signpost of this consensus has been the passage of the

Adoption and Safe Families Act 1997 (ASFA). This legislation formalized desired outcomes for child welfare services and created the Child and Family Services Review, a federal oversight procedure for monitoring outcomes in each state in terms of child safety, permanent living arrangements and well-being. State child welfare agencies are required to reach 'substantial compliance' with the outcomes specified by the ASFA. If this is not achieved, agencies are required to develop a 'program improvement plan' and, if these efforts fail over time, financial consequences are applied to the organization. The creation of standards and the implementation of a federal oversight process have set the stage for a new approach to managing child welfare programmes.

A similar initiative in the UK has led to the articulation of a range of desired outcomes and performance assessment ratings for social services in England and Wales; these form part of a comprehensive performance assessment programme for all local government services (Social Services Inspectorate 2003). Star ratings for social services are based on ten key performance indicators, as well as on reviews of strategic plans and reports from bodies such as the Social Services Inspectorate and the Audit Commission. Star ratings have implications for freedom of action rather than finances:

> The best performing councils have an increased level of freedom in the way they use centrally provided grant funds. They also have a reduced programme of inspection and monitoring and reduced requirements for planning information. Councils with zero stars receive additional support, return fuller information, and are subject to more frequent monitoring. (Social Services Inspectorate 2003, p.2)

Key indicators for children's services for the most recent ratings include stability of placements and educational qualifications of looked after children, reviews of child protection cases, adoptions of looked after children and results of an audit of children's services in response to the Climbié Inquiry (Laming 2003). They form part of a comprehensive and detailed programme that requires statutory child welfare organizations to measure performance and reach specific targets with the aim of optimizing outcomes for children and families.

As Chapter 16 has demonstrated, such a programme presents major challenges, for it demands a sophisticated approach to identifying goals at local as well as national levels and monitoring progress towards them. The complex, changing and variable nature of child welfare provision, together with pressures such as high turnover and a decreasing workforce, mean that it is often difficult for organizations to define clear, achievable goals. In their absence, the need to comply with procedures and to avoid censure can become the major focus of management. As Chapter 16 has also shown, there are concerns that to focus singularly on performance indicators imposed by central government as the standard for the success of programmes or initiatives is problematic. Practice standards can be abandoned or greatly diminished in the process. Too narrow a focus on arbitrary targets can inhibit the accumulation of knowledge and expertise (Casey Family Foundation 1999) and draw attention away from the best practices supported by research evidence (Poertner 2001). Performance indicators may be further limited if data is outdated or only available in aggregate form.

In order to improve the delivery of services to children and families in the community and to develop processes that make sense to practitioners, it is also necessary to develop standards for evidence-based practice. Setting standards can be complex; few practice interventions have withstood the test of randomized trials, systematic reviews or meta-analysis (Macdonald 1998), although there are some examples in this book (see for instance Chapters 5, 12, 13 and 15). However, in addition to specific programmes such as these, the complexities of delivering more general social care services also require evidence-based practice, defined as 'the conscientious, explicit and judicious use of current best evidence in making decisions about individuals' (Sackett, Straus and Richardson 1997 cited in Poertner 2001, p.97). Professional judgements need to be informed by and inform current best practice.

This is not to promote the view that attention should be directed away from optimizing the outcomes for children and families, but that both evidence-based practice, which includes professional judgement and expertise, and good quality data should play a role in guiding, shaping and developing services and the systems required to support them. Three requirements for using data to improve performance through such a results- or outcome-based approach have been identified:

1. An organizational culture that supports learning.

2. Sufficient managerial skills to analyse and use information.

3. An information system to store, retrieve and produce reports which enhance the understanding of what is happening on a daily basis to individual and groups of children.

(Rapp and Poertner 1992, p.93)

An organizational culture that supports learning

The culture in the organization

Those developing policy or working with vulnerable children and families should understand the future implications of unmet need (see Chapters 2 and 4). When governments recognize this and take steps to tackle some of these issues, there can be a greater drive and impetus to deliver such policies locally. When the focus from government is absent it is easy for policies to become fragmented and be considered a lower priority at a local level (see Chapter 7).

However, setting the scene nationally does not, in itself, ensure that policies or programmes continue to be delivered locally. As Chapter 16 demonstrates, practitioners and managers in local child welfare organizations need to develop a shared understanding for working collaboratively, and to be clear about where they are coming from, where they want to get to and how they might reach their goals.

In any organization, the culture shapes the attitudes, values and behaviours of its members and is communicated through formal (performance reviews, training, management meetings) and informal (observation, 'grapevine', mentors, supervision) channels (Leichtman 1996). The culture of an organization is difficult to recognize, let alone change.

Historically, social services both in the UK and US have lacked a culture of systematic analysis (Bamford 1996). The reasons for this need to be addressed before practitioners and managers will use an outcome-based approach effectively. The overwhelming needs of children and families, limited resources, a constantly changing workforce, the number of high profile inquiries into the deaths of children in public care or known to child welfare agencies, and the views of the press and public have all contributed to a defensive mentality of staff and managers delivering welfare services. This makes it difficult to admit problems or to create a safe environment in which to address them.

There are also concerns about the poor quality of data collected by practitioners and their frequent failure to understand its potential both in the management of individual cases as well as in the evaluation of the service as a whole. In England and Wales, the increasing requirements placed on child welfare organizations by government have led some practitioners to view collecting information as a separate, irrelevant activity, undertaken for someone else's benefit rather than their own or that of the service users for whom they have responsibility; a means of measuring performance which has certain consequences if standards are not met. Practice tools that accompany programmes such as Looking After Children or the Framework for the Assessment of Children in

Need and their Families are designed to structure social work interactions with service users and ensure that necessary information is collected as a result. However, they are frequently viewed as preventing practitioners from engaging with service users rather than as a means of guiding key social care processes.

There are also concerns that data can be used as a basis for criticism and punitive action, nationally, through the inspection of child welfare agencies by government, and locally, through managers targeting teams or individual members of staff. The challenge is therefore to develop learning organizations that are 'skilled at creating, acquiring and transferring knowledge and at modifying [their] behaviour to reflect new knowledge and insights' (Garvin 2000, p.11).

As Chapter 16 has shown, such organizations engage in systematic problem-solving, experiment with new approaches, learn from their own experience and that of others, and develop robust systems for disseminating and transferring knowledge. Encouraging a free flow of rewards within an organization helps to establish trust and balances the need to examine data critically. Managers must also address performance problems by engaging staff and other stakeholders in developing improvement strategies. Evaluating past performance is necessary, but more productive if it is done in the spirit of informing future practice and services delivery. This focus on a better future avoids the act of blaming which often results in inaction. Managers promote learning by reviewing performance regularly, encouraging and pursuing curiosity, creating opportunities to exchange knowledge, and engaging expertise both inside and outside the organization.

Child welfare practitioners and managers also need to have easy access to the evidence-based practice research documented in the literature. If managers are to focus more on results, information is required not only on outcomes, but also on practice and interventions that might help achieve them.

Involvement of key participants

Since implementation of the Children Act 1989 in England and Wales and the Children (Scotland) Act 1995, involving users in the design and evaluation of public services has gained currency and is now an integral part of government policy. Although their involvement has been emphasized by policymakers and politicians, there is still concern that service users are on the periphery of engagement and participation. This is more likely to indicate that the processes of involving children, young people and their families are more complex than many perceive rather than a lack of interest in doing so.

In the US user involvement in the design of programs and services has become increasingly prevalent in the child social services sectors for developmentally disabled and mental health. Child welfare programs are just beginning to recognize the value of service user involvement as recently recognized through federally funded Systems of Care demonstration projects.

Skuse and Ward (2003) have argued that an analysis of quantitative data is not sufficient to evaluate services. Users' views provide a very different picture of those elements that contribute to successful outcomes than that shown by the more formal, quantitative performance indicators. Both elements need to be incorporated into any evaluation of effectiveness.

Chapters 7 and 15 have shown that, in Canada and Australia, engagement has resulted in some highly effective and imaginative services that meet the particular needs of very vulnerable communities. However, there is a balance to be achieved between fruitful engagement and exploitation (see Chapter 11).

Skills to analyse and use information

Understanding the data

To use information effectively, managers and practitioners need to have the analytical skills necessary to make sense of the data and be able to ask critical questions (Bamford 1996). To understand outcome data one needs to understand how the measure is constructed in order to derive its meaning. For example, in the US one federal outcome measure – timely adoption – is based on the number of children adopted within 24 months of admission, expressed as a percentage of the total number for whom adoption orders are made. Before one uses data derived from this measure, it is important to understand that children must be adopted to be included in the population being measured. Thus, the measure does not reflect the population of children for whom adoption efforts failed or who either age out or stay in long term foster care.

A key target for managers of social services departments in England and Wales is to reduce the number of placements in any year experienced by children and young people looked after away from home. Data submitted to central government now shows that improvements have been made, but a closer analysis demonstrates that stability for some children tends to mask constant changes for others, particularly during the first year of a care episode (Ward *et al.* 2002).

Data can also be difficult to interpret when there are tensions between outcome measures. Sometimes maximizing performance on one indicator may reduce performance on another. For example, high rates of timely reunification can lead to high re-entry rates if children and young people are being returned home prematurely. Similarly, too close a focus on a single measure may lead to a reduction rather than an improvement in well-being: there is evidence, for instance, that some children in the UK are remaining in placements that do not meet their needs in order to ensure that stability targets are met (Skuse and Ward 2003).

Managers therefore need to be skilled in identifying and verifying factors that impact on outcome performance. Making these connections informs actions to improve outcomes. The search for explanations of outcome performance is at the heart of targeting improvements in the quality of services. The numerous factors that impact on client outcomes, and therefore need to be taken into account in analysis, generally fall within one of the following categories:

- Client characteristics: identifying how successful the agency is with different groups of clients against a certain outcome or groups of outcomes.

- Service factors: identifying the impact of different services, or the quality of services on achieving certain outcomes.

- Organizational factors: the impact of certain agency policies or procedures, staffing, available resources.

- Community factors: identifying the differences between outcomes in different communities and community systems.

Lastly, managers must be able to reach tentative conclusions by putting these various pieces of information together. This serves as a basis to develop an action plan to improve performance.

An information system to enhance understanding

Using information effectively

We live in an 'information age' where information can be exchanged across continents at the touch of a button and conversations can take place via the internet without a word being spoken. Rarely, however, can child welfare managers or practitioners access information in a form that enables them to monitor outcomes performance and use the data to aid decision-making or to improve service or programme delivery (Moore, Rapp and Roberts 2000; Schoech, Quinn and Rycraft 2000).

Research undertaken in the UK has identified practical, technical and cultural obstacles to the use of information systems to support the work of child welfare agencies. Practical obstacles include too few computers so that practitioners have to share, limited access to email and the internet, and malfunctioning or incompatible printer programmes. Technical problems reflect how systems have been designed to record and store data, with little attention being given to the question of how it might be used to support practice or strategic planning and evaluation of services. Outputs are often ignored in the design of the system so that a separate reporting application is often needed; these are expensive to deploy, require special skills to use and frequently can only generate printed reports. These obstacles are reflected in cultural attitudes to the use of information technology. Many practitioners view computers as being of little value in their work. Electronic record keeping is thus seen as an added imposition that, far from supporting their practice, takes valuable time away from interactions with service users. Such perceptions mean that insufficient attention is often given to recording data accurately or to updating it. One unfortunate consequence has been that information about outcomes for groups of service users required for national returns, such as educational qualifications of care leavers, is often obtained in the aggregate, directly from agencies and cannot be related back to individual case files (Gatehouse, Statham and Ward 2004).

In the both the UK and the US, specific problems have also been identified in the reports produced for managers. These include information overload, lack of relevant or accurate information about specific groups of children or exceptions reports for individuals, and insufficient analytic tools to aid hypothesis identification and testing (Fluke *et al.* 2000; Gatehouse, Statham and Ward 2004). Of particular value would be reports that allow managers and other professionals to make useful comparisons of performance over time or between different teams or areas. Although some comparisons can now be made in the UK at national level (see for example Department for Education and Skills 2003b) few local systems are sufficiently flexible to allow managers to produce their own customised reports (Gatehouse, Statham and Ward 2004).

Concerns have also been raised about the duplication of data required by the many agencies working with children in need and their families; in particular, service users have regarded repeated requests for the same information, each made by a different professional, as intrusive and confusing (Ward and Peel 2002). Initiatives to improve inter-agency working, currently the subject of legislation in the UK (Department for Education and Skills 2003d), pose both challenges and opportunities for rationalizing the way in which information is recorded and shared (Cleaver *et al.* forthcoming).

Related to concerns over the duplication of data is the integration of data systems. The US federal government has introduced requirements for state-wide automated child welfare information systems. This legislation requires bi-directional interfaces with such programs as Temporary Assistance to Needy Families and Child Support systems. This interface has the potential to reduce duplicate data; however, it is largely used to look up information on the use of services from other systems.

Development of the Integrated Children's System

In England and Wales, one initiative has tried to address some of these issues. The Integrated Children's System (ICS) incorporates three inter-related themes, each of which reflects a key element of the government agenda to improve the quality of social care (Department of Health 2003). First, the ICS is a recording system for use by practitioners, linking together Looking After Children and the Framework for the Assessment of Children in Need and their Families (see Chapter 1, pp.15–16). It is based on the same concepts of optimizing children's opportunities for successful development that run through the earlier initiatives, and forms part of the government's wider agenda for improving outcomes for all children by promoting and safeguarding their well-being. The system provides a unified methodology for assessing the impact of adverse factors within the three domains of the Assessment Triangle (child development, parenting capacity and family and environmental factors, see Chapter 3, p.51), for planning appropriate interventions and for monitoring their effectiveness throughout contact with social care services. The emphasis on articulating outcomes in terms of children's well-being means that the same theoretical framework can underpin all social care interventions for children and their families, whether support is offered in the form of services within the home or through placement in foster or residential care, and whatever the elements of the package of interventions provided.

Second, the Integrated Children's System forms part of the current government initiative on Information for Social Care (www.doh.gov.uk/scg/information.htm). As part of this initiative, the core data requirements (data model) for children's social care services have been mapped out, refined and related to the key social care processes (process model) from point of first contact through referral, assessment, planning, intervention and review to case closure. In the UK, these processes are underpinned by the regulatory requirements that guide practice in working with children in need under the Children Act 1989. The Integrated Children's System covers both the data model and the process model, and also a series of recording tools (exemplars) which illustrate how the requisite data can be captured as each of these processes is undertaken.

The Integrated Children's System has been developed as an electronic system, and will eventually be incorporated into the e-social care record for children. The data and process models are used by local authorities as templates for the design and commissioning of management information systems for children's services. The ICS exemplars provide, in electronic format, the screens through which social workers gather and store the information they need for the case management of individual children, as well as the point at which outcome-based data can be harvested and aggregated for strategic planning purposes. Thus the third theme addressed by the ICS is the collection of data on key indicators that informs the programme of performance management at a strategic level and case management at an individual level.

One of the expectations is that, because the ICS has been developed as an electronic system, the link between individual and aggregate data will be restored. Information collected by social workers in the course of their interactions with individual children will no longer be divorced from the data from which national returns are compiled.

Further work has recently been undertaken to develop a framework for describing and categorizing those outputs that can be retrieved from information systems in order to support the work of a child welfare organization at every level. Such outputs range from automatic alerts to social workers, signifying, for instance, that a review is due, to trend reports to managers, showing how performance compares over time and between different areas of the authority (see www.dfes.gov.uk/qualityprotects/pdfs/outputs.pdf; Gatehouse, Statham and Ward 2004). This is yet another element in a comprehensive strategy, linked to the Integrated Children's System, and is aimed at facilitating more effective use of information in child welfare agencies.

The ICS aims to produce a comprehensive methodology for assessing need, making plans and introducing interventions and evaluating outcomes for all children who are identified as being 'in need' under the Children Act 1989 (Section 17). Within this overall objective it aims to address numerous more detailed issues that have, so far, emerged as practical, cultural or technical obstacles to assessing the effectiveness of child welfare interventions. These include the duplication of assessments undertaken by different agencies, poor recording which means that information about wraparound services is rarely available, practitioners' insufficient skills in analysing information and in using information technology, and current problems with the accessibility and structure of electronic information systems, particularly their ability to produce outputs that can genuinely support practice.

In the UK, policy for children in need is developed and strictly regulated by central government. At the time of writing, the Integrated Children's System is due to be implemented in all local authorities in England and Wales as part of the government's wider agenda for electronic record keeping. There is an expectation that, at least in theory, it will eventually to be possible to make valid comparisons of the effectiveness of different interventions in meeting needs in different localities.

With a less centralized system, the US federal government has nevertheless established two client level datasets that states must submit semi-annually. The National Child Abuse and Neglect Data System (NCANDS) provides data on abuse/neglect allegations and findings, and the Adoption and Foster Care Analysis and Reporting System (AFCARS) provides data on the status of children in out of home care (looked after children). National outcome measures are computed using these data and reported to Congress. While debates continue over data comparability between states, noteworthy improvements have been made in data quality and standardization. This has advanced outcome measurement, report systems development and the idea of managing for outcomes. Likewise, commonly defined data has reduced barriers to undertaking research that has the potential to advance knowledge development.

Conclusion

This book has explored a range of interventions aimed at safeguarding and promoting the well-being of children, families and communities. The increasing literature on the different approaches adopted by child welfare organizations and on measures of performance is helping to clarify our understanding of the complexities of measuring outcomes in this area. There have been numerous strategies to devise electronic systems designed to structure the data upon which outcomes can be assessed and to facilitate analysis. It is clear that such developments can only be effective in organizations that support a learning culture, and develop the analytical skills of staff to use data in a way that contributes to continuous program improvements. Successful organizations also need to develop a culture of outcome-based accountability and genuine partnership working.

Systems such as the Integrated Children's System may resolve some of the technical and practical obstacles to recording accurate data and using it effectively to monitor outcomes. However, it is the approach taken by the organization that will bring together the skill, judgement and experience of the practitioner and the data that can inform evidence-based practice. In doing so, the organization should develop a better understanding of the extent of need and the range of services required and eventually be able to monitor their effectiveness as a routine process, thereby safeguarding and promoting the well-being of children, families and their communities.

Glossary

Association of Directors of Social Services (UK)
The professional body for local authority directors of social services in England, Wales and Northern Ireland. It was set up in 1971 following the implementation of the Local Authority Social Services Act 1970 and superseded the Associations of Children's, Mental Health and Welfare Officers.

Audit Commission (UK)
A non-departmental public body responsible for ensuring that public money is well spent. In charge of local government's best value inspection regime and responsible for auditing the finances of councils and NHS organisations.

Census tracts (US)
Geographically defined districts (of roughly similar size) within which residents are counted for the census.

Child and Adolescent Mental Health Services (UK)
The aim of this service is to provide a high-quality specialist and multi-disciplinary diagnostic assessment, treatment, advisory and consultative service for children and adolescents suffering psychiatric disorders, or where behaviour, emotional state or development is causing serious concern to themselves or those caring for them.

Child maltreatment (US)
Child maltreatment is defined by Federal law as serious harm (neglect, physical abuse, sexual abuse, and emotional abuse or neglect) caused to children by parents or primary caregivers, such as extended family members or babysitters. Child maltreatment can also include harm that a caregiver *allows* to happen (or does not *prevent* from happening) to a child. In general, child welfare agencies do not intervene in cases of harm to children caused by acquaintances or strangers. These cases are the responsibility of law enforcement.

Child protection (UK)
The term 'significant harm' was introduced in England and Wales through the Children Act 1989. Local authorities were given the duty to protect a child (up to 17th birthday or 16th if married) who is suffering significant harm, or likelihood of harm, attributable to care given, or likely to be given to the child, not being what it would be reasonable to expect a parent to give him or her, or the child is beyond parental control.

Child welfare system (UK)

The child welfare system is a group of services designed to promote the well-being of children by ensuring safety, achieving permanency, and strengthening families to care for their children successfully.

Children's Aid Societies (Canada)

The Children's Aid Society (CAS), also known as Family and Children's Services (F&CS), is a non-profit agency working in local communities to provide help and support to children and their families. Established under the authority of the Child and Family Services Act, the CAS is operated by a board of directors elected from the local community and by the membership at large. Programs and services are developed in response to the needs of children and families in the local community.

Children's National Service Framework (UK)

The NSF lays down standards to improve the lives and health of children and young people through the delivery of appropriate, integrated, effective, evidence-based and needs-led services, and to improve the experiences and satisfaction of children, young people and their carers in a number of key areas: children needing acute/hospital services; maternity; mental health and psychological well-being; children in special circumstances; disabled children; and healthy children and young people.

Children's panels (Scotland)

A panel of lay persons empowered under Scots law to make decisions to secure and progress the welfare of children referred to it. Children up to the age of 16 may be referred on a number of 'grounds' including having been the subject of abuse or neglect, failure to attend school, or for offending behaviour.

Connexions (UK)

An all-encompassing youth service launched in April 2001 to replace the careers service and other statutory youth services. It is aimed at giving 13- to 19-year-olds 'the best transition to adulthood' and involves personal advisers going into schools, colleges and communities to steer young people towards goals and guide them to relevant services.

Family centres (UK)

The term 'family centre' refers to a wide range of community-based services for supporting parents and families. The services share a holistic and problem-solving approach based on ideas of partnership, but are otherwise diverse in funding, financial stability, size, the breadth or narrowness of purpose, policies on access and patterns of referral.

Family preservation (US)

Family preservation refers to a systematic determination of those families in which children could remain in their homes or be returned home safely, and provision of the services needed to ensure that safety.

Family support services (UK)
Family support services provide a range of services that promote and safeguard the welfare of families and young children. Staff work with parents or carers to help them understand and meet the needs of children in safe, supported and caring environments. Each offers a specific service to a local community.

Food stamps (US)
The United States' premier anti-hunger program. It helps low-income households buy the food they need to stay healthy. The program is funded by the United States Department of Agriculture and administered in New York State by the Office of Temporary and Disability Assistance, local county departments of social services and, in New York City, the Human Resources Administration. In order to be eligible for food stamps, a household must meet income and resource guidelines, as well as citizenship/legal alien requirements and employment standards.

Foster care (UK)
The term 'foster care' refers only to children placed away from their birth parents in another family. This is a more restricted usage than in some other countries.

Foster carers (UK)
Foster parents look after and promote the growth and development of a child or young person in place of the natural or adoptive parents.

Graduate Equivalency Diploma (GED) (US)
The Graduate Equivalency Diploma (GED) is a degree for people who do not finish high school. It is equal to a high school diploma.

Green Paper (UK)
A Green Paper is a government consultative document, which usually leads to a 'white' paper and thence to legislation.

Health visitors (UK)
Registered nurses with specialist training in the assessment of the health needs of children under five, their families and their community.

Link workers and key workers (UK)
These terms are sometimes used interchangeably. Link workers operate to help people with multiple needs make contact with the various services they need. Link workers often have a more advisory and information-giving role. The term 'key worker' is more common within the health services. They often have a role as advocates on behalf of the service users with whom they work.

Local Government Association (UK)

This organization represents around 400 councils in England and Wales. It lobbies central government on behalf of its members and advises on policy.

Local/unitary authority (UK)

A publicly elected and accountable body which has a range of statutory powers and responsibilities to obtain or provide particular services.

Looked after and accommodated children (UK)

In England and Wales, this term refers to children who are either in care (subject to a care order) or accommodated by a local authority. Children become looked after if, for example, their birth parents are temporarily unable to care for them, or they have been neglected or abused. For the most part this corresponds with children described in Scotland under the Children (Scotland) Act 1995 as looked after and accommodated. There are some differences, however; for example, a young person counts as looked after in England and Wales even when placed at home under a Care Order, while a child on home supervision in Scotland is looked after but not looked after and accommodated.

Looked after children reviews (UK)

All children looked after and accommodated by the local authority are required by the Guidance attached to the Children Act 1989, which covers England and Wales, and the Children (Scotland) Act 1995, to have their circumstances reviewed no less frequently than six monthly. Reviews can be undertaken more frequently than this.

Mental health development fund (UK)

This central government funding scheme fosters the development of innovative models of practice and intervention in mental health services. The fund provides 'seed' monies and is awarded on the understanding that the receiving agencies commit to the ongoing funding of the provision.

NHS Primary Care Trust (UK)

Primary care is the care provided by those health professionals normally seen at the initial stages of health problems or concerns. This might include routine visits to a doctor or NHS Walk-in Centres, or calls to the phone-line service, NHS Direct. All these services are managed by local Primary Care Trusts (PCT). PCTs work with local authorities and other agencies to provide health and social care locally to meet the needs of the local community.

Regional health boards (UK)

Regional health authorities, such as the Greater Glasgow Health Board, are responsible for the strategic planning and development of all health services across the specific area.

Scottish Executive (Scotland)
The Scottish Executive is responsible to the newly established Scottish Parliament, and is heritor to the powers and duties of the former Scottish Office. Among its delegated areas of responsibility are health, education and social work.

Section 8 (US)
This program gives rental assistance for low- and very low-income households by providing direct payments through public housing authorities to landlords.

Sober housing (US)
Sober housing involves living with people in residences that require and support sobriety. Although these programs are often helpful, few of these residences allow children.

Spending reviews (UK)
Spending reviews set firm and fixed three-year Departmental expenditure limits and, through Public Service Agreements, define the key improvements that the public can expect from these resources. Successive spending reviews have targeted resources at the Government's priorities, have matched these resources with reforms, and have set ambitious targets for improvements in key public services: in education, health, transport and criminal justice.

Temporary Assistance for Needy Families (US)
Temporary Assistance for Needy Families (TANF) provides assistance and work opportunities to needy families by granting states the federal funds and wide flexibility to develop and implement their own welfare programs. TANF is a block grant program designed to make dramatic reforms to the nation's welfare system by moving recipients into work and turning welfare into a program of temporary assistance.

Transitional housing (US)
A time-limited, subsidized apartment or home for homeless individuals or families that is intended to precede residence in a more permanent self-sufficient housing situation.

Who Cares? Trust (UK)
A national campaigning organization for children and young people in care throughout the UK. It provides a range of direct services to looked after and accommodated children including advice and advocacy.

Women Infants and Children (US)
WIC provides nutritious foods, nutrition counselling, and referrals to health and other social services to participants at no charge. WIC serves low-income pregnant, postpartum and breastfeeding women, and infants and children up to age five who are at nutrition risk. WIC is a Federal grant program for which Congress authorizes a specific amount of funding each year for program operations.

References

Abandoned Infants Assistance (AIA) Resource Center (1996) *Shared Family Care Program Guidelines*. Berkeley, CA: AIA Resource Center. http://ist-socrates.berkeley.edu/~aiarc/information_ resources/shared_ family_care/program_guideline.html.

Abidin, R.R. (1995) *Parenting Stress Index (PSI)* (3rd edn). Charlottesville, VA: Pediatric Psychology Press.

Achenbach, T.M., Edelbrock, C. and Howell, C.T. (1987) 'Empirically based assessment of the behavioral/ emotional problems of 2–3-year-old children.' *Journal of Abnormal Child Psychology 15*, 629–50.

Adelman, L., Middleton, S. and Ashworth, K. (2003) *Britain's Poorest Children: Severe and Persistent Poverty and Social Exclusion*. London: Save the Children.

Adoption and Children Act (2002) London: HMSO.

Adoption and Safe Families Act (1997) Washington, DC: US Department of Health and Human Sciences.

Almgren, G., Ymashiro, G. and Ferguson, M. (2002) 'Beyond welfare to work: Teen mothers, household subsistence strategies, and child development outcomes.' *Journal of Sociology and Social Welfare 29*, 3, 125–49.

Anderson-Butcher, D., Khairallah, A.O. and Race-Bigelow, J. (2004) 'Mutual support groups for long-term recipients of TANF.' *Social Work 49*, 1, 131–40.

Association of Directors of Social Services (2002) *Tomorrow's Children: A Discussion Paper on Child Care Services in the Coming Decade*. London: ADSS.

ATD Fourth World (1996) *Talk With Us Not At Us*. London: ATD Fourth World.

Atkinson, L. (1993) 'Aboriginal youth, police and the juvenile justice system in Western Australia.' *Children Australia 18*, 1, 14–19.

Audit Commission (1994) *Seen But Not Heard: Co-ordinating Child Health and Social Services for Children in Need*. London: Audit Commission.

Audit Commission (2002) *Recruitment and Retention: A Public Sector Workforce for the Twenty-first Century*. London: Audit Commission.

Australian Government (2004) *Australian Employment Services News*, retrieved on 16 September 2004 www.workplace.gov.au.

Australian Institute of Health and Welfare (2001) *Australia's Welfare 2001*. Canberra: Australian Institute of Health and Welfare.

Axford, N., Little, M. and Morpeth, L. (2003) 'Children's services in the UK 1997–2003: Problems, developments and challenges for the future.' *Children and Society Special Issue: New Labour Policy and its Outcomes for Children 17*, 3, 205–14.

Bahktin, M.M. (1986) *Speech Genres and Other Late Essays* (trans. V.W. McGee). Austin, TX: University of Texas Press.

Bamford, T. (1996) 'Information Driven Decision Making: Fact or Fantasy?' In A.K.N. Gould (ed) *Information Management in Social Services*. Aldershot: Avery Ashgate Publishers Ltd.

Banerjee, M. (2002) 'Voicing realities and recommending reform in PRWRA.' *Social Work 47*, 3, 315–28.

Barber, J. and Gilbertson, R. (2001) *Foster Care – The State of the Art*. Adelaide: Australian Centre for Community Services Research.

Barclay, P. (1995) *Inquiry into Income and Wealth, vol. 1*. York: Joseph Rowntree Foundation.

Bardach, E. (2000) *A Practical Guide for Policy Analysis: The Eightfold Path to More Effective Problems Solving*. New York: Chatham House.

Barlow, M. and Campbell, B. (1995) *Straight Through the Heart: How the Liberals Abandoned the Just Society*. Toronto: HarperCollins.

Barnes, C. (1991) *Disabled People in Britain and Discrimination: A Case for Anti-Discrimination Legislation*. Belper: British Council of Organisations of Disabled People.

Barnes, H. (2001) 'How other countries monitor the wellbeing of their children.' In J. Bradshaw (ed) *Poverty: The Outcomes for Children*. London: Family Policy Studies Centre and NCB Books.

Barnes, J., Broomfield, K., Frost, M., Harper, G., McLeod, A., Knowles, J. and Leyland, A. (2003) *Characteristics of Sure Start Local Programme Areas: Rounds 1–4.* London: Department for Education and Skills.

Barrera, M. (1980) 'A method for the assessment of social support networks in community survey research.' *Connections 3,* 8–13.

Barrington Research Group Inc. (2002a) *Canada Prenatal Nutrition Program 2000–2001 IPQ Evaluation Summary Report.* Unpublished report prepared for Health Canada, Calgary.

Barrington Research Group Inc. (2002b) *Canada Prenatal Nutrition Program: Participant Summary, 1996–2002.* Unpublished report prepared for Health Canada, Calgary.

Barth, R.P., Landsverk, J., Chamberlain, P., Reid, J., Hurlburt, M., James, S., McCabe, K. and Kohl, P. (in press) 'Parent training programs in child welfare services: The current evidence reviewed.' *Research on Social Work Practice.*

Barth, R.P. and Price, A. (1999) 'Shared family care: Providing services to parents and children placed together in out-of-home care.' *Child Welfare 78,* 88–107.

Bastien, M-F., Pomerleau, A., Malcuit, G., Moreau, J., Bouchard, C., Denis, É., Goulet, J., Gratton, G. and Blanchard, D. (2002) 'Conditions de vie, milieux, parentage et développement des enfants.' Communication présentée dans le cadre du congrès Bâtisseurs D'avenirs, Québec. 25 novembre.

Bates, B.C., English, D.J. and Kouidou-Giles, S. (1997) 'Residential treatment and its alternatives: A review of the literature.' *Child and Youth Care Forum 26,* 1, 7–61.

Bath, H.I. and Haapala, D.A. (1993) 'Intensive family preservation services with abused and neglected children: An examination of group differences.' *Child Abuse and Neglect 17,* 213–25.

Bayley, N. (1993) *Bayley Scales of Infant Development* (2nd edn). San Antonio, TX: Psychological Corporation.

Beauvais, C. and Jenson, J. (2003) *The Wellbeing of Children: Are There 'Neighbourhood Effects'?* Discussion paper F/31. Canadian Policy Research Networks.

Bebbington, A. and Miles, J. (1989) 'The background of children who enter local authority care.' *British Journal of Social Work 19,* 349–68.

Becker, S. (1997) *Responding to Poverty: The Politics of Cash and Care.* London: Longman.

Becker, S. and Ward, H. (undated) Presentation about work of Centre for Child and Family Research (personal correspondence).

Beresford, P. (2002) 'User involvement in research and evaluation: Liberation or regulation?' *Social Policy and Society 1,* 2, 95–106.

Beresford, P., Green, D., Lister, R. and Woodard, K. (1999) *Poverty First Hand: Poor People Speak for Themselves.* London: Child Poverty Action Group.

Berkowitz, B. (2001) 'Studying the outcomes of community-based coalitions.' *American Journal of Community Psychology 29,* 213–29.

Berrick, J.D., Needell, B., Barth, R.P. and Jonson-Reid, M. (1998) *The Tender Years: Toward Developmentally Sensitive Child Welfare Services.* New York: Oxford University Press.

Berthoud, R. (2001) 'A childhood in poverty: Persistent versus transitory poverty.' *New Economy 8,* 2.

Biehal, N. (2005) *Working with Adolescents. Supporting Families, Preventing Breakdown.* London: BAAF.

Biehal, N., Clayden, J. and Byford, S. (2000) *Home or Away? Supporting Young People and Families.* London: National Children's Bureau.

Biehal, N., Clayden, J., Stein, M. and Wade, J. (1995) 'Leaving care in England: A research perspective.' *Children and Youth Services Review 16,* 3, 231–54.

Biehal, N. and Wade, J. (2000) 'Going missing from residential and foster care.' *British Journal of Social Work 30,* 211–25.

Billings, P., Moore, T.D. and McDonald, T.P. (2003) 'What do we know about the relationship between public welfare and child welfare?' *Child and Youth Services Review 25,* 8, 633–50.

Blackstock, C. (2003) 'First Nations child and family services: Restoring peace and harmony in First Nations communities.' In K. Kufeldt and B. McKenzie (eds) *Child Welfare: Connecting Research, Policy and Practice.* Ontario: Wilfrid Laurier University.

Boswell, G. and Wedge, P. (2001) *Imprisoned Fathers and their Children.* London: Jessica Kingsley Publishers.

Bouchard, C. (1999) 'The community as a participative learning environment. The case of Centraide of Greater Montreal 1,2,3, GO! Project.' In D.P. Keating and C. Hertzman (eds) *Developmental Health and the Wealth of Nations.* New York: The Guilford Press.

Boyle, M.H., Offord, D.R., Racine, Y., Fleming, J.E., Szatmari, P. and Sanford, M. (1993) 'Evaluation of the revised Ontario Child Health Study scales.' *Journal of Child Psychology and Psychiatry 16,* 771–91.

Bradshaw, J. (ed) (2001a) *Poverty: The Outcomes for Children.* London: Family Policy Studies Centre and NCB Books.

Bradshaw, J. (2001b) 'Child poverty under Labour.' In G. Fimister (ed) *An End in Sight? Tackling Child Poverty in the UK.* London: Child Poverty Action Group.

Bradshaw, J. (ed) (2002) *The Well-being of Children in the UK.* London: Save the Children.

Brewer, M., Clark, T. and Goodman, A. (2002) *The Government's Child Poverty Target: How Much Progress Has Been Made?* London: Institute for Fiscal Studies.

Briskman, L. (2001) 'Beyond apologies: The stolen generations and the churches.' *Children Australia 26,* 3, 4–8.

Brodie, I., Berridge, D., Ayre, P., Barrett, D., Burroughs, L., Porteous, D. and Wenman, H. (1998) *Family Support for Adolescents: An Evaluation of the Work of the Adolescent Community Support Team.* Luton: University of Luton.

Bronfenbrenner, U. (1979) *The Ecology of Human Development. Experiments in Nature and Design.* Cambridge: Harvard University Press.

Brooks-Gunn, J., Duncan, G. and Aber, J.L. (eds) (1997) *Neighborhood Poverty: Context and Consequences for Children (Vol. I); Policy Implications for Studying Neighborhoods (Vol. II).* New York: Russell Sage Foundation.

Brown, Rt Hon. G., Chancellor of the Exchequer (1999) 'A scar on the nation's soul.' *Poverty 104,* autumn, 8–10.

Brown, J. (1998) *Family and Adolescent Support Service* (discussion paper). London: National Institute for Social Work.

Buckner, J.C. (1988) 'The development of an instrument to measure neighborhood cohesion.' *American Journal of Community Psychology 16,* 771–791.

Budgell, R. and Robertson, L. (2003) 'Evaluating miracles: Challenges in evaluating the Aboriginal Head Start Program.' In K. Kufeldt and B. McKenzie (eds) *Child Welfare: Connecting Research, Policy and Practice.* Waterloo, ON: Wilfrid Laurier University Press.

Burns, B.J. and Hoagwood, K. (2002) *Community Treatment for Youth: Evidence-based Interventions for Severe Emotional and Behavior Disorders.* New York: Oxford University Press.

Cameron, G. (2003) 'Promoting positive child and family welfare.' In K. Kufeldt and B. McKenzie (eds) *Child Welfare: Connecting Research, Policy and Practice.* Waterloo, ON: Wilfrid Laurier Press.

Canadian Institute for Health Information (2004) 'Improving the Health of Canadians.' www.cihi.ca.

Canadian Intergovernmental Conference Secretariat (2000) 'First Ministers' Meeting Communiqué on Early Childhood Development.' www.scics.gc.ca/cinfo00/800038005_e.html.

Carnevale, A.P. and Desrochers, D.M. (1999) ' Getting down to business: Matching welfare recipients' skills to jobs that train.' *Policy and Practice 57,* 1, 18–24.

Carter, J. (2002) *Towards Better Foster Care: Reducing the Risks in Caring for Other People's Children.* Melbourne: The Children's Foundation.

Casey Family Foundation (1999) *Improving the Quality of Children's Services: A Working Paper on Outcome-Based Models of Service Delivery and Managed Care.* Englewood, CO: The Casey Outcomes and Decision-Making Project.

Casey Foundation, Annie. E. (1995) *The Path of Most Resistance: Reflections on Lessons Learned from New Futures.* Baltimore, MD: Annie E. Casey Foundation.

Center on Budget and Policy Priorities (1999) *The Poverty Despite Work Handbook* (2nd edn). Washington, DC: Center on Budget and Policy Priorities.

Chambless, D. and Hollon, S.D. (1998) 'Defining empirically supported therapies.' *Journal of Consulting and Clinical Psychology 36,* 9–17.

Chambless, D. and Ollendick, T.H. (2001) 'Empirically supported psychological interventions: Controversies and evidence.' *Annual Review of Psychology 52,* 685–716.

Chetwynd, P. and Robb, W. (1999) *Psychological Difficulties in Young People in Residential Care in Glasgow.* Glasgow: Greater Glasgow Health Board.

Child and Family Canada (2001) *All the Rage!: A Proven Programme to Reduce Incidences of Parent Rage and Increase Social Capital.* www.cfc-efc.ca/docs/fscan/00001364.htm.

Child and Family Welfare Association of Australia (CAFWAA) (2002) *A Time to Invest in Australia's Most Disadvantaged Children, Young People and Their Families.* Canada: CAFWAA.

Children Act (1989) London: HMSO.

Children (Leaving Care) Act (2000) London: HMSO.

Children (Scotland) Act (1995) London: HMSO.

Children and Young People's Unit (2001) *Building a Strategy for Children and Young People.* Nottingham: Department for Education and Skills.

Children's Defense Fund Minnesota (2003) 'Number of poor children in American rises second straight year: Black and Latino children bear the brunt of increase.' *A Child's Voice 10*, 1–3.

Cicchetti, D., Rappaport, J., Sandler, I. and Weissberg, R.P. (eds) (2000) *The Promotion of Wellness in Children and Adolescents*. Washington, DC: Child Welfare League of America Press.

City of Toronto (2000) *Toronto Report Card on Homelessness*. Toronto: City of Toronto.

Clare, M. and Noonan, J. (2002) *Developments in Child Welfare Policy and Practice in Australia: A Review of Programmes to Improve the Health and Well-Being of Aboriginal Children in Australia*. Paper presented at the 5th International Seminar of the Looking After Children Project held at Worcester College, Oxford.

Clare, M. and Peerless, H. (1996) *An Evaluation Study of the UK Looking After Children Materials for the Out-of-Home, Preventative and Alternative Care Committee*. University of Western Australia: Department of Social Work and Social Policy.

Clarke, A. and Clarke, A. (2003) *Human Resilience: A Fifty Year Quest*. London: Jessica Kingsley Publishers.

Cleaver, H., Pithouse, A., Rose, W., Scott, J., Walker, S. and Ward, H. (forthcoming) *A Pilot Study to Assess the Development of a Multi-agency and Integrated Approach to the Delivery of Services to Children and their Families*. London: Royal Holloway.

Cleaver, H., Unell, I. and Aldgate, J. (1999) *Children's Needs – Parental Capacity: The Impact of Parental Mental Illness, Problem Alcohol and Drug Use and Domestic Violence on Children's Development*. London: The Stationery Office.

Cleaver, H. and Walker, S. (2004) *Assessing Children's Needs and Circumstances*. London: Jessica Kingsley Publishers.

Cliffe, D. and Berridge, D. (1991) *Closing Children's Homes. An End to Residential Child Care?* London: National Children's Bureau.

Coburn, D. (2000) 'Income inequality, social cohesion and health status of populations: The role of neo-liberalism.' *Social Science and Medicine 51*, 135–46.

Cohen, R., Coxall, J., Craig, G. and Sadiq-Sangster, A. (1992) *Hardship Britain: Being Poor in the 1990s*. London: CPAG Ltd.

Cohen-Schlanger, M., Fitzpatrick, A., Hulchanski, J.D. and Raphael, D. (1995) 'Housing as a factor in admissions of children to temporary care.' *Child Welfare 74*, 3, 547–62.

Coleman, J. and Hendry, L. (1999) *The Nature of Adolescence*. London: Routledge.

Commission on Poverty, Participation and Power (2000) *Listen Hear! The Right To Be Heard*. Bristol: The Policy Press.

Community Services Commission (2001) *A Question of Safeguards – Inquiry into the Care and Circumstances of Aboriginal and Torres Strait Islander Children and Young People in Care*. New South Wales: Community Services Commission.

Connors, C. and Stalker, K. (2003) *The Views and Experiences of Disabled Children and their Siblings: A Positive Outlook*. London: Jessica Kingsley Publishers.

Corlyon, J. and McGuire, C. (1999) *Pregnancy and Parenthood: The Views and Experiences of Young People in Public Care*. London: National Children's Bureau.

Cowen, E.L. (2000) 'Community psychology and routes to psychological wellness.' In J. Rappaport and E. Seidman (eds) *Handbook of Community Psychology*. New York: Kluwer Academic/Plenum Publishers.

CREATE Foundation (2002) *Australian Children and Young People in Care – Report Card – December 2002*. Brisbane: The Create Foundation.

Crewe, S.E. (2003) 'Behind the numbers: Welfare reform from an ecological perspective.' *International Journal of Public Administration 26*, 7, 753–71.

Crichton, L.I. (2003) *The Welfare Time Limit in Minnesota: A Survey of Families Who Lost MFIP Eligibility as a Result of the Five Year Time Limit*. St Paul, MN: Minnesota Department of Human Services.

Crichton, L.I. and Meyer, V.A. (2003) *Minnesota Family Investment Program Longitudinal Study: Three Years After Baseline*. St Paul, MN: Minnesota Department of Human Services. Retrieved on 2/5/04 from http://edocs.dhs.state.mn.us/lfserver/Legacy/DHS-3974-ENG (see also www.dhs.state.mn.us/ecs/Reports/default.htm).

Currie, C. (2001) 'Socioeconomic circumstances among school-aged children in Europe and North America.' In K. Vleminckx and T.M. Smeeding (eds) *Child Well-being, Child Poverty and Child Policy in Modern Nations: What Do We Know?* Bristol: The Policy Press.

Deacon, A. (2002) *Perspectives on Welfare*. Buckingham: Open University Press.

Department for Education and Skills (2001) *Learning to Listen: Core Principles for the Involvement of Children and Young People*. Nottingham: DfES Publications.

Department for Education and Skills (2002) *Getting Sure Start Started.* Nottingham: DfES Publications.

Department for Education and Skills (2003a) *Children in Need in England: Results of a Survey of Activity and Expenditure as Reported by Local Authority Social Services Children and Families Teams for a Survey Week in February, 2003.* London: DfES Publications.

Department for Education and Skills (2003b) *Children Looked After by Local Authorities, Year Ending 31st March 2003.* London: DfES Publications.

Department for Education and Skills (2003c) *Children Act Report.* Nottingham: DfES Publications.

Department for Education and Skills (2003d) *Every Child Matters: Green Paper on Children's Services,* Cm5860. London: The Stationery Office.

Department for Education and Skills and HM Treasury (2003) *National Framework for Parenting Support.* Nottingham: DfES Publications.

Department for Work and Pensions (2002) *Measuring Child Poverty: A Consultation Document.* London: HMSO.

Department for Work and Pensions (2003a) *Households Below Average Income: An Analysis of the Income Distribution from 1994/95–2001/02.* Leeds: Corporate Document Services.

Department for Work and Pensions (2003b) *Opportunity for All: Fifth Annual Report 2003,* Cm 5956. London: The Stationery Office.

Department of Health (1998a) *Partners in Planning: Approaches to Planning Services for Children and their Families.* London: Department of Health.

Department of Health (1998b) *Quality Protects Circular: Transforming Children's Services (LAC (99) 29).* London: Department of Health.

Department of Health (1999) *The Government's Objectives for Children's Social Services.* London: Department of Health.

Department of Health (2000a) *Social Services Performance in 1999–2000: The Personal Social Services Performance Assessment Framework Indicators.* London: Department of Health.

Department of Health (2000b) *The National Health Service Plan: A Plan for Investment, A Plan for Reform.* London: Department of Health.

Department of Health (2002a) *Compendium of Clinical Health Indicators.* London: Department of Health.

Department of Health (2002b) *Integrated Children's System. Working with Children in Need and Their Families: Consultation Document.* London: Department of Health.

Department of Health (2002c) *National Standards for the Provision of Children's Advocacy Services.* London: Department of Health.

Department of Health (2003) *Getting the Right Start: The National Service Framework for Children. Emerging Findings.* London: Department of Health.

Department of Health and Human Services (2002) *Status Report on Research on the Outcomes of Welfare Reform.* Washington, DC: United States Department of Health and Human Services. www.aspe.hhs.gov/hsp/welf-ref-outcomes02/index.htm.

Department of Health, Department for Education and Skills (2004) *National Service Framework for Children, Young People and Maternity Services.* wwww.dh.gov.uk/PolicyAndGuidance/HealthAndSocialCareTopics/ChildrenServices/ChildrenServicesInformation/fs/en.

Department of Health, Department for Education and Skills and Home Office (2000) *Framework for the Assessment of Children in Need and their Families.* London: HMSO.

Department of Social Security (2001) *Households Below Average Income 1994/95–1999/00.* Leeds: Corporate Document Services.

Disability Discrimination Act (1995) London: HMSO.

Dixon, J. and Stein, M. (2002) *A Study of Throughcare and Aftercare Services in Scotland, Research Findings No 3.* Edinburgh: Scottish Executive.

Dobson, B., Beardsworth, A., Keil, T. and Walker, R. (1994) *Diet, Choice and Poverty.* York: Joseph Rowntree Foundation.

Duncan, G.J. and Chase-Lansdale, P.L. (eds) (2001) *For Better and For Worse: Welfare Reform and the Well-Being of Children and Families.* New York: Russell Sage Foundation.

Duncan, G.J., Young, I.W., Brooks-Gunn, J. and Smith, J. (2001) 'How much does childhood poverty affect the life chances of children?' *American Sociological Review 63,* 406–23, 1998, cited in I. Plewis, G. Smith, G. Wright and A. Cullis (2001) *Linking Child Poverty and Child Outcomes: Exploring Data and Research Strategies.* Department for Work and Pensions Research Working Paper No. 1. London: HMSO.

Dunifon, R., Kalil, A. and Danziger, S.K. (2003) 'Maternal work behavior under welfare reform: How does the transition from welfare to work affect child development?' *Children and Youth Services Review 25,* 1, 55–82.

Dunst, C.J., Trivette, C.M. and Deal, A.G. (eds) (1994) *Supporting and Strengthening Families. Vol.1 Methods, Strategies and Practice.* Cambridge, MA: Brookline Books.

Eisen, A. (1994) 'Survey of neighborhood-based, comprehensive community empowerment initiatives.' *Health Education Quarterly 21,* 235–52.

Elliott, D. and Mayadas, N. (1999) 'Infusing global perspectives into social work practice.' In C.S. Ramanathan and R.J. Link (eds) *All Our Futures: Principles and Resources for Social Work Practice in a Global Era.* New York: BrooksCole.

EPPE (2004) *The Effective Provision of Pre-school Education Project.* London: Institute of Education. www.ioe.ac.uk/cdl/eppe/.

Epstein, N., Baldwin, L. and Bishop, D. (1983) 'The McMaster family assessment device.' *Journal of Marital and Family Therapy 9,* 2, 171–80.

Ermisch, J., Francesconi, M. and Pevalin, D. (2001) *Outcomes for Children of Poverty.* Leeds: Corporate Document Services.

Etzioni, A. (1994) *The Spirit of Community: The Reinvention of American Society.* New York: Touchstone.

Eurostat (2000) *European Social Statistics: Income, Poverty and Social Exclusion, Theme 3: Population and Social Conditions.* Luxembourg: Office for Official Publications of the European Communities.

Evans, M. and Boothroyd, R. (1997) 'Family preservation services for families with children who have mental health problems.' In S. Henggeler and A. Santos (eds) *Innovative Approaches for Difficult to Treat Populations.* Washington, DC: American Psychiatric Press.

Farmer, E., Moyers, S. and Lipscombe, J. (2004) *Fostering Adolescents.* London: Jessica Kingsley Publishers.

Febbraro, A. (1994) 'Single mothers "at risk" for child maltreatment: An appraisal of person-centred interventions and a call for emancipatory action.' *Canadian Journal of Community Mental Health 13,* 2, 47–60.

Feinstein, L. (1998) *Pre-school Education Inequality?* London: Centre for Economic Performance, London School of Economics.

Feldman, L.K. (1991) *Assessing the Effectiveness of Family Preservation Services in New Jersey.* New Jersey: Division of Youth and Family Services, Bureau of Research, Evaluation and Quality Assurance.

Finegold, K. and Staveteig, S. (2002) 'Race, ethnicity and welfare reform.' In A. Weil and K. Finegold (eds) *Welfare Reform: The Next Act.* Washington, DC: Urban Institute.

Fluke, J.D., Edwards, M., Kutzler, P., Kuna, J. and Tooman, G. (2000) 'Safety, permanency and in-home services: Applying administrative data.' *Child Welfare LXXIX,* 5, 573–95.

Flynn, R., Lemay, R., Ghazal, H. and Hébert, S. (2003). 'P3M: A performance measurement, monitoring and management system for child welfare organizations.' In K. Kufeldt and B. McKenzie (eds) *Child Welfare: Connecting Research, Policy and Practice.* Waterloo, ON: Wilfrid Laurier Press.

Forman, R., Klein, J., Meta, D., Barks, J., Greenwald, M. and Koren, G. (1994) 'Prevalence of fetal exposure to cocaine in Toronto 1990–1991.' *Clinical Investigative Medicine 17,* 3, 206–11.

Foster-Fishman, P., Salem, D.A., Allen, N.A. and Fahrbach, K. (2001) 'Facilitating interorganizational collaboration: The contribution of interorganizational alliances.' *American Journal of Community Psychology 29,* 875–905.

Fraser, M.W., Nelson, K.E. and Rivard, J.C. (1997) 'Effectiveness of family preservation services.' *Social Work Research 21,* 3, 138–53.

French, S. (1993) 'Disability, impairment or something in between?' In J. Swain, V. Finkelstein, S. French and M. Oliver (eds) *Disabling Barriers – Enabling Environments.* London: Sage.

Friday, E. (1998) *Listen Up: Young People Talk About Mental Health Issues in Residential Care.* Edinburgh: Who Cares? Scotland.

Friedman, M. (2000) *Results Accountability for First Five Commissions: A Planning Guide for Improving the Well-being of Young Children and Their Families.* Los Angeles, CA: The UCLA Center for Healthier Children, Families and Communities.

Frost, N. (1997) 'Delivering family support: Issues and themes in service development.' In N. Parton (ed) *Child Protection and Family Support.* London: Routledge.

Fuller, R. (1989) 'Problems and possibilities in studying preventive work.' *Adoption and Fostering 13,* 9–13.

Furstenberg, F.F. and Hugues, M.E. (1997) 'The influence of neighborhoods on children's development: A theoretical perspective and a research agenda.' In J. Brooks-Gunn, J.G. Duncan and J.L.Aber (eds) *Neighborhood Poverty. Vol. 2.* New York: Russell Sage Foundation.

Garbarino, J. and Kostelny, K. (1992) 'Child maltreatment as a community problem.' *Child Abuse and Neglect 16,* 3, 455–64.

Gardner, R. (1992) *Supporting Families: Preventative Social Work in Practice.* London: NCB.

Garvin, D.A. (2000) *Learning in Action: A Guide to Putting the Learning Organization to Work.* Boston, MA: Harvard Business School Press.

Gatehouse, M., Statham, J. and Ward, H. (2004) *Information Outputs for Children's Social Services, CCFR Evidence Issue 9.* Loughborough: Centre for Child and Family Research.

Gelles, R.J. (1996) *The Book of David: How Preserving Families Can Cost Children's Lives.* New York: Basic Books.

Gennetian, L.A. and Miller, C. (2002) 'Children and welfare reform: A view from an experimental welfare program in Minnesota.' *Child Development 73,* 2, 601–20.

Ghate, D. and Hazel, N. (2002) *Parenting in Poor Environments: Stress, Support and Coping.* London: Jessica Kingsley Publishers.

Gibbons, J. (1991) 'Children in need and their families: Outcomes of referral to social services.' *British Journal of Social Work 21,* 217–27.

Gibbons, J., Conroy, S. and Bell, C. (1995) *Operating the Child Protection System.* London: HMSO.

Gibbons, J., Thorpe, S.A. and Wilkinson, P. (1990) *Family Support and Prevention: Studies in Local Areas.* London: NISW.

Goddard, M. and Smith, P.C. (2001) 'Performance management in the new NHS.' *Health Policy Matters 3.* York: Centre for Health Economics, University of York.

Goldberg, D. and Williams, P. (1988) *A User's Guide to the General Health Questionnaire.* Windsor: NFER-Nelson.

Goldberg, G.S. (2002) 'More than reluctant: The United States of America.' In G.S. Goldberg and M.G. Rosenthal (eds) *Diminishing Welfare: A Cross-National Study of Social Provision.* Westpoint, CT: Auburn House.

Goldberg, G.S. and Rosenthal, M.G. (eds) (2002) *Diminishing Welfare: A Cross-National Study of Social Provision.* Westpoint, CT: Auburn House.

Goode, J., Callender, C. and Lister, R. (1998) *Purse or Wallet? Gender Inequalities and Income Distribution within Families on Benefits.* London: Policy Studies Institute.

Goodman, R. (1997) 'The strengths and difficulties questionnaire: A research note.' *Journal of Child Psychology and Psychiatry 38,* 5, 581–86.

Gordon, D., Adelman, A., Ashworth, K., Bradshaw, J., Levitas, R., Middleton, S., Pantazis, C., Patsios, D., Payne, S., Townsend, P. and Williams, J. (2000) *Poverty and Social Exclusion in Britain.* York: Joseph Rowntree Foundation.

Government of Canada (1991) *The Child Development Initiative of Brighter Futures.* Ottawa: Government of Canada.

Greenberg, M. (2001) 'Developmental and ecological considerations in implementing community action strategies for children and youth.' In A. Booth and A.C. Crouter (eds) *Does it Take A Village? Community Effects on Children, Adolescents and Families.* Mahwah, NJ: Lawrence Erlbaum Associates.

Gregg, P., Harkness, S. and Machin, S. (1999) *Child Development and Family Income.* York: Joseph Rowntree Foundation.

Gregg, P. and Machin, S. (2001) 'Childhood experiences, educational attainment and adult labour market performance.' In K. Vleminckx and T.M. Smeeding (eds) *Child Well-being, Child Poverty and Child Policy in Modern Nations: What Do We Know?* Bristol: The Policy Press.

Gresham, F.M. and Elliott, S.N. (1990) *Social Skills Rating System Manual.* Circle Pines, MN: American Guidance Services.

Guardian (2002) '100,000 children are homeless, shelter report says.' 19 September.

Guardian (2003) 'Lifted out of the worst poverty.' 5 August.

Haebich, A. (2001) *Broken Circles: Fragmenting Indigenous Families 1800–2000.* Fremantle, Western Australia: Fremantle Arts Centre Press.

Hage, D. (2004a) 'Welfare reform that made work pay: Can't Congress learn from Minnesota's success?' *Star Tribune 22,* 352, AA9.

Hage, D. (2004b) *Reforming Welfare by Rewarding Work: One State's Successful Experiment.* London: G.K. Hall and Co.

Hardina, D. (2003) 'Book review: Maeve Quaid's workfare: Why good social policy ideas go bad.' *Social Service Review 77,* 3, 481–84.

Harker, L. and Kendall, L. (2003) *An Equal Start: Improving Support During Pregnancy and the First Twelve Months.* London: Institute for Public Policy Research.

Harris, J. (2003) *The Social Work Business.* London and New York: Routledge.

Haskins, R. (2001) 'Effects of welfare reform at four years.' In G.J. Duncan and P.L. Chase-Lansdale (eds) *For Better and For Worse: Welfare Reform and the Well-being of Children and Families*. New York: Russell Sage Foundation.

Hatton, C., Akram, Y., Shah, R., Robertson, J. and Emerson, E. (2004) *Supporting South Asian Families with a Child with Severe Disabilities*. London: Jessica Kingsley Publishers.

Havighurst, R. (1972) *Developmental Tasks and Education* (3rd edn). New York: McKay.

Hawkins, J.D., Catalano, R.F. and Associates (1992) *Communities that Care: Action for Drug Abuse Prevention*. San Francisco: Jossey Bass.

Hawthorn, H.B. (ed) (1967) *A Survey of the Contemporary Indians of Canada: A Report on Economic, Political, Educational Needs and Policies in Two Volumes*. Ottawa: Indian Affairs Branch. www.ainc-inac.gc.ca.

Hays, S. (2003) *Flat Broke with Children: Women in the Age of Welfare Reform*. New York: Oxford University Press.

Health Canada (1997) *Community Action Program for Children and the Canada Prenatal Nutrition Program*. www.hc-sc.gc.ca/english/media/releases/1997/capce.htm.

Health Canada (1998) *CPNP: Reaching Canadian Communities – Overview of the Canada Prenatal Nutrition Program's Individual Project Questionnaire Report*. Ottawa: Minister of Public Works and Government Services Canada.

Health Canada (2000a) *Children Making a Community Whole: A Review of Aboriginal Head Start in Urban and Northern Communities*. Ottawa: Minister of Public Works and Government Services Canada.

Health Canada (2000b) *CPNP: A Portrait of Participants – Highlights of the Canada Prenatal Nutrition Program's Individual Client Questionnaire*. Ottawa: Minister of Public Works and Government Services Canada.

Health Canada (2001) *CAPC/CPNP Renewal: 2000 Final Report*. Unpublished report.

Health Canada (2002a) *Aboriginal Head Start in Urban and Northern Communities: Program and Participants 2001*. Ottawa: Minister of Public Works and Government Services Canada.

Health Canada (2002b) 'The Government of Canada announces early childhood development initiative for Aboriginal children.' News release, October 31. www.hc-sc.gc.ca.

Henggeler, S.W., Melton, G.B. and Smith, L.A. (1992) 'Family preservation using multi-systemic therapy: An effective alternative to incarcerating serious juvenile offenders.' *Journal of Consulting and Clinical Psychology 60*, 6, 953–61.

Hetherington, R., Cooper, A., Smith, P. and Wilford, G. (1997) *Protecting Children: Messages from Europe*. Dorset: Russell House Publishing Ltd.

Hicks, L. (1997) *Drug Addiction and Pregnant/Parenting Women: Factors Affecting Client Engagement*. Toronto: Breaking the Cycle and the University of Toronto.

Higgins, G.O. (1994) *Resilient Adults: Overcoming A Cruel Past*. San Francisco, CA: Jossey-Bass.

Hills, J., Le Grand, J. and Piachaud, D. (eds) (2002) *Understanding Social Exclusion*. Oxford: Oxford University Press.

Himmelman, A.T. (1992) *Communities Working Collaboratively for a Change*. Minneapolis, MN: The Himmelman Consulting Group.

HM Treasury (1998) *Modern Public Services for Britain: Investing in Reform. Comprehensive Spending Review: New Public Service Plans 1999–2002*. London: The Stationery Office.

HM Treasury (1999a) *The Modernisation of Britain's Tax and Benefit System no. 4: Tackling Poverty and Extending Opportunity*. London: HMSO.

HM Treasury (1999b) *The Modernisation of Britain's Tax and Benefit System no. 5: Supporting Children through the Tax and Benefit System*. London: HMSO.

HM Treasury (2001) *Tackling Child Poverty: Giving Every Child the Best Possible Start in Life*. A pre-budget report document. London: HMSO.

HM Treasury (2002) *Opportunity and Security for All: Investing in an Enterprising, Fairer Britain, New Public Spending Plans 2003–2006*. (White Paper.) London: HMSO.

Hobcraft, J. (1998) *Intergenerational and Life-Course Transmission of Social Exclusion: Influences of Child Poverty, Family Disruption and Contact with the Police*. Case paper 15. London: Centre for Analysis of Social Exclusion, London School of Economics.

Hollins, S. and Sinason, V. (2000) 'Psychotherapy, learning disabilities and trauma: new perspectives.' *British Journal of Psychiatry 17*, 32–6.

Hollister, D., Martin, M., Toft, J., Yeo, J. and Kim, Y. (2003) *The Well-being of Parents and Children in the Minnesota Family Investment Program in Hennepin County, Minnesota, 1998–2002*. St Paul, MN: University of Minnesota School of Social Work Center for Advanced Studies in Child Welfare.

Home Office (1998) *Supporting Families*. (Green Paper.) London: HMSO.

Howard, M., Garnham, A., Fimister, G. and Veit-Wilson, J. (2001) *Poverty: The Facts* (4th edn). London: Child Poverty Action Group.

Human Resources Development Canada (2001) 'The school to work transition of post-secondary graduates in Canada.' *Applied Research Bulletin*, Special Edition Summer 2001. Ottawa: Human Resources Development Canada.

Humphreys, C. and Mullender, A. (undated) *Children and Domestic Violence*. Dartington: Research in Practice.

Hunter, B.H., Kinfu, Y. and Taylor, J. (2003) *The Future of Indigenous Work: Forecasts of Labour Force Status to 2011*. Canberra: Centre for Aboriginal Economic Policy Research, Australian National University Publications.

Huston, A.C., McCloyd, V.C. and Garcia Coll, C.T. (1994) 'Children and poverty' Special issue. *Child Development 65*, 2.

Huxley, P.J., Evans, S., Burns, T., Fahy, T. and Green, J. (2001) 'Quality of life outcome in a randomized controlled trail of case management.' *Social Psychiatry and Psychiatric Epidemiology 36*, 249–55.

Indian and Northern Affairs Canada (2000) *Information Sheet Definitions March 2000*. www.ainc-inac.gc.ca.

Indian Residential Schools Resolution Canada (2003) *Residential School Historical Overview*. www.irsr-rqpi.gc.ca.

Institute for Social Research (1977, 1979, 1981) *Social Change in Canada Series*. Downsview, ON: York University.

Institute of Medicine (1994) *Reducing Risks for Mental Disorders: Frontiers for Preventive Intervention Research*. Wanshington, DC: National Academy Press.

Jackson, S. (ed) (2001) *Nobody Ever Told Us School Mattered*. London: BAAF.

Jean Yeung, W., Linver, M.R. and Brooks-Gunn, J. (2002) 'How money matters for young children's development: Parental investment and family processes.' *Child Development 73*, 1629–43.

Johnston, C.E. and Mash, E.J. (1989) 'A measure of parenting satisfaction and efficacy.' *Journal of Clinical Child Psychology 18*, 167–75.

Jones, H., Chant, E. and Ward, H. (2003) 'Integrating children's services: a perspective from England.' In N. Trocme, D. Knoke and C. Roy (eds) *Community Collaboration and Differential Response: Canadian and International Research and Emerging Models of Practice*. Ottawa: Centre of Excellence for Child Welfare.

Jones, L. (2003) *An Evaluation of a Dedicated Service for Looked After and Accommodated Young People for Greater Glasgow Health Board and East Dunbartonshire Council by Scottish Health Feedback*. Edinburgh: Scottish Health Feedback.

Joseph Rowntree Foundation (2002) *The Youth Divide*. York: Joseph Rowntree Foundation.

Kaplan, R. and Norton, D. (1992) 'The balanced scorecard: Measures that drive performance.' *Harvard Business Review* Jan–Feb.

Katz, M. (2001) *The Price of Citizenship: Redefining the American Welfare State*. New York: Henry Holt.

Kempson, E. (1996) *Life on a Low Income*. York: Joseph Rowntree Foundation.

Kent, R. (1998) *Children's Safeguards Review*. Edinburgh: HMSO.

Kirk, S. and Glendinning, C. (1999) *Supporting Parents Caring for a Technology-Dependent Child*. Research report. Manchester: National Primary Care Research and Development Centre, University of Manchester.

Kleinman, M. (1999) 'There goes the neighbourhood: Area policies and social exclusion.' *New Economy 6*, 88–192, 1999, cited in I. Plewis, G. Smith, G. Wright and A. Cullis (2001) *Linking Child Poverty and Child Outcomes: Exploring Data and Research Strategies*. Department for Work and Pensions Research Working Paper no. 1. London: HMSO.

Knapp, M. (2000) 'The cost consequences of conduct disorder.' *Mental Health Research Review 7*, 8–11.

Kohen, D.E., Brooks-Gunn, J.B., Leventhal, T. and Hertzman, C. (2002) 'Neighborhood income and physical and social disorder in Canada: Associations with young children competencies.' *Child Development 73*, 1844–60.

Kreuter, M.W., Lezin, N.A. and Young, L.A. (2000) 'Evaluating community-based collaborative mechanisms: Implications for practitioners.' *Health Promotion Practice 1*, 49–63.

Kubisch, A.C. and Connell, J.P. (1998) 'Applying a theory of change approach to the evaluation of comprehensive community initiatives: Progress, prospects, and problems.' In K. Fulbright-Anderson, A.C. Kubisch and J.P. Connell (eds) *New Approaches to Evaluating Community Initiatives, Volume 2: Theory, Measurement, and Analysis*. Washington, DC: The Aspen Institute.

Kufeldt, K. (2003) 'Graduates of guardianship care: Outcomes in early adulthood.' In K. Kufeldt and B. McKenzie (eds) *Child Welfare: Connecting Research, Policy and Practice*. Waterloo, ON: Wilfrid Laurier Press.

Kufeldt, K., Armstrong, J. and Dorosh, M. (1989) 'In care, in contact?' In J. Hudson and B. Galaway (eds) *The State as Parent*. Dordrecht: Kluwer Academic Publishers.

Kufeldt, K. and Burrows, B. (1994) *Issues Affecting Public Policies and Services for Runaway and Homeless Youth.* Calgary: The University of Calgary.

Kufeldt, K., Durieux, M., McDonald, M. and Nimmo, M. (1992) 'Providing shelter for street youth: Are we reaching those in need?' *Child Abuse and Neglect, The International Journal 16,* 2, 187–99.

Kufeldt, K., Simard, M., Tite, R. and Vachon, J. (2003) 'The looking after children in Canada project: Educational outcomes.' In K. Kufeldt and B. McKenzie (eds) *Child Welfare: Connecting Research, Policy and Practice.* Waterloo, ON: Wilfrid Laurier Press.

Kufeldt, K., Simard, M., Vachon, J. and Andrews, T. (2000) *Looking After Children in Canada: Final Report.* Fredericton: University of New Brunswick, Canada.

Kurtz, Z. (2003) 'Outcomes for children's health and wellbeing.' *Children and Society Special Issue: New Labour Policy and its Outcomes for Children 17,* 3, 173–83.

Laming, Lord (2003) *The Victoria Climbié Inquiry.* London: The Stationery Office.

Law, C. and Joughin, C. (2005) *Standard 5, Safeguarding and Promoting the Welfare of Children and Young People.* London: Department of Health.

Lazar, I. and Darlington, R. (1982) 'Lasting effects of early education: A report from the consortium for longitudinal studies.' *Monographs of the Society for Research in Child Development 47,* 2, 195.

Leichtman, H.M. (1996) *Helping Work Environments Work.* Washington, DC: Child Welfare League of America Inc.

Lengyel, T.E. (ed) (2001) *Faces of Change: Personal Experiences of Welfare Reform in America.* Milwaukee, WI: Alliance for Children and Families.

Lens, V. (2002) 'TANF: What went wrong and what to do next.' *Social Work 47,* 3, 279–90.

Leslie, M. (2002) *Breaking the Cycle Pregnancy Outreach Program: Renewal Report 2002.* Toronto: Health Canada.

Leventhal, T., Brooks-Gunn, J. and Kamerman, S.B. (1997) 'Communities as place, face and space: Provision of services to poor, urban children and their families.' In J. Brooks-Gunn, J.G. Duncan and J.L. Aber (eds) *Neighborhoods Poverty. Vol. 2.* New York: Russell Sage Foundation.

Levinas, E. (1989) *Humanisme van de Andere Mens.* Kampen: Kok Agora.

Link, R.J. and Bibus, A.A. (2000) *When Children Pay: US Welfare Reform and its Implications for UK Policy.* London: Child Poverty Action Group.

Lipsey, M.W. and Wilson, D.B. (2001) *Practical Meta-analysis.* Thousand Oaks, CA: Sage.

Lister, R. (2002) 'A politics of recognition and respect: Involving people with experience of poverty in decision making that affects their lives.' *Social Policy and Society 1,* 1, 37–46.

Littell, J. and Schuerman, J. (1999) 'Innovations in Child Welfare.' In D. Biegel (ed) *Innovations in Practice and Service Delivery across the Life Span.* New York: Oxford University Press.

Loprest, P. (2003) *Fewer Welfare Leavers Employed in Weak Economy.* Washington, DC: Urban Institute. 21 August, 2003 report, retrieved on 30 December 2003 from http://www.urban.org/url.cfm?ID=310837.

Lucas, P. (2003) 'Home visiting can substantially reduce childhood injury.' *What Works for Children Group Evidence Nugget.* Retrieved April 2003 from www.whatworksforchildren.org.uk ESRC, University of York, City University, Barnardos: Evidence Network.

Macdonald, G. (1998) 'Promoting evidence-based practice in child protection.' *Clinical Child Psychology and Psychiatry 3,* 1, 71–85.

Macdonald, G. (2001) *Effective Interventions for Child Abuse and Neglect: An Evidence-Based Approach to Planning and Evaluating Interventions.* Chichester: Wiley.

Macdonald, G. and Williamson, E. (2002) *Against the Odds: An Evaluation of Child and Family Support Services.* London: National Children's Bureau.

MacLeod, J. and Nelson, G. (2000) 'Programs for the promotion of family wellness and the prevention of child maltreatment: A meta-analytic review.' *Child Abuse and Neglect 9,* 1127–49.

Marsh, A., McKay, S., Smith, A. and Stephenson, A. (2001) *Low Income Families in Britain: Work, Welfare and Social Security in 1999.* Department of Social Security Research Report 138. Leeds: Corporate Document Services.

Marsh, A. and Perry, J. (2003) *Families and Children Study: Family Change 1999–2001.* DWP Research Report 180. London: HMSO.

Martin, F. (1998) 'Tales of transition: Self-narrative and direct scribing in exploring care-leaving.' *Child and Family Social Work 3,* 1, 1–12.

Maslow, A.H. (1970) *Motivation and Personality* (2nd edn). New York: Harper and Row.

Mason, J., Falloon, J., Gibbons, L., Spence, N. and Scott, E. (2002) *Understanding Kinship Care.* NSW: Association of Children's Welfare Agencies.

Mathematica Policy Research (2003) 'Mathematica welfare research.' Retrieved on 2 December 2003 from http://www.mathematica- mpr.com/welfarefinding.htm.

McCann, J.B., James, A., Wilson, S. and Dunn, G. (1996) 'Prevalence of psychiatric disorders in young people in the care system.' *British Medical Journal 313,* 1529–30.

McCauley, C., Knapp, M., Beecham, J., McCurry, N. and Sleed, M. (2002) *Evaluating the Outcomes and Costs of Home-Start Support to Young Families Experiencing Stress: A Comparative Cross Nation Study.* York: Joseph Rowntree Foundation.

McCulloch, A. and Joshi, H.E. (1999) *Child Development and Family Resources: An Exploration of Evidence from the Second Generation of the 1958 British Birth Cohort.* Colchester: Institute for Social and Economic Research, University of Essex.

McCulloch, A. and Joshi, H.E. (2001) 'Neighbourhood and family influences on the cognitive ability of children in the British National Child Development Study.' *Social Science and Medicine 53,* 579–91, cited in I. Plewis, G. Smith, G. Wright and A. Cullis (2001) *Linking Child Poverty and Child Outcomes: Exploring data and research strategies.* Department for Work and Pensions Research Working Paper No. 1. London: HMSO.

McDonald, R.-A.J., Ladd, P. *et al.* (2000) *First Nations Child and Family Services Joint National Policy Review Final Report June 2000.* Ottawa: Assembly of First Nations/Department of Indian and Northern Affairs.

McHugh, M. (2002) *The Costs of Caring: A Study of Appropriate Foster Care Payments for Stable and Adequate Out-of-Home Care in Australia.* NSW: Association of Child Welfare Agencies.

McPhee, D.M. and Bronstein, L.R. (2003) 'The journey from welfare to work: Learning from women living in poverty.' *Affilia 18,* 1, 34–48.

MDRC (2003) *Minnesota Family Investment Program (MFIP) Evaluation.* New York: MDRC. http://www.research forum.org/project_general_20.html.

Meltzer, H., Gatward, R., Corbin, T., Goodman, R. and Ford, T. (2003) *The Mental Health of Young People Looked After by Local Authorities in England.* London: HMSO.

Meltzer, H., Smyth, M. and Robus, N. (1989) *OPCS Surveys of Disability in Great Britain Report 6: Disabled Children: Services, Transport and Education.* London: HMSO.

Middleton, S., Ashworth, K. and Braithwaite, I. (1997) *Small Fortunes: Spending On Children, Childhood Poverty and Parental Sacrifice.* York: Joseph Rowntree Foundation.

Millar, J. and Ridge, T. (2001) *Families, Poverty, Work and Care: A Review of the Literature on Lone Parents and Low Income Couple Families with Children.* Department for Work and Pensions Research Report 153. Leeds: Corporate Document Services.

Minnesota Department of Human Services (2000) *Minnesota Family Investment Program (MFIP) Evaluation: Reforming Welfare and Rewarding Work: A Summary of the Final Report on the Minnesota Family Investment Program.* St Paul, MN: Minnesota Department of Human Services. http://www.researchforum.org/project_printable_20.html.

Minnesota Department of Human Services (2001) *Successes and Challenges for MFIP Families: A Progress Report for the Minnesota Family Investment Program.* St Paul, MN: Minnesota Department of Human Services.

Minnesota Department of Human Services (2003) *Measuring Minnesota Investment Program Performance for Racial/Ethnic and Immigrant Groups: Study Brief.* St Paul, MN: Minnesota Department of Human Services.

Minnesota Department of Human Services (2004) 'Minnesota Family Investment Program home page.' Retrieved on 2 January 2004 from http://www.dhs.state.mn.us/ecs/ Reports/default.htm.

Modood, T. and Berthoud, R. (eds) (1997) *Ethnic Minorities in Britain: Diversity and Disadvantage.* London: Policy Studies Institute.

Moore, T., Rapp, C. and Roberts, B. (2000) 'Improving child welfare performance through supervisory use of client data.' *Child Welfare LXXIX,* 5, 475–97.

Moore, T.E., Pepler, D.J. and Motz, M. (1998) *Breaking the Cycle: The Evaluation Report (1995–1997).* Toronto: Health Canada.

Morris, J. (1992) 'Personal and political: A feminist perspective on researching physical disability.' *Disability, Handicap and Society 7,* 2, 157–66.

Morris, J. (1998) *Still Missing? Disabled Children and The Children Act.* London: Who Cares? Trust.

Morris, P.A. and Gennetian, L.A. (2003) 'Identifying the effects of income on children's development using experimental data.' *Journal of Marriage and Family 56,* 716–29.

Moyers, S. and Mason, A. (1995) 'Identifying standards of parenting.' In H. Ward (ed) *Looking After Children: Research Into Practice.* London: The Stationery Office.

Mustard, C., Derksen, S., Berthelot, J.-M., Wolfson, M., Roos, L.L. and Carriere, K.C. (1995) *Socio-Economic Gradients in Mortality and the Use of Health Care Services at Different Stages in the Life Course.* Winnipeg: Manitoba Centre for Health Policy and Evaluation.

National Center for Health Statistics (2003) *Health, United States 2003 with Chartbook on Trends in Health of Americans.* Hyattsville, MA: National Center for Health Statistics.

National Health Advisory Service (1995) *Together We Stand: Thematic Review on the Commissioning, Role and Management of Child and Adolescent Mental Health Services.* London: HMSO.

National Longitudinal Survey of Children and Youth (1994, 1996, 1998) *Child Behaviour Problems and Parenting Scale.* Ottawa, ON: Human Resources Development Canada.

National Statistics (2003) *Census 2001 National Report for England and Wales.* London: The Stationery Office.

Needell, B., Webster, D., Barth, R.P. and Armijo, M. (1996) *Performance Indicators for Child Welfare Services in California: 1995.* Berkeley, CA: Child Welfare Research Center, School of Social Welfare, University of California.

Nelson, G., Amio, J., Prilleltensky, I. and Nickels, P. (2000) 'Partnerships for implementing school and community prevention programs.' *Journal of Educational and Psychological Consultation 11,* 121–45.

Nelson, G., Laurendeau, M.-C. and Chamberland, C. (2001) 'A review of programs to promote family wellness and prevent the maltreatment of children.' *Canadian Journal of Behavioural Science 33,* 1–13.

Nelson, G., Pancer, S.M., Hayward, K. and Kelly, R. (2004) 'Partnerships and participation of community residents in health promotion and prevention: Experiences of the Highfield community enrichment project (better beginnings, better futures).' *Journal of Health Psychology 9,* 2, 213–27.

Nelson, G., Pancer, S.M., Hayward, K. and Peters, R. DeV. (in press) *Partnerships for Prevention: The Story of the Highfield Community Enrichment Project (Better Beginnings, Better Futures).*

Nelson, G., Westhues, A. and MacLeod, J. (2003) 'A meta-analysis of longitudinal research on preschool prevention programs for children.' *Prevention and Treatment 6* (December). Available at http://journals.apa.org/prevention/volume6/toc-dec18-03.html

Nelson, R.J. (1973) 'An evaluation of child protection caseloads.' Speech to child welfare workers in New Brunswick, unpublished.

Newman, T. and Blackburn, S. (2002) *Transitions in the Lives of Children and Young People: Resilience Factors.* Edinburgh: Scottish Executive.

Nightingale, D.S. (2002) 'Work opportunities for people leaving welfare.' In A. Weil and K. Finegold (eds) *Welfare Reform: The Next Act.* Washington, DC: The Urban Institute Press.

Noble, M., Evans, M., Dibben, C. and Smith, G. (2001) *Changing Fortunes: Geographic Patterns of Income Deprivation in the Late 1990s.* London: Department for Transport, Local Government and the Regions.

Norris, D. (Director General, Census and Demographic Statistics, Statistics Canada) (2003) 'Evidence presented to Special Subcommittee on Children and Youth at Risk of the Standing Committee on Human Resources Development and the Status of Persons with Disabilities.' Retrieved on 29 January 2004. www.parl.gc.ca.

Northern Ireland Children's Order (1995) London: HMSO.

Observer (2002) 'Benefits cut for truancy shelved.' 1 December.

Office of the Legislative Auditor (2002) *Economic Status of Welfare Recipients.* St Paul, MN: Office of the Legislative Auditor.

Oliver, M. (1990) *The Politics of Disablement.* London: Macmillan.

Olsen, R. and Clarke, H. (2003) *Parenting and Disability: Disabled Parents' Experiences of Raising Children.* Bristol: Policy Press.

O'Neal, M.E. and Marano, M. (2003) '(Re)development or gentrification: critically assessing housing patterns in the inner-city.' Unpublished paper to be presented at SSSP Annual Conference.

O'Neill, O. (2002) 'A question of trust.' The 2002 Reith Lecture. London: BBC, www.bbc.co.uk/radio4/reith2002/lectures.shtml.

Packman, J. and Hall, C. (1998) *From Care to Accommodation.* London: The Stationery Office.

Pancer, S.M., Nelson, G., Dearing, B., Dearing, S., Hayward, K. and Peters, R. DeV. (2003) 'Highfield Community Enrichment Project (Better Beginnings, Better Futures): A community-based project for the promotion of wellness in children and families.' In K. Kufeldt and B. McKenzie (eds) *Child Welfare: Connecting Research, Policy, and Practice.* Waterloo, ON: Wilfrid Laurier University Press.

Parker, H. (ed) (1998) *Low Cost but Acceptable: A Minimum Income Standard for the UK.* Bristol: The Policy Press.

Parker, R., Ward, H., Jackson, S., Aldgate, J. and Wedge, P. (eds) (1991) *Looking After Children: Assessing Outcomes in Child Care.* London: HMSO.

Patton, M.Q. (2002) *Qualitative Evaluation and Research Methods* (3rd edn). Thousand Oaks, CA: Sage Publications.

Pecora, P.J., Fraser, M.W. and Haapala, D.A. (1991) 'Client outcomes and issues for programme design.' In K. Wells and D. Biegel (eds) *Family Preservation Services.* Newbury Park, CA: Sage.

Peirson, L., Laurendeau, M.-C. and Chamberland, C. (2001) 'Context, contributing factors, and consequences.' In I. Prilleltensky, G. Nelson and L. Peirson (eds) *Promoting Family Wellness and Preventing Child Maltreatment: Fundamentals for Thinking and Action* (pp.41–123). Toronto: University of Toronto Press.

Pelton, L.H. (1992) 'A functional approach to reorganizing family and child welfare interventions.' *Children and Youth Services Review 14,* 3–4, 289–303.

Pepler, D.J., Moore, T.E., Motz, M.H. and Leslie, M. (2003) *Breaking the Cycle: The Evaluation Report (1995–2000).* Toronto: Health Canada.

Peters, R. DeV., Arnold, R., Petrunka, K., Angus, D.E., Brophy, K., Burke, S.O., Cameron, G., Evers, S., Herry, Y., Levesque, D., Pancer, S.M., Roberts-Fiati, G., Towson, S. and Warren, W.K. (2000) *Developing Capacity and Competence in the Better Beginnings, Better Futures Communities: Short-term Findings Report.* Kingston, ON: Better Beginnings, Better Futures Research Coordination Unit Technical Report, www.bbbf.queensu.ca.

Peters, R. DeV., Peters, J., Laurendeau, M.-C., Chamberland, C. and Peirson, L. (2001) 'Social policies for promoting the wellbeing of Canadian children and families.' In I. Prilleltensky, G. Nelson and L. Peirson (eds) *Promoting Family Wellness and Preventing Child Maltreatment: Fundamentals for Thinking and Action.* Toronto, ON: University of Toronto Press.

Piachaud, D. (2001) 'Child poverty, opportunities and quality of life.' *Political Quarterly 72,* 4, 446–53.

Piachaud, D. and Sutherland, H. (2001) 'Child poverty.' In J. Hills, J. Le Grand and D. Piachaud (eds) *Understanding Social Exclusion.* Oxford: Oxford University Press.

Pinnock, M. and Dimmock, B. (2003) 'Managing for outcomes.' In J. Henderson and D. Atkinson (eds) *Managing Care in Context.* London: Open University/Routledge.

Pinto, R.M. (2002) 'Social work values, welfare reform, and immigrant citizenship conflicts.' *Families in Society 83,* 1, 85–92.

Platt, L. (2002) *Parallel Lives? Poverty Among Ethnic Minority Groups in Britain.* London: Child Poverty Action Group.

Plewis, I., Smith, G., Wright, G. and Cullis, A. (2001) *Linking Child Poverty and Child Outcomes: Exploring Data and Research Strategies.* Department for Work and Pensions research working paper no.1. London: HMSO.

Poertner, J. (2001) 'Linking Child Welfare Training and Child Outcomes.' Paper presented at the fourth annual National Human Services Training Evaluation Symposium, Berkeley, CA.

Power, M. (1997) *The Audit Society: Rituals of Verification.* Oxford: Oxford University Press.

Price, A. and Barth, R.P. (1997) 'Shared family care: Child protection without parent–child separation.' *Protecting Children 13,* 3, 15–16.

Prilleltensky, I., Nelson, G. and Peirson, L. (eds) (2001) *Promoting Family Wellness and Preventing Child Maltreatment: Fundamentals for Thinking and Action.* Toronto, ON: University of Toronto Press.

Probert, A. and Poirier, R. (2003) 'The health status of first nations people in Canada.' *Health Canada Policy Research Bulletin no. 5.* www.hc-sc.gc.ca.

Pugh, G. (2003) 'Early childhood services: evolution or revolution?' *Children and Society Special Issue: New Labour Policy and its Outcomes for Children 17,* 3, 184–94.

Pugh, G. and Parton, N. (eds) (2003) *Children and Society Special Issue: New Labour Policy and its Outcomes for Children 17,* 3, 157–260.

Quinton, D. (2004) *Supporting Parents: Messages from Research.* London: Jessica Kingsley Publishers.

Rabiee, P., Priestley, M. and Knowles, J. (2001) *Whatever Next? Young Disabled People Leaving Care.* Leeds: First Key.

Rae-Grant, N.I. and Russell, C.C. (1989) *Better Beginnings, Better Futures: An Integrated Model of Primary Prevention of Emotional and Behavioural Problems.* Toronto, ON: Queen's Printer for Ontario.

Ramey, C.T. and Landesman Ramey, S. (1998) 'Early intervention and early experience.' *American Psychologist 53,* 109–20.

Rank, M.R. (1994) *Living on the Edge: The Realities of Welfare in America.* New York: Columbia University Press.

Rapp, C.A. and Poertner, J. (1992) *Social Administration: A Client-centered Approach.* White Plains, NY: Longman Publishing Group.

Regehr, C., Leslie, B., Howe, P. and Chau, S. (2000) 'Stress and trauma in child welfare practice.' *Canada's Children,* Summer edition, 12–14.

Riddell, S. (2001) 'New bill to ensure greater access.' *Children In Scotland,* November, 5–7.

Ridge, T. (2002) *Childhood Poverty and Social Exclusion: From a Child's Perspective.* Bristol: The Policy Press.

Robinson, P., Auckland, K., Crawford, H. and Nevison, C. (1999) *Care Sick?: The Physical and Mental Health Needs of a Sample of Young People in Local Authority Residential Care.* Edinburgh: Lothian Health Board.

Rubin, L. (1996) *The Transcendent Child: Tales of Triumph Over the Past.* New York: Basic Books.

Rushton, A. and Dance, C. (in press) 'Negative parental treatment of the singled out child: Responses to the problem by Health Visitors, Social Services Departments and Child and Adolescent Mental Health Services.' *Clinical Child Psychology and Psychiatry.*

Rushton, A. and Minnis, H. (2002) 'Residential and foster family care.' In M. Rutter and E. Taylor (eds) *Child and Adolescent Psychiatry.* Oxford: Blackwell Science.

Russell, P. (2003) 'Access and achievement or social exclusion? Are the government's policies working for disabled children and their families?' *Children and Society Special Issue: New Labour Policy and its Outcomes for Children 17,* 3, 215–25.

Rutter, A., Giller, H. and Hagell, A. (1998) *Antisocial Behaviour by Young People.* Cambridge: Cambridge University Press.

Ruxton, S. and Bennett, F. (2002) *Including Children? Developing a Coherent Approach to Child Poverty and Social Exclusion Across Europe.* Brussels: Euronet.

Sackett, D.L., Straus, S.E. and Richardson, W.S. (1997) *Evidence-based Medicine: How to Practice and Teach EBM.* New York: Churchill Livingston.

Safe on the Streets Research Team (1999) *Still Running. Children on the Streets in the UK.* London: The Children's Society.

Sampson, R.J. (2001) 'How do communities undergird or undermine human development? Relevant contexts and social mechanisms.' In A. Booth and A.C. Crouter (eds) *Does it Take a Village? Community Effects on Children, Adolescents and Families.* Mahwah, NJ: Lawrence Erlbaum Associates.

Sampson, R.J., Raudenbush, S. and Earls, F. (1997) 'Neighborhoods and violent crime. A multilevel study of collective efficacy.' *Science 277,* 918–24.

Sandywell, B. (1998) 'The shock of the old: Mikhail Bakhtin's contribution to the theory of time and alterity.' In M.M. Bell and M. Gardiner (eds) *Bakhtin and the Social Sciences.* London: Sage.

Schoech, D., Quinn, A. and Rycraft, J.R. (2000) 'Data mining in child welfare.' *Child Welfare LXXIX,* 5, 633–50.

Schofield, G. (2001) 'Resilience in family placement, a lifespan perspective.' *Adoption and Fostering 25,* 3, 6–19.

Schoor, L.B. (1997) *Common Purpose: Strenghtening Families and Neighborhoods to Rebuild America.* New York: Doubleday.

Schorr, E. (1995) *The Case for Shifting to Results-based Accountability.* Washington, DC: Center for the Study of Social Policy.

Schuerman, J., Rzepnicki, T. and Littell, J. (1994) *Putting Families First: An Experiment in Family Preservation.* New York: Aldine de Gruyter.

Schwartz, I., Au Claire, P. and Harris, L. (1991) 'Family preservation services as an alternative to the out-of-home placement of adolescents: the Hennepin County experience.' In K. Wells and D. Biegel (eds) *Family Preservation Services.* Newbury Park, CA: Sage.

Scott, S. and Sylva, K. (2002) *The 'SPOKES' Project: Supporting Parents on Kids' Education, Final Report.* London: Department of Health.

Scottish Consortium for Learning Disability (undated) *Top Marks for Good Practice: Getting the Most for Your Child's Schooling, A Checklist for Parents.* Glasgow: Scottish Consortium for Learning Disability.

Seccombe, K. (1999) *'So You Think I Drive a Cadillac?' Welfare Recipients' Perspective on the System and its Reform.* Boston, MA: Allyn and Bacon.

Sharpe, S. (2002) *Sort it Out! Revisited.* London: Office of Children's Rights Commissioner for London.

Shaw, L. (1998) 'Childrens' Experiences of School' in C. Robinson and K. Stalker (eds) *Growing up with Disability.* London: Jessica Kingsley Publishers.

Shelton, E. and Roy, C. (2001) *Filling the Gaps in Welfare Reform.* St Paul: McKnight Foundation and Wilder Research Center.

Sherman, A. (1999) 'Children's poverty in America.' *Forum for Applied Research and Public Policy 14,* 4, 68.

Shonkoff, J.P. and Phillips, D.A. (eds) (2000) *From Neurons to Neighbourhoods: The Science of Early Childhood Development.* Committee on Integrating the Science of Early Childhood Development, Board on Children, Youth and Families, National Research Council and Institute of Medicine. Washington, DC: National Academy Press.

Shropshire, J. and Middleton, S. (1999) *Small Expectations: Learning to Be Poor?* York: Joseph Rowntree Foundation.

Sinclair, I., Baker, C., Wilson, K. and Gibbs, I. (2003) *What Happens to Foster Children?* Report to the Department of Health. York: University of York.

Sinclair, I., Wilson, K. and Gibbs, I. (2000) *Supporting Foster Placements.* Report to the Department of Health. York: Social Work Research and Development Unit.

Sinclair, R., Garnett, L. and Berridge, D. (1995) *Social Work and Assessment with Adolescents.* London: National Children's Bureau.

Skinner, A. (1992) *Another Kind of Home: A Review of Residential Child Care.* Edinburgh: HMSO.

Skuse, T. and Ward, H. (2003) *Outcomes for Looked After Children: Children's Views of Care and Accommodation. An Interim Report to the Department of Health.* Loughborough: Centre for Child and Family Research.

Smith, D. (2003) 'New Labour and youth justice.' *Children and Society Special Issue: New Labour Policy and its Outcomes for Children 17*, 3, 226–35.

Smith, M. (2003) 'New stepfamilies – A descriptive study of a largely unseen group.' *Child and Family Law Quarterly 15*, 2, 185–98.

Smith, P. (1993) 'Outcome-related performance indicators and organisational control in the public sector.' *British Journal of Management 4*, 135–51.

Smith, T. (1992) *Family Centres and Bringing Up Young Children.* London: HMSO.

Smith, M., Boddy, J., Hall, S., Morse, C., Pitt, C. and Reid M. (unpublished) *A Study of Normal Injuries.* Thomas Coram Research Unit, Institute of Education, University of London.

Social Exclusion Unit (2001) *A New Commitment to Neighbourhood Renewal: National Strategy Action Plan.* London: HMSO.

Social Exclusion Unit (2003) *A Better Education for Children in Care.* London: Social Exclusion Unit.

Social Services Inspectorate (2003) *Performance Ratings for Social Services in England.* London: Social Services Inspectorate.

Special Educational Needs and Disability Act (2001) London: HMSO.

St Pierre, R.G. and Layser, J.I. (1998) 'Improving the life chances of children in poverty: Assumptions and what we have learned.' Social Policy Report. *Society for Research in Child Development 12*, 1–25.

Stalker, K. and Connors, C. (2003) 'Communicating with disabled children.' *Adoption and Fostering 27*, 1, 26–35.

Statistics Canada (2002) *Births and Deaths.* Ottawa: Ministry of Industry, Government of Canada.

Statistics Canada (2003) *2001 Census Analysis Series: Aboriginal Peoples of Canada: A Demographic Profile.* www.statcan.ca.

Stein, M. (1997) *What Works in Leaving Care?* Ilford: Barnardos.

Stein, M. (2002) 'Leaving care.' In D. McNeish, T. Newman and H. Roberts (eds) *What Works For Children?* Buckingham: Open University Press.

Stein, M. (forthcoming) *Overcoming the Odds: Resilience and Young People Leaving Care.* York: Joseph Rowntree Foundation.

Stein, M. and Carey, K. (1986) *Leaving Care.* Oxford: Blackwell.

Strawn, J. (1998) 'Beyond job search or basic education: Rethinking the role of skills in welfare reform.' *Policy and Practice 56*, 2, 49–54.

Sultmann, C.-M. and Testro, P. (2001) *Directions in Out-of-Home Care – Challenges and Opportunities.* Queensland: Peakcare Queensland Inc.

Sutherland, H. (2001) *Five Labour Budgets (1997–2001): Impacts on the Distribution of Household Incomes and on Child Poverty.* Microsimulation Unit Research Note no. 41. Cambridge: University of Cambridge.

Tanner, E., Bennett, F., Churchill, H., Ferres, G., Tanner, S. and Wright, S. (2003) *The Costs of Education: A Local Study.* London: Child Poverty Action Group.

Tardieu, B. (1997) 'The human rights of children growing up in extreme poverty: What lacks of basic securities?' In A. Ben-Arieh and H. Wintersberger (eds) *Monitoring and Measuring the State of Children – Beyond Survival. Eurosocial Report 62/1997.* Austria: European Centre for Social Welfare Policy and Research.

Terling-Watt, T. (2000) 'A communitarian critique of the child protection system.' *Journal of Sociology and Social Welfare 27*, 4, 3–23.

Tessier, R., Pilon, N. and Fecteau, D. (1985) 'Étude méthodologique d'un instrument de mesures des conduites de contrôle parental: Fiabilité et validité de construit.' *Revue Canadienne des Sciences du Comportement 17*, 62–73.

Thomas, C. (1999) *Female Forms: Experiencing and Understanding Disability.* Buckingham: Open University Press.

Thompson, M.J.J., Raynor, A., Cornah, D., Stevenson, J. and Sonuga-Barke, E.J.S. (2002) 'Parenting behaviour described by mothers in a general population sample.' *Child Care Health and Development 28*, 2, 149–55.

Tomison, A.M. (1996) *Child Maltreatment and Mental Disorder. National Child Protection Clearinghouse, Discussion Paper No. 3.* Melbourne: Australian Institute of Family Studies.

Tomlinson, S. (2003) 'New Labour and education.' *Children and Society Special Issue: New Labour Policy and its Outcomes for Children 17*, 3, 195–204.

Toulmin, S. and Gustavsen, B. (1996) *Beyond Theory: Changing Organisations Through Participation.* Amsterdam: Benjamins Publishing Company.

Triseliotis, J., Borland, M., Hill, M. and Lambert, L. (1995) *Teenagers and the Social Work Services.* London: The Stationery Office.

Trocmé, N., Fallon, B., MacLaurin, B., Daciuk, J., Bartholomew, S., Ortiz, J., Thompson, J. and Helfrich, W. (2002) *1998 Ontario Incidence Study of Reported Child Abuse and Neglect.* Toronto, ON: Centre of Excellence for Child Welfare, Faculty of Social Work, University of Toronto.

Trocmé, N., MacLaurin, B., Fallon, B., Daciuk, J., Billingsley, D., Tourigny, M., Mayer, M., Wright, J., Barter, K., Burford, G., Hornick, J., Sullivan, R. and McKenzie, B. (2001) *Canadian Incidence Study of Reported Child Abuse and Neglect: Final Report.* Ottawa, ON: Ministry of Public Works and Government Services Canada.

Tunstill, J. and Aldgate, J. (2000) *Services for Children in Need. From Policy to Practice.* London: The Stationery Office.

Tunstill, J., Hughes, M. and Aldgate, J. (in press) *Family Support at the Centre: The Role of Family Centres in Local Service Networks.* London: Jessica Kingsley Publishers.

Tweedie, J. (2001) 'Sanctions and exits: What states know about families that leave welfare because of sanctions and time limits.' In G.J. Duncan and P.L. Chase-Lansdale (eds) *For Better and For Worse: Welfare Reform and the Well-being of Children and Families.* New York: Russell Sage Foundation.

UNICEF (1997) *Children and Families of Ethnic Minorities, Immigrants and Indigenous Peoples.* Innocenti Global Seminar Summary Report. Florence: UNICEF.

United Nations (2002) *A World Fit for Children.* www.unicef.org/specialsession/wffc/.

United States Census Bureau (2003) 'American community survey change profile: Table 3 Selected economic characteristics.' Retrieved on 30 December 2003 from www.census.gov/acs/www/.

Utting, D. (1995) *Family and Parenthood: Supporting Families, Preventing Breakdown.* York: Joseph Rowntree Foundation.

Utting, D. (1998) 'Suggestions for the UK: An overview of possible action.' Paper for cross-departmental review on provision for young children (unpublished).

Utting, D., Rose, W. and Pugh, G. (2001) *Better Results for Children and Families: Involving Communities in Planning Services Based on Outcomes.* London: The National Council of Voluntary Child Care Organisations.

Utting, W. (1997) *People Like Us: The Report of the Review of Safeguards for Children Living Away from Home.* London: The Stationery Office.

van Beinum, M., Martin, A. and Bonnett, C. (2002) 'Catching children as they fall: Mental health promotion in residential care in East Dunbartonshire.' *Scottish Journal of Residential Child Care 1*, 19–20.

Vandivere, S., Gallagher, M. and Moore, K.A. (2004) *Changes in Children's Well-being and Family Environment.* Washington, DC: Urban Institute. Retrieved on 2 May 2004 from www.urban.org/url.cfm?ID=310912

Vleminckx, K. and Smeeding, T.M. (eds) (2001) *Child Well-being, Child Poverty and Child Policy in Modern Nations: What Do We Know?* Bristol: The Policy Press.

Wahler, R.G. and Dumas, J.E. (1989) 'Attentional problems in dysfunctional mother–child interactions: An interbehavioral model.' *Psychological Bulletin 105*, 116–130.

Wakefield, Jerome C. (1996) 'Does social work need the eco-systems perspective?' *Social Services Review 70*, 1, 1–32.

Walker, D. (2003) Personal communication, 15 April.

Walker, R. (1999) 'Lifetime poverty dynamics.' In Centre for Analysis and Social Exclusion/HM Treasury *Persistent Poverty and Lifetime Inequality: The Evidence.* London: CASE, London School of Economics.

Ward, H. (ed) (1995) *Looking After Children: Research Into Practice.* London: HMSO.

Ward, H., Holmes, L., Soper, J. and Olsen, R. (2004) *The Costs and Consequences of Different Types of Child Care. Report to the Department of Health.* Loughborough: Centre for Child and Family Research.

Ward, H., Macdonald, I., Pinnock, M. and Skuse, T. (2002) 'Monitoring and improving outcomes for children in out of home care.' In K. Kufeldt and B. McKenzie (eds) *Child Welfare: Connecting Research, Policy and Practice.* Waterloo, ON: Wilfrid Laurier Press.

Ward, H. and Peel, M. (2002) 'An inter-agency approach to needs assessment.' In H. Ward and W. Rose (eds) *Approaches to Needs Assessment in Children's Services*. London: Jessica Kingsley Publishers.

Wedeven, T., Pecora, P.J., Hurwitz, M., Howell, R. and Newell, D. (1997) 'Examining the perceptions of alumni of long-term family foster care: A follow-up study.' *Community Alternatives 9*, 1, 89–105.

Wedge, P. and Prosser, H. (1973) *Born to Fail?* London: Arrow Books for the National Children's Bureau.

Weil, A. and Finegold, K. (eds) (2002) *Welfare Reform: The Next Act*. Washington, DC: The Urban Institute Press.

Whitbourne, S.K. and Weinstock, C.S. (1979) *Adult Development: The Differentiation of Experience*. New York: Holt, Rinehart and Winston.

Whittaker, J.K. and Maluccio, A.N. (2002) 'Rethinking child placement: A reflective essay.' *Social Service Review*, March, 108–33.

Wilder Research Center (2003) *The Issues Behind the Outcomes for Somali, Hmong, American Indian, and African American Welfare Participants*. St Paul, MN: Wilder Research Center.

Willinsky, J. (2003) 'Policymakers' online use of academic research.' Education Policy Analysis Archives. Retrieved 29 April from http://epaa.asu.edu/epaa/v11n2/.

Willitts, M. and Swales, K. (2003) *Characteristics of Large Families*. In-house research report no. 118. London: Department for Work and Pensions.

Wilson, H. (2002) 'Brain science, early intervention and "at risk" families: Implications for parents, professionals and social policy.' *Social Policy and Society 1*, 3.

Winnicott, D.W. (1985) *The Maturational Processes and the Facilitating Environment*. London: Hogarth Press.

Wise, S. (2003) 'An evaluation of a trial of Looking After Children in the state of Victoria, Australia.' *Children and Society 17*, 1, 3–17.

Wolfe, D.A. (1987) *Implications for Child Development and Psychopathology*. Newbury Park, CA: Sage.

Zaslow, M., Moore, K.A., Trout, K., Scarpa, J.P. and Vandivere, S. (2002) 'How are children faring under welfare reform?' In A. Weil and K. Finegold (eds) *Welfare Reform: The Next Act*. Washington, DC: The Urban Institute Press.

Zedlewski, S.R. (2003) *Work and Barriers to Work Among Welfare Recipients in 2002*. Washington, DC: The Urban Institute Press. www.urban.org.

Zuravin, S.J. (1989) 'The ecology of child abuse and neglect: Review of the literature and presentation of data.' *Violence and Victims 4*, 2, 101–20.

Zuravin, S.J. and Taylor, R. (1987) 'The ecology of child maltreatment: Identifying and characterizing high-risk neighbourhoods.' *Child Welfare 66*, 6, 497–506.

The Contributors

Richard P. Barth is the Frank A. Daniels Professor of Human Services at the University of North Carolina at Chapel Hill.

Michael van Beinum is a consultant in child and adolescent psychiatry and honorary senior clinical lecturer at Glasgow University, with an attachment to the Medical Research Council Social and Public Health Sciences Research Unit, Glasgow University.

Fran Bennett is a senior research fellow at the Department of Social Policy and Social Work, University of Oxford.

Anthony Bibus is Professor and Chair at Augsburg College Social Work Department, US.

Nina Biehal is a senior research fellow at the Social Work Research and Development Unit (SWRDU) at the University of York and editor of the journal *Child and Family Social Work*.

Chris Bonnett is a consultant clinical psychologist for looked after children, South of Tyne and Wearside Mental Health NHS Trust, Sunderland.

Camil Bouchard was a professor at the University of Quebec. He is now Vice Chair of the Committee on Social Affairs at the National Assembly Quebec and official opposition critic for employment, social solidarity and family welfare.

Richard Budgell is Senior Analyst, Indian Affairs and Health Division in Treasury Board Secretariat, Government of Canada.

Mike Clare is Associate Professor in Social Work and Social Policy at the University of Western Australia.

Clare Connors is Honorary Research Fellow at the Centre for Applied Social Studies at Durham University.

Mark Friedman founded and currently directs the Fiscal Policy Studies Institute in Santa Fe, New Mexico.

Louise Garnett manages a small team of information and research officers which supports two Local Strategic Partnerships in North Lincolnshire and North East Lincolnshire.

Kathleen Kufeldt is an adjunct professor, coordinating the Child Abuse and Neglect team for the Muriel McQueen Fergusson Centre for Family Violence Research at the University of New Brunswick.

Bruce Leslie was the Research and Quality Improvement Analyst at the Children's Aid Society of Toronto when this research was conducted. He is now the Manager of Quality Assurance at the Catholic Children's Aid Society of Toronto.

Margaret Leslie is Director of Early Intervention Programs at Mothercraft, and Program Manager of Breaking the Cycle, Canada.

Rosemary Link is Professor of Social Work at Augsburg College, Minneapolis, Minnesota.

Andy Martin is Planning and Commissioning Manager for East Dunbartonshire Social Work Services.

Terry Moore is a research associate at the University of Kansas School of Social Welfare.

Geoffrey Nelson is Professor of Psychology at Wilfrid Laurier University, Waterloo, Ontario.

Jennifer Noonan is a recently graduated social worker.

Michael E. O'Neal is a former faculty member in the Sociology Department and Urban Studies Program at Augsburg College, Minneapolis, Minnesota.

Mike Pinnock is Head of Learning, Development and Support for North Lincolnshire Council.

Amy Price is Associate Director of the National Abandoned Infants Assistance (AIA) Resource Center at the University of California, Berkeley.

Gillian Pugh DBE was formerly Chief Executive of Coram Family and an advisor to the Children and Families directorate within the Department for Education and Skills. Dr Pugh is chair of the Parenting Education and Support Forum, a trustee of the National Family and Parenting Institute, a member of the Children's Workforce Development Council and a visiting Professional Fellow at the Institute of Education.

David Quinton is Emeritus Professor of Psychosocial Development in the School for Policy Studies as the University of Bristol.

Lynne Robertson is the Health Canada Aboriginal Head Start National evaluation analyst.

Jane Scott is a research fellow in the Centre for Child and Family Research within the Department of Social Sciences at Loughborough University, and a lecturer in the Department of Social Work, Dundee University.

Kirsten Stalker is Reader at the Social Work Research Centre, Stirling University.

Mike Stein is Professor of Social Work and Co-director of the Social Work Research and Development Unit at the University of York.

Harriet Ward is Director of the Centre for Child and Family Research and a Professor in the Department of Social Sciences at Loughborough University.

Judy Watson is the Manager of Community Based Programs with the Centre for Healthy Human Development, Health Canada.

Author Index